94

"You won't always ag   .olds barred' approach to so many .... issues will keep you reading all night long."

Dick Ebersol, Chairman, NBC Sports and Olympics

"The Olympic Games exist for the benefit of the athletes and not the IOC. Many IOC members still don't get it; however, Dick Pound (a former Olympic swimmer) certainly does. His unique view from inside the Olympic Movement is told in his usual straightforward manner, with his special blend of idealism and cynicism."

Brian Williams, CBC, Veteran Broadcaster and Olympic Host

"The only man who could have written this book has done it with candor and style. A lucid and penetrating look at the five-ringed world, filled with Dick Pound's customary insight, frankness and wit. *Inside The Olympics* wins gold, silver and bronze."

John Powers, Boston Globe

"Pound takes us through the Olympic landscape with insight and opinion and on one of the biggest problems we all face: drugs in sport, he has always stood shoulder to shoulder with the good guys."

Sebastian Coe, OBE, double Olympic Gold 1500-meter champion

"Pound captures both the spirit and complexity of life in sport—from athlete to administrator—through his bold, candid, and always relevant observations of life inside the rings. A must read for anyone intrigued by sports and the passionate pursuit of excellence."

Charmaine Crooks, IOC Member, Silver Medallist and Five-Time Olympian, Executive Board Member of the World Olympians Association

"Sharp, insightful, witty and honest are my first reactions to this book. It offers a level of insight and critique, touched with a continued sense of hope and caring for sport. A must read for anyone who is interested in sport and the many influences that impact it."

Karen O'Neill, Chief Executive Officer, Commonwealth Games Canada

About the Author

Author photo: Kant Photo

Richard W. Pound has been a member of the International Olympic Committee (IOC) for over 25 years. He has served on the IOC Executive Board, and in 1987 was elected vice-president for a four-year term and served a second term from 1996 to 2000. During the 2000 Summer Games in Sydney, he was acting president, and in 2001 ran unsuccessfully in the election to replace Juan Antonio Samaranch as the eighth president of the IOC.

Pound is the founding chair of the World Anti-Doping Agency, which was established in 1999. He was also Chairman of the IOC Television Negotiation Committee (1983-2001), and Chairman of the IOC Marketing Committee until 2001. Pound served as the Chair of the Coordination Commission for the 1996 Olympic Games, and as a director of the Organizing Committee for the 1988 Olympic Winter Games in Calgary, Alberta. It was partly because of Pound's investigation of the Salt Lake City bribery scandal that new regulations and an ethics watchdog to oversee interaction between IOC members and bidding cities were created. He is a past president, director, and executive committee member of the Canadian Olympic Committee.

Born in Canada in 1942, Pound began his athletic career as a competitive swimmer. At the 1960 Olympic Games in Rome, he was a double Olympic finalist, finishing fourth in the 400 meter medley relay and sixth in the 100 meter freestyle. He went on to win four medals—a gold, a bronze, and two silvers—at the 1962 Commonwealth Games in Australia.

Pound was educated in Montreal, receiving degrees in commerce and law from McGill. He is currently a partner in the law firm Stikeman Elliott. In 1999, he was made the seventeenth chancellor of McGill University.

INSIDE THE OLYMPICS

A BEHIND-THE-SCENES LOOK AT THE POLITICS, THE SCANDALS, AND THE GLORY OF THE GAMES

RICHARD W. POUND

John Wiley & Sons Canada Ltd.

National Library of Canada Cataloguing in Publication Data

Pound, Richard W.
 Inside the Olympics : a behind-the-scenes look at the politics,
 the scandals, and the glory of the games / Richard W. Pound.

Includes index.

ISBN-13 978-0-470-83454-1 (bound)

ISBN-10 0-470-83454-4 (bound)

ISBN-13 978-0-470-83870-9 (pbk.)

ISBN-10 0-470-83870-1 (pbk.)

1. Olympics – Political aspects – History. 2. International Olympic
Committee – History. 1. Jeux olympiques – Aspect politique – Histoire.
2. Comité international olympique – Histoire. I. Title.

GV721.5.P69 2004   796.48   C2004-901563-X

GV721.5

Production Credits:
Concept developers and editors: Adrianna Edwards & Ron Edwards, Focus
                                Strategic Communications Incorporated
Cover design: Sputnik Design Partners Inc.
Interior text design: Adrian So R.G.D.
Front cover photo: Dave Black Photography
Printer: Tri-Graphic Printing Ltd.

Printed in Canada

1 2 3 4 5 TRI 10 09 08 07 06

Dedication

To athletes who play fair,
to those who teach them,
and to those who
ensure the playing field is level.

RWP

Contents

Preface

Many people have urged me to write an Olympic book that would be directed at general readers who already have some understanding of how the world works. They said I should write to give the readers some idea of the issues that are faced by those who choose and direct the organization of the great phenomenon known as the Olympic Games, but without becoming so detailed that only specialists would be willing to make the effort. Knowing my proclivities, they assured me that I could always do a detailed and scholarly study of particular events or problems at some later date. Having been thus freed from having to record the entire history and devlopment of the Olympic movement, my purpose became to focus on modern issues and personalities and I did not feel compelled to keep all my opinions to myself.

I have an interesting perspective for such a work, having competed as an Olympic athlete; worked as a national sports administrator, first in the position of secretary and then president of the Canadian Olympic Association (now the Canadian Olympic Committee); and become a member of the International Olympic Committee (IOC). The span of years covered from the time of my first competitions is now well over a half century and I have witnessed and been party to many significant changes in the world of sport and politics. As an athlete, I competed under the presidency of the terrifying Avery Brundage. As a national sports administrator, I worked under Brundage and Lord Killanin; and as a member of the IOC, I served in the latter part of Killanin's term, the entire era of Juan Antonio Samaranch and into the presidency of Jacques Rogge. There has been much to observe and even more to learn.

This work is, deliberately, not a personal memoir or chronicle. That, too, can wait until I finally acknowledge that I am getting "old," a state that always seems to be a decade or more ahead. The book does not explore all the nuances and the interpersonal tensions, positive and negative, that created some of the events that are described. I have tried to provide enough background to bring the events into a context, while cutting out the trivia that would impede the main story. Friends and colleagues who come to read this book in the usual fashion of insiders (turning immediately to the index to see how often they are identified) may experience some disappointment that they are not as prominent as they might have hoped. I assure them they will get their full due in future memoirs or specific treatments of events in which we acted together.

I should declare, if not a bias, at least a mental set. I am convinced that the Olympic Games and the ethical practice of sport are wonderful contributors to the fulfilment of the youth of all countries. They assist in the development of social skills and abilities, and in the creation of a healthier society that does not draw on the social net as much as an unhealthy one and that can make genuine contributions to peace in the world. I am, in that respect, a self-confessed and unrepentant idealist. I am not, however, devoid of skepticism, especially as it relates to individuals and certain groups, some of whom appear to embrace the idealistic view but in fact do not. I have learned to look beyond bland assertions of commitment to ethical sport—grist for the public relations mill—and to compare what is said with what is actually done. In the process, I often find myself astonished at the degree of hypocrisy I encounter both within sport itself and in statements by public authorities.

The contents of this work reflect the interaction of all three Olympic goals—personal fulfilment, the development of social skills, and a healthier and more peaceful society—and the conduct arising from them. The Olympics represent an ideal for everyone, where the finest athletes from throughout the world can come in peace to compete at the highest level, with mutual respect, for the glory of becoming Olympic champions. There is no event like this in the world. It reflects the dream of a nineteenth-century French educator who would be astonished—and delighted—to see what his dream for the first modern Olympic Games in 1896 has become more than a century later.

It is in pursuit of the ideal that some of the failures begin, and the challenge to uphold the ideal in the face of evident imperfection becomes more difficult. The Games are the event that drives a vast and complex international sports movement spread across more than two hundred countries, involving, one way or another, hundreds of millions of athletes, coaches, officials and spectators. The pressures to host the Olympics have increased in recent years as the economic model for the Games has changed to make them a very profitable as well as prestigious event. Bidding cities have been tempted to cross the line from acceptable competition for the prize to inappropriate conduct and have been met halfway (if not further) by some members of the IOC. This has brought disgrace on themselves and their cities, as well as on the IOC.

Sport officials, leaving aside those who may merely be incompetent, have shown that they are often not the disinterested arbiters whose role is to validate the competitions taking place on the field of play. All too often it appears that they have their own undisclosed "games" running parallel to the competitions for which they are responsible. Collusion between judges has blackened the reputation of officials in general. By acting this way, they have completely destroyed the integrity of their sport through their contemptuous treatment of athletes who have trained for years and sacrificed much, in the expectation that they will be judged impartially. Such conduct is a disgrace.

Others work, just as clandestinely and just as assiduously, to undermine the integrity of sport by cheating through the use of prohibited drugs and prohibited methods of performance enhancement, such as blood doping. Although the occasional athlete may take something by accident that could produce a positive doping test result, the great majority of cases involve the assistance, support or knowledge of other persons who have deliberately set out to achieve a better result in the competition by cheating. These may be coaches, friends (spare me such "friends"), doctors, scientists, agents and others in the entourage of the athlete. Whoever they may be, their objective is to cheat other athletes out of the results they achieve by competing fairly.

It is in relation to this kind of practice that the idealist needs to become cynical and to think like a cheat, to anticipate what cheaters might do and to take preemptive preventive action where possible. Where prevention proves not to be possible in all cases, then there must be procedures to detect cheaters and deal with them appropriately. The vast majority who play fair must have confidence in the system. I regard doping as the single most important problem facing sport today. Quite apart from the risks to athletes' health, the clandestine use of drugs and methods for performance enhancement subverts the ethical underpinnings of sport. Cheaters are forced into hiding what they have done and compete in fear that some day, somehow, their deception will be disclosed and that disgrace will follow. What should be a triumph of human achievement becomes, instead, a hollow pretence. Heroes become exposed as shallow cheaters. This is offensive to the ideal that motivates almost everyone regarding sport.

The Olympic movement and Olympic Games are so huge that they seem to create their own myths and they are surrounded by mysteries. Most can be explained, although there always seems to be some magic that defies full articulation and that draws the world into an inexorable fascination with what the next Games will bring and who the next Olympic legends will be. One of the most persistent concerns about the Olympics has been the so-called commercialism associated with them. It has become almost dogma for the media to bemoan any commercial connection with the Olympics, and this concern is shared by many members of the IOC and the sports movement generally. For most of my years in the IOC, my primary responsibility was the generating of the revenues necessary to run the IOC and the Olympic movement, principally from television rights and international sponsorships. It was a series of exciting challenges to constantly increase the revenues and to balance this against the delicate sensibilities of those who loved the money but who did not wish to be seen actually earning it.

We had tremendous fun inventing marketing programs as we went along, persuading sponsors on the one hand that there was commercial value in being associated with the Olympic movement. On the other hand, we had to convince the Olympic movement that it was not compromising any of its values as a result of such association. The television and sponsorship revenues provided us with the chance to act as redistributors of funds, making it possible to channel much-needed financial sport to the developing countries that had little, if any, access to hard currency. There is not enough money to make everyone equal, but the expansion of the number of countries able to produce Olympic medal-winning athletes is a direct result of the funds given to talented athletes who might otherwise never have been able to realize their full potential.

It has always been a matter of great satisfaction to know that many of the athletes who reach Olympic finals or semifinals have done so because we have been able to generate support from the private sector. One of the ideas I had hoped to implement if I became president of the IOC in 2001 was to set aside the first dollars from those earned in connection with each edition of the Games—say US$50 million from the IOC and from the organizing committees—into a fund that would help improve sport development in countries that cannot afford such investment. In addition, I would seek ways to leverage such funding, with matching programs from governments and the private sector. I am convinced that we must do what we can to narrow the gap between the developed and developing worlds, not to allow it to widen.

I also examine the leadership of the IOC, especially that of Juan Antonio Samaranch, since I was present throughout his term and close to the center of the action. The organization is quite unique in structure and mandate. It consists of volunteers who meet very seldom and the personality of the president is imposed on it almost as a matter of course, given both the statutory powers vested in the president and the fact that he is the only member continuously involved in the business of the IOC. More than almost any international organization, the IOC will rise, fall or drift along in direct relation to the strengths, abilities and convictions of its presidents. There has been a remarkable stability in the leadership provided by the IOC presidents, whose terms have generally been quite lengthy and three of whom (Pierre Frédy, Baron de Coubertin; Brundage; and Samaranch) account for more than half of modern Olympic history.

The most difficult aspect of writing a book of this nature is having to leave out much of what I consider to be interesting material. The publishers assure me that if potential readers get hernias from trying to lift a heavy tome, they will not buy it and, therefore, the material that is in the work will also not be known. So, while there may be more on the proverbial cutting-room floor than I might have wished, it has also been a good exercise for me to concentrate on the essentials and to try to make a good read that will accomplish the real objective of making the Olympic movement more accessible to more readers.

Montreal
April 2004

 Going Home

Arriving in Greece is a delight. As the plane circles for its approach into the Athens airport, the view is stupendous—a rocky, convoluted coast jutting out into the Mediterranean. A beautiful airport, built by German construction experts, adds to the impression of modern Greece as a country that has arrived. This positive impression fades as the visitor experiences the notorious Athens traffic, and it becomes increasingly clear as you get closer to the center of the city that not all of modern Greece has been modernized. Security is both visible and invisible. For those of us with Olympic experience, it's the invisible kind that's especially important. Thousands of people are about to descend on Athens for the 2004 Olympic Games, and although amateur would-be terrorists may be impressed with the obvious security, the professionals on either side of the security line play their deadly games out of the public eye.

The Olympic Games are the most important sporting event the world has ever known. Many are drawn by its irresistible magnet—some to compete, some to watch, some to organize, some to destroy and others to protect. The Games have become a special and compelling drama, offering a unique set of heroes, moments of glory and disaster, and a lifelong set of extraordinary memories. It's one of the largest peaceful gatherings of young people on the face of the planet.

Eleven thousand athletes from more than two hundred countries will compete in twenty-eight sports at the Athens Games and be watched by more than four billion spectators. But what really sets the summer of 2004 apart is that the Olympic Games are finally returning home.

• • •

The ancient Olympics were an invention of the Greeks. There are records of Games being held in honor of Zeus as early as 776 BC, and they were celebrated every four years at Olympia for more than a millennium before Roman Emperor Theodosius banned them in AD 393, during the Roman occupation of Greece. By then, Games for the Romans had degenerated from sporting matches into disruptive entertainment and declined along with the empire itself. Wars were the only games during the Dark Ages and the Middle Ages, and it was not until the late nineteenth century that society had evolved to the point where organized sport had any following.

Although there were signs of interest in the ancient Greek Games in a number of quarters, such as Britain, it fell to the young French nobleman and educator Pierre Frédy, Baron de Coubertin, to conceive the idea of renovating the Olympic Games, but this time on an international basis. After studying the problem of physical fitness for several years, partly as a result of the trouncing of the French by the Germans in one of their regular exchanges of hostilities, de Coubertin concluded that physical fitness through sport, combined with education and culture, could enhance society. He traveled throughout Europe and eastern North America to study how sport was practiced and, more importantly, integrated into the educational and social systems of each country. These observations confirmed his own thinking and propelled him to organize an international conference at the Sorbonne in 1894. Out of that came the decision to hold the first modern Olympic Games in Athens in 1896. Another decision that would have a lasting impact on international sport was to create the International Olympic Committee (IOC), now headquartered in Switzerland. The first committee was made up of acquaintances of de Coubertin and men chosen from the international conference.

It was a modest beginning, with twelve countries and some four hundred athletes represented. The 1896 Games were financed largely by a gift from a wealthy Greek architect (one million drachma, a significant amount) and the proceeds from the sale of souvenirs. The Greek royal family, especially the Crown prince, was actively involved and made some land available for the stadium. There were competitions in track and field, weightlifting, swimming, cycling, Greco-Roman wrestling, lawn tennis, shooting, fencing and gymnastics. The Greeks did fairly well, partly because, as the host country, there were more of them, and they took several medals including golds in gymnastics, shooting and fencing. But the great moment for the hosts occurred when Spyridon Louis, a twenty-four-year-old Greek shepherd, won the marathon. This was naturally the highlight for the country that had originated and named this long-distance event, and so the regular cycle of the modern Games was started.

The two succeeding editions of the Games, in Paris in 1900 and in St. Louis in 1904, were organizational shambles, so much so that the future of the Games was in serious doubt. The Greeks were called upon to salvage the situation with further Games in 1906. These were decidedly better and led to the official 1908 Games in London (after Italy bailed out for financial reasons), which were better still. In the years since, they have evolved into the extraordinary spectacle that we see today. The Greeks have not been given the full credit for their between-Games effort in 1906, though; the Olympic establishment has resolutely refused to recognize that year's event as official Games.

The Games are an integral part of Greece's history, culture, mythology and psyche. The Greeks have always claimed a degree of ownership in the Games that is deeply felt and aggressively expressed. At various times when the Olympics have come under political attack and pressure, Greece has offered to become the permanent host for the Games, to be centered near ancient Olympia, in the Peloponnesus region, several hours by car from Athens on largely indifferent roads. This is a generous but completely impracticable idea that the IOC has always gently refused. The size and scope of the infrastructure needed to host the modern Games would have been a strain on Greece that it could not have afforded. In addition, all the facilities, including the major broadcast center and the hotels needed for Olympic visitors, would have had to be maintained, even though they would have been largely empty for all but one month out of every four years between the Games. These are massive facilities that can be used only by major cities. This would all have been well beyond the financial means of the country. The huge fees and other service charges for television broadcasting rights and sponsorship go toward the costs of organizing the Games and building some installations, but not the ongoing maintenance. Apart from that, there is no enthusiasm at all by the

IOC to turn over ongoing responsibility for the Games to Greece, a country in which political instability is a principal characteristic. Even had that not been a feature, the Games now belong to the world at large and many countries wish to be the hosts. There are nine candidates for the 2012 Games: Havana, Istanbul, Leipzig, London, Madrid, Moscow, New York, Paris and Rio de Janeiro. Some of these cities, such as Leipzig and New York, went through extensive internal processes in their countries before emerging as the selections endorsed by the national Olympic committees for submission to the IOC as official candidates.

Athens has tried many times to have the Games, but even though it has often been the emotional favorite, it has never won the bidding to host the Games. There has long been a feeling, almost entirely sentimental, that the Games should go back to Greece someday. Several other countries have hosted them more than once, and the same honor was one that the Greeks should also have—someday.

However, it was only in the latter part of the twentieth century that this became even a remote possibility. Greece's political situation took a serious detour in 1967 when the military took control and exiled King Constantine, an Olympic champion whose grandfather had played a large role in the original modern Games in 1896. The presence of such a regime would have had an adverse impact on any plan to award the Games to Greece, although the IOC has occasionally granted the Games in circumstances that have drawn criticism, such as the 1980 Games to Moscow and the 2008 Games to Beijing, where human rights records have been less than exemplary. In all such cases, the IOC has opted for expanding the Games, so that when the Games were awarded to Moscow in 1974, the prospect of getting behind the Iron Curtain for the first time and balancing the East–West considerations outweighed the existence of a repressive regime. The decision in 2001 to give the Games to China was made in the hope of improvement in human rights and, indeed, the Chinese themselves said that having the Games would accelerate progress in such matters. Time will tell, but the full glare of the world media is bound to be on Beijing the moment the Athens Games are finished

As the centenary of the modern Games approached in 1996, Athens had managed to convince itself of its right to host the Centennial Games. Of course, this view was not shared by the other candidates, including Australia (Melbourne, the host of the 1956 Games), Britain (Manchester), Canada (Toronto), the United States (Atlanta) and Yugoslavia (Belgrade). The Greeks angrily dismissed these other candidates, but a majority of the IOC members were sensible enough to know that, given the existing economic and political difficulties faced by the small country, it would have been impossible for Greece to succeed. The whole conduct of the Athens campaign showed that there was no unified commitment to making the Games a success. I believed that, if the bid from Toronto (which I personally thought was the best of the five we had to consider) failed, then it should be an Anyone-but-Athens contest.

At the IOC session in Tokyo in 1990, Athens placed a noisy second to Atlanta for the 1996 Games. Its support came from the older IOC members and those Mediterranean countries, but there was a prevailing view that, instead of celebrating the past, the Centennial Games should look forward to the second century of modern Olympism—a philosophy combining the qualities of body, will and mind, blending sport with culture and education. It would have been a disaster for Greece to get the 1996 Games, and I am sure, in their heart of hearts, thinking

Greeks secretly thank the gods that they did not win. Atlanta had its own set of problems, but at least there was never any doubt that the Centennial Games would, in fact, take place, something that would never have been certain had Athens been selected. (Even now, with a different economic model for the Games and access to the credits provided by the European Community, it will be a close-run venture.)

In 1997, seven years after losing out to Atlanta for the 1996 Games, Athens was back in the hunt—this time for the 2004 Games. Greece was better organized for the contest; it was on the verge of admission into the European Community; and it had access to additional infrastructure funding. While no less proud of its Olympic heritage, Greece was now at least aware that it would have to win the right to host the Games, not simply trumpet some self-proclaimed right to do so. That arrogant assumption was both annoying and entirely dismissed by competitors. With some misgivings, which have turned out to be fully justified, the IOC chose Athens over its chief rival, Rome, with all of the historical irony implicit in the choice.

It was an interesting election. By eliminating Stockholm before Cape Town, the IOC sent a signal that some day the Games would go to Africa. Almost no one in the IOC thought, expected or wanted Cape Town to win, but it was important to show the world that Africa was not being ignored. It has long been the dream of the IOC that the Games be celebrated on all continents, but we have not managed to do so in either Africa or South America. There are few countries in Africa that could realistically aspire to host the Games. The most obvious are Egypt and South Africa, but it would be a major political and economic stretch for both countries. Cairo has major infrastructure challenges, and South Africa, now that it is finally free of the destructive apartheid regime, undoubtedly has more press-ing short-term problems than hosting Olympic Games. Nor does it have the moral leadership that was provided by Nelson Mandela, so there may yet be more tears in its future. South America has several cities that could be hosts, but the countries have been burdened by political and economic instability and the IOC has been reluctant to take the risk of going there. Buenos Aires had been a candidate for the 2004 Games. Now that we've seen the degree of economic insta-bility that was coming, imagine if we had, in an abundance of misguided goodwill, given Argentina the Games!

The main contest, however, was between Rome and Athens, with the elimination of the others as mere warm-up exercises. IOC president Juan Antonio Samaranch still wanted Athens, as he had eight years earlier, but had many of his sport-political connections with Rome, so he was particularly anxious about the outcome. As we were walk-ing into the room where the announcement was to be made, he asked me who I thought would win. "Athens," I said. "Do you think it will be close?" he asked. I said my guess was that the victory would be convincing enough, with sufficient votes separating the two, that there would be no recriminations. The result in the final round was 66–41. A very close vote would have shown a deep split and likely an emotional decision, so with this margin there could be no complaint.

•   •   •

Greece is still a small country that is obsessed by politics, which perhaps befits the cradle of Western democracy. But these politics impede the ability to move decisively on a long-term agenda. It is said, only partly in jest, that if you have three Greek cabinet ministers in a meeting, there will be at least four opinions.

With the growing list of financial successes associated with hosting the Games, the IOC enjoyed the luxury of having several candidates in the race for 2004. To simplify the process and to keep down the expenses of candidates that would have no realistic possibility of winning, we established a sort of electoral college to select a limited number of finalists. I was part of this preliminary selection committee that reduced the many candidates to five. The evaluation commission reported on the strengths and weaknesses of the candidates, but failed to mention one of the major obstacles to having the Games in Greece—the terrible air pollution that is part of life in Athens. I was astonished and remember commenting that, according to the media, hundreds of people died in Athens each summer, just trying to breathe, never mind competing athletically. To this day, when I hear the word "Athens," my visceral memory dating back to my first visit is the stench of diesel fumes. The conditions in Athens made the much-vaunted smog of Los Angeles appear to be a breath of fresh air. The commission blithely assured us that, in the late summer, when the Games would be held, the winds normally change to come off the Mediterranean and would carry away all the pollution. I am sure we all look forward to this miracle.

In political terms, it was clear that the evaluation commission had been charged by Samaranch with making sure that Athens got through the eye of the Olympic needle. He had, inexplicably, also favored Athens for 1996 and had no intention of allowing a mere electoral college to stand in its way on this occasion. And so Athens moved into the final round.

The infrastructure demands for the Games and the community as a whole are considerable and require significant construction, but the political and other considerations in Greece make the planning as well as the execution of the

9

work difficult. At the time of the bid for 1996, and still at the time of the 2004 bid, the airport at Athens was Third World quality, and the security was woefully inadequate. It was generally regarded as one of the most unsafe airports in all of Europe. By 1997, at least there were definite plans for a modern airport. It has now been opened and, with difficulty, connected to a road system that is also in the process of becoming tolerable for a capital city. More ambitious plans for a subway system have not jelled, and only portions of it will be open by the time of the Games. Moving large crowds at Games time (as well as any other rush-hour period) will be highly problematic.

Greece can build well and fairly quickly, but the whole situation is extremely complex. Quite apart from the politics, every time a shovel is put in the ground, archaeological artifacts are encountered and lawyers appear with briefs to generate delay. The magnificent subway station at Syntagma Square, in the center of Athens, is a veritable archaeological museum. And in a small country such as Greece, there are only so many workers and only so much equipment that can be mobilized on a single project.

The result has been significant internal strife and major delays in proceeding with the necessary construction. There is no guarantee that all will be completed on time. The inability to have access to the Olympic sites in sufficient time to test all the systems remains a major operational worry. The problem with the Olympics is that everything has to work perfectly, the first time. You cannot tell the winner of the 100 meters, "That was a great race, but would you mind doing it over again because our timing system did not work?" Everyone understands that, in a Mediterranean country, one is considered to be in plenty of time if ready at 11:59:59, but the complexity and integration of timing, communications and broadcasting systems require time to test and test again to reduce the possibilities of failure. Athens will not have enough time to do this, so it will be interesting to see what happens.

The IOC bears its share of responsibility for this state of affairs, having waited far too long before blowing the whistle on the lack of progress in the early stages of the preparations. Far more was said than was done. It was only when Samaranch said that Athens was now operating on a yellow light that was very close to being red that Greece began to get serious. The image was quite powerful and had the effect of putting the Greeks on notice that they had significant problems. The IOC was not going to take any of their promises or progress reports at face value. In the old days, the IOC generally announced the winner of the Games and then left it to the organizing committee established by the host city to deliver the Games. The IOC kept itself informed by requiring that its member in the country and the president and secretary-general of the national Olympic committee be members of the organizing committee, but the IOC did not get involved in any of the organizational details. Now we have much more expertise and keep close tabs on progress.

No one was ever entirely sure what would have happened had Samaranch given the red light. It is, as a practical matter, almost impossible to change the site of the Games once they have been awarded. Host cities are generally chosen seven years before the Games because that is about how long it takes to organize them. Probably the only alternative would be to cancel them altogether, and most would prefer badly organized Games to no Games at all. The only comparable recent example involved the 1976 Winter Games, when Denver backed out in 1972, well after winning the Games, and Innsbruck, the 1964 host, was called upon to rescue the situation. For 2004, we were stuck with Athens and with whatever influence we had to spur them along. In the Greek community, where political issues dominate every aspect of public life and effort, this meant constantly urging cabinet ministers, the prime minister and the president to get things moving, to get the permits to build, to choose the right contractors rather than cronies, to get all-party consent to important initiatives, and to impress on them that the world perception of Greece would be heavily influenced by how well they delivered the Games. It gave us new understanding of the myth of Sisyphus, although it seemed more like pushing a giant ball of Jell-O up each hill, only to see it wobble down again.

Not the least of our worries was getting the Greeks to focus early enough and seriously enough on the vital question of security. This is an important, but nevertheless delicate, matter for the IOC in its relations with governments. The IOC is a private, sports-related organization of volunteers, assisted by a professional staff. We have no qualifications to advise or counsel governments on this issue, but have to raise it with sufficient determination to make the highest authorities aware that the host government has a special responsibility. Since 1972, when Black September terrorists infiltrated the Olympic Village in Munich, capturing and killing eleven Israeli athletes, security has been a major concern for Games organizers. Up to that time, in the more innocent days, Olympic Village security had focused mainly on keeping the male athletes out of the female section.

It is no secret that serious security concerns have been heightened in Greece, not only because of an apparent inability or unwillingness of the Greek government to deal effectively with local terrorists, but also because of the country's proximity to several hot spots of international instability. The major domestic terrorist organization was one calling itself November 17, after the date in 1973 when student protest was crushed by the military dictatorship that then ruled Greece. Over a period of years, it carried out a number of assassinations and other terrorist acts, but had never been caught. The very equivocal approach of the Greek authorities to the continuing existence of the November 17 terrorist group was extremely troubling to the international community. It is probably fair to conclude that this concern was what led to the recent "breakthrough" that resulted in the capture, trial and conviction of some of its members.

The official Greek view is that the November 17 problem has now been solved. If it has, so much the better. In any event, I personally came to believe that—much like the Basque-separatist-dominated ETA terrorists at the time of the 1992 Barcelona Olympics—these domestic terrorists were not likely to prove to be a problem at the Greek Games. Such groups depend on some degree of at least tacit acceptance by the population for their survival, and the Greeks' emotional feeling for the Games is such that, if local terrorists disrupt the event, such support will disappear. But the region itself is far more problematic, and other terrorists may not have the same qualms. The security effort will be the most extensive in modern Olympic history and will call upon unprecedented international cooperation, including that of the United States, which, in the post-September 11 environment, is concerned that it and its interests may be a far more convenient target abroad than at home.

●　●　●

Even with all the inherent problems arising from the IOC's choice of Athens, I confess to a soft spot for Games in Greece. It is an emotional response, but nevertheless real. I first went to Greece in 1971, when I was secretary of the Canadian Olympic Association, far too young to even dream of becoming its president. I went to ancient Olympia, saw the original Olympic stadium, and put my feet into the gouges in the marble that served as the starting blocks centuries ago for the original Olympic athletes. It was an unforgettable experience, and I still get a tingle thinking of the ghosts of the athletes who must haunt the site of their own glory. Maddening as it is to try to do business in Greece, the Greeks themselves are warm, proud, short-fused and delightful. On that 1971 visit, my wife and I could not wheel the baby stroller, noisily occupied by our sixteen-month-old blond child, more than twenty-five yards without someone stopping to admire him (wonderful judgment, we thought) and to give him treats or break off a portion of their bread for him to chew. That just does not happen in most large cities. If they pull everything together, the Greeks will be so excited about showing off their Olympic heritage that the Athens experience will be wonderful. I hope they succeed.

Life is filled with coincidence. It was at a session in Athens in 1978 that I was co-opted as a member of the IOC at the tender (in IOC terms) age of thirty-six. To be part of Games in that city, less than 200 kilometers from where the ancient Games were held in Olympia, has long been my dream. All that said, I did not vote for Athens in 1997, despite the brilliantly organized campaign led by Gianna Angelopoulos-Daskalaki (who was later brought back to put an end to the early organizational "chaos"—a word that was appropriately invented by the Greeks). I was still not persuaded that Athens was ready to take on the many challenges of a modern Olympic Games, and in the final round, I voted for my other favorite Olympic city, Rome, where I had competed as a swimmer in 1960.

All this aside, in my opinion there is an even more compelling reason for returning to Greece to stage the Olympic Games—renewal. Within the IOC, until I inherited the anti-doping portfolio in 1999, I was most identified with marketing, television and the commercial or business activities of the IOC. Although important, even essential, these activities tended to be regarded as somehow separate from the main philosophical elements of the Olympic movement. That was fine, in some respects, since it gave me a reasonably free hand to help generate the resources needed within an international sports system and to offset many of the costs of organizing the Games themselves. People were constantly bemoaning the commercialization of the Games, but that actually gave me the benefit of being able to do what I wanted to do anyway, because it is easier to ask for forgiveness than for permission. On the other hand, while no one enjoyed the early poverty of the Olympic movement, it was at least the devil they knew, and many IOC members were diffusely uncomfortable with the new economic model that we had invented through marketing and television.

Many expressed considerable fear that, in the process of developing our financial resources—which gave us a much-needed autonomy, freeing us from domination by governments—we were, somehow, compromising the ethical values of the Olympic movement. The feeling was that commercial or private sector support of the Games was incompatible with the Olympic values of self-respect, respect for others and respect for the rules; fair play; self-discipline; teamwork; and fulfilment through the joy of effort. These are essentially ethical values, to which competitive results or measurable achievement are subordinate. It is these values that differentiate the Olympic movement (the aggregation of the IOC, international sports federations, national Olympic committees, athletes, officials and organizers) from other organized sport. In the entertainment or gladiator sports, the owners, competitors and even the public neither expect these qualities nor care that they are missing. All that matters at a football match is the spectacle; what the performers do, on or off the field, to be ready to perform on command is of no importance. Commercial, moneymaking interests dominate the agenda. But the more money the IOC had, so the mantra went, the more we had sold out to commercial interests. Some went as far as to suggest that these interests dominated the IOC so much that we might be prepared to cover up such matters as doping offenses, in order not to tarnish the Olympic image and thereby reduce its commercial attractiveness. In fact, nothing was further from the truth.

What we were selling, what the sponsors and broadcasters wanted, and what the public demanded, were precisely those ethical values that differentiate the Olympics from professional entertainment sports. We delivered pure sport, in which every event, every match, every bout meant something. It was not, as in commercial sport, a matter of watching endless, meaningless games in a season that went on and on, to be followed by interminable play-offs. For example, by the time ice hockey finishes, spectators are in serious danger of contracting sunstroke. What we delivered was sportsmanship, the youth of the entire world, each the best that his or her country had to offer, competing for the most intangible but most prized reward imaginable, the dream that if, on the day, everything were to go absolutely right, a competitor might, just might, become an Olympic champion.

I don't care how many Super Bowl rings someone may have won, along with the bonus money. Nothing in the world can compare with the magic of the Olympic dream.

It was for those very reasons that the sponsors and broadcasters wanted to be involved. They recognized that there would be the occasional failure to deliver on everything the Olympic movement stood for, but the most important aspect was that we were committed to trying to do the right thing for the athletes from all over the world. We had an ethical base that was different from other sports. The success of this differentiation was one of the reasons for such a violent reaction by the world when the Salt Lake City scandals burst in 1998 and 1999, exposing certain IOC members as having asked for and accepted money and other personal benefits from the bidding committee for the 2002 Winter Games. The IOC itself had failed to live up to the ethical expectations it had created for the Olympic movement.

Holding the Games in Athens has provided us with the opportunity to return to our roots—to refresh and renew our commitment to the Olympic values that should be the foundation of all sport, but particularly Olympic sport. The Athens Games will not be the most extravagant in Olympic history. There will be no attempt to stage the "best Games ever" in competition with the Sydneys of the world, with bigger and better stadiums and other excesses. This is both a physical and philosophical consideration for one of the smallest countries ever to host the Games. But these Games will provide us with the opportunity to reflect on the ethical foundation of sport, in the crucible that gave rise to the ancient and modern Games. In a world that is deeply troubled and in search of ethical platforms, where business, professional and political leaders have drifted away from acceptable standards in their pursuit of money and power, sport can provide a model that is transferable to many walks of life. The principles are universal and uncomplicated. Sport is also guilty of having strayed from the path, and its leaders, participants and supporters can benefit from a return to basic values. The Olympic Games in Athens in 2004 could not have come at a better time for everyone.

Even if the delivery of the Games falls well short of perfect—and it probably will—this won't interfere with the rejuvenation of the Olympic spirit. Some degree of failure could even serve to illustrate the indomitable will to succeed—on honorable terms—in a noble endeavor. In the Olympic Games, as in life, the most important thing is not the triumph but the struggle. The Greeks have taken on a huge challenge, arguably too big for their capacity, but they are nevertheless going to do everything they can to pull it off. And if they miss by a bit, it will still have been a heroic effort. You *can* go home again.

02 Who Guards the Guards: Judging

The performance ended. The audience was ecstatic and all but brought the house down. Everyone awaited the results impatiently; they had been watching the competition for three hours. After a couple of minutes, the scores were posted. The spectators went wild—with rage. The performance they had witnessed was obviously different from the one officials had seen. Something had to be wrong—tragically wrong. It was an affront to the competition itself and a complete travesty to the athletes who had competed. When the medals for pairs figure skating were announced, Canadians Jamie Salé and David Pelletier were awarded silver and the Russian pair got gold. That was one of the scandals of the 2002 Salt Lake City Olympics. It opened up a Pandora's box.

●　●　●

The world has a vision of the Olympics as an event that brings out the best in everyone, most of all the athletes who have trained for years for this unique opportunity to represent their countries. Not everyone has the ability to aspire to a medal, or even to reach the finals, but that is not as important as the fact that they are there in this wonderful crucible of competition, where emotion, striving and fair play are honored as much as victories. For the athletes to do well, so must the officials who organize and judge the competitions. The officials are all expected to adhere to the same high standards that are set for the athletes. At the opening ceremony of each Games, just as the athletes take an oath to compete fairly, the judges take one to officiate impartially. It was all too clear that some of the judges in the figure skating at Salt Lake City had deliberately betrayed that oath.

This is, unfortunately, all too common in sports events, even at the Olympic Games. It is hard to imagine any competitive sport that does not require at least some element of judging by independent officials. Of course, some sports are easier to judge than others. In a race, it is generally fairly simple to determine who arrives at the finish line first. In a throwing event, it is pretty easy to see who threw the shot, the discus, the javelin the farthest. In contact sports, there can be a mixture of pure result and application of rules, such as offsides or interference. But when you get to sports like diving, gymnastics or figure skating, the problems become more acute. Judging "artistic merit" inevitably involves some element of subjective opinion. And subjective opinion can be manipulated to produce results that can destroy the integrity of the competition.

Athletes and their performances are the main focus of ___ ___ ___ ___itcome of a sporting contest should be determined he rules agreed upon for each sport, the those rules by the athletes in the competition al application of those rules by the officials at the competition. Sports officials are bound by duty to act fairly and there are inherent dangers that flow from their failure to do so. First and foremost, sports officials need to have the knowledge and experience to be able to apply the rules. Most sports have a hierarchy of officials, based on their exposure to the sport at increasingly higher levels of competition. Many sports organizations offer regularly organized educational sessions, where officials can learn the finer points of the rules. Some have developed classification systems for officials, so that they can draw on a panel of qualified officials for competitions as required. So, there can be officials authorized to act at local competitions, school sports, state or provincial events, national championships, world championships and Olympic Games. Typically officials start at local or provincial levels and, if they demonstrate capability and enthusiasm, can move up to the national level. The best of them can be nominated by their national associations, or be chosen by the technical committees of the international federation, to officiate at international events—perhaps even the Olympic Games. Professionally organized sports, such as ice hockey, basketball, soccer and football, have the same arrangements.

Assuming that the underlying knowledge and experience exist, now comes the most important part: sports officials must act in a completely disinterested fashion (in the sense of having no stake in the outcome of the event) and be free of any actual or perceived conflict of interest. There can be nothing more fundamental to the conduct of a sports event than the impartiality of the officials. The players and the public must be confident that the judging is fair and reasonable. The rules generally provide officials with all the authority that's needed to enforce them and to discipline those participating. Competitors can be penalized for rule infractions and ejected for serious breaches, including a refusal to accept the final authority of the presiding officials. Power, however, is one thing; respect for the officials who exercise the power is quite another. The one is conferred; the other must be earned.

Decisions by officials in the course of an event can often determine the eventual outcome and are made, in many cases, under difficult conditions that require split-second judgment in a rapidly unfolding series of actions. There is no question that there will be the occasional error, and most athletes accept and understand that this is one of the random factors inherent in sport. They, too, make errors of judgment during the course of the competition and can accept the same failings of officials. The officials may have had a bad angle on the play or have had their vision blocked. Or the play may have been so close to compliance or infraction that it would have been anyone's good-faith call. The notorious "Hand of God" goal scored by Argentina's Diego Maradona in football's 1986 World Cup in Mexico is an example. The official could not see that the goal had been scored off Maradona's hand, rather than as a header, and could not, therefore, disallow the goal. It brings into question, of course, the ethical standards of Maradona, who certainly knew what had happened, but who refused to acknowledge it at the time and later shrugged his shoulders and pronounced it a miracle of sorts.

Other decisions are more deliberate, and officials have time to consider before rendering them. In sports such as synchronized swimming, diving, figure skating and weightlifting, officials rarely have to make split-second decisions under pressure. Although not faced with the time, speed and visual constraints affecting officials in other sports, they have their own judgmental challenges of evaluating performances against defined performance criteria. Their goldfish bowls are even clearer, since the spectators have seen exactly what the officials saw and, chauvinism aside, many spectators are very knowledgeable about both performance and rules.

The Olympic Games bring together the best athletes from around the globe every four years. Billions watch the Games, and almost everyone in the world is fascinated by the performances of the remarkable individuals who participate. Results are often measured in milliseconds or millimeters and hundredths of a point. Olympic officials' abilities should match the performances they are judging and, above all, because of the international character of the competitions, their ability to act impartially should be beyond question.

A fact that often goes unnoticed with respect to Olympic officials is that they are selected by the international sports federations (IFs) governing each sport. Thus, ice hockey officials are chosen by the International Ice Hockey Federation (IIHF), gymnastics officials by the International Gymnastics Federation (known by its French acronym, FIG), diving by the Fédération Internationale de Natation (FINA), figure skating by the International Skating Union (ISU), and so on. No officials, even for Olympic competitions, are selected by the International Olympic Committee. This is a matter of tradition in the organization of the Games. The IFs are responsible for all technical aspects of each sport, including the rules of play, equipment and officiating. It is also a matter of practicality, since each IF knows the most about its own sport and is responsible for the organization of events for the three years, eleven months and two weeks out of every four years between the Olympics.

It is especially important during the Olympics that the best officials be selected and that they behave in accordance with the highest ethical standards of the Olympics. If they fail to do so, this reflects badly on the Olympics, not on the IF that selected the officials. If there are obvious officiating failures, people will think the Olympics are crooked. They do not make the distinction between the IF officials who are responsible for the failures and the Olympic Games they are watching. The judging controversy during the 2002 Salt Lake City Olympic Winter Games in the pairs figure skating event illustrates this. Spectators saw the effects of collusion and cheating by French and Russian officials, but it was the IOC and the Olympic movement in general that took the heat.

• • •

Artistic figure skating is an archetypal judgment sport. Skaters are required to perform a series of figures and movements. There used to be three segments of a singles figure skating competition: compulsory figures (such as figure eights and other prescribed shapes, in which the skaters had to reproduce the figures as exactly as possible) for 30 percent of the marks; a short program with specified elements for 20 percent; and a long freestyle program for the remaining 50 percent of the marks. The latter permitted more flexibility, but still contained a certain number of movements and jumps that were determined in advance. There were no compulsory figures for pairs. Marks were always on a 6-point scale, but each judge also ranked the skaters from best to worst, in what are called ordinal rankings. The marks only served to break a tie in the ordinal rankings or where no majority of such rankings was given to a particular athlete. So, if a judge awards 5.6 to two athletes, he or she also determined which 5.6 was the better of the two. It should have been painfully obvious that a 6-point scale was not sufficient to allow for the nuances, but the ISU persisted with its tradition.

The compulsory figures were boring beyond belief—to athletes, spectators and officials alike—and the last competitions that used this portion of the program occurred in 1990. Now, 30 percent of the marks are for the short program and 70 percent for the long (but if a preliminary competition is held to determine who gets to the finals, 10 percent of the final mark comes forward from the preliminaries and the short and long are then split 30–60). In both the short and the long segments, competitors (or pairs) come out, one after the other, and perform their routines. They are wonderful athletes who have worked for years to perfect their skills and develop routines that will display their talents and appeal to judges and spectator alike.

Judges are nominated by the national skating federations, so countries in the competition nominate judges and referees. Panels of judges are appointed for each competition. It is quite common for judges representing countries that have athletes in that event to be judging their own athletes—and their major competitors, as well. It was an ongoing matter of disgrace that, in competition after competition, national judges were seen as persisting in over-marking their own athletes and under-marking their strongest opponents. The ISU did nothing about it and, in fact, those officials who complained about such conduct were disciplined or dropped. The national federations were equally guilty, since it was clear that if a national judge did not follow the directions given regarding scoring—to mark high for your own and low for certain of the others, or to mark higher for "friends" who would be well disposed for other events—he or she would not be reappointed for future competitions.

To deal with the situation, about all that the ISU could think of was to drop the one or two highest and lowest marks (depending on the number of judges assigned to a competition) in order to take some of the excesses out of the process. It had also allowed itself to fall into the intellectual trap of believing that only countries with a figure skating tradition could produce first-class judges and referees. This is nonsense, but it suited the stronger skating countries, who could keep control of the judging process. Therefore, the ISU had no alternative but to accept judges named by those countries and to allow them to judge the competitions. Presumably there was some misguided anticipation of mutual assured destruction or, perhaps, the view that, in the long run, things would balance out. The skating union seemed never to grasp the idea that it should appoint its own judges, who would be responsible to the ISU itself and not be beholden to the national federations.

Even more important, it did not comprehend the enormous damage that the conduct of its officials caused to the integrity of its sport and to the athletes. They participated in good faith on the basis that the grown-ups charged with officiating would judge the performances they saw on the ice spontaneously, not with reference to agreements made out of sight in the committee rooms or corridors. It is all very well to say that things may balance out in the long run, but in the long run, as John Maynard Keynes noted, we will all be dead. What about the athlete who started figure skating at age eight; who practiced alone on cold rinks early in the morning for years; who spent a fortune on coaching, choreography, costumes, renting ice time and traveling to competitions? These athletes may have delayed studies and made many other personal sacrifices, all in pursuit of finding out just how good they might be against all the other athletes in the world, only to have this trivialized as a result of some secret offstage deal made by judges.

Over the quarter century or so prior to Salt Lake City, the ISU appeared to have been making some progress with the most flagrant of the abuses, especially in the singles and pairs events. People began to believe, cautiously, that the final outcome would be based more on what the judges saw on the ice, although the glaring national judging biases continued, and no country was without fault in this shameful practice. The sole holdout was ice dancing; its technical committee operated as a self-controlled fiefdom. I remember being introduced to its chair of the day, Kurt Kunz, in Japan during the 1998 Winter Games in Nagano. I think I was supposed to gush about how wonderful the ice dancing was. Instead, I told him that I thought ice dancing had major problems. He was offended. "What problems?" I said, "The judging is a farce." Now he was really offended. "What do you mean?" I said that, at that very moment—before a single team had put a skate to ice—I could tell him the exact order of finish of at least the first six teams, and would probably be very close with the next four. I proposed that each of us write down our "guesses" and put them in a sealed envelope with $100, the winner to keep the $200. My hunch was that we would each get our $100 back. We would both have been right. That's how stacked the cards were.

One of the reasons the ice dancing committee is so arrogant is that it believes its event is too popular to ever be taken off the Olympic program, because it fills at least one evening with major television audiences. I told the same official that my solution (I was negotiating the television contracts for the IOC at the time) would be to replace ice dancing with a team event, somewhat similar to the gymnastics competition, with partial results carried forward from the singles and pairs competition and leading to an overall team result and Olympic medals. I thought that such a competition would be just as satisfying as ice dancing and more popular. Furthermore, despite the beauty and grace of ice dancing, many people do not, in the end, seriously regard it as a sport. Avery Brundage, who was president of the IOC at the time ice dancing was introduced for the 1976 Games, had personally opposed it precisely on the basis that it was not really a sport. But several years later, when the IOC was reviewing the overall Olympic program, the ice dancing committee pooh-poohed the possibility of removal, believing, correctly, that the IOC—by then under a new president, Juan Antonio Samaranch—would never be inclined to make such waves. The committee might have been more nervous had I succeeded him as IOC president in the 2001 election.

Amusingly enough, the only time I really got onto their radar scope was in Salt Lake City, after I had lost the IOC election. At that time, I was the newly appointed chair of the Olympic Games Study Commission (OGSC), in charge of finding ways to cut down on the cost and complexity of the Games. They suddenly thought that I might be in a position to eliminate their discipline, and their new president—the Russian Alexander Gorshkov—made a point of approaching me, begging me not to do anything so drastic. Unfortunately, the mandate of the OGSC did not extend to recommending changes to the Olympic program, but I gave them no comfort whatsoever. I said, enigmatically, "We are looking at all aspects of the Games." I hope they had at least some anticipatory heartburn. I feel strongly enough about the irresponsibility of the ice dancing committee that I intend to continue to be a thorn in its side until it is able to rid itself of arbitrary judging.

Another extraordinary aspect of figure skating judging is that the judges are allowed to attend the practice sessions. They can therefore watch the routines that the athletes will be skating in the competitions. They see the athletes experimenting with, for example, quadruple jumps (quads) instead of triples. They see where certain athletes have difficulties with movements, jumps or transitions. As a result, when they sit as judges in the competitions, instead of simply seeing what is done in front of them, each also sees, in his or her mind's eye, what might have happened, based on the practice sessions. Thus, for example, instead of seeing a brilliant triple jump, they may see a missed quad, and mark "down" for a missed quad instead of marking for the actual jump that they witnessed. I would not permit any judge in a competition to attend practice sessions immediately before the competition. Let them judge what they see, not what they may expect.

• • •

Fast forward to Salt Lake City. It was generally clear that the pairs gold medal would go to either the Canadian pair of Jamie Salé and David Pelletier or the Russians Elena Berezhnaya and Anton Sikharulidze. Both pairs were excellent skaters, and, barring a fall or some other major error, they were expected to be the leaders in the event. The competition was everything that could be expected. Both pairs were in the final group, which is reserved for the best skaters, based on the preliminary results. The order of skating is determined by a draw. Salé and Pelletier were to skate after the Russians.

The Russians did a fine job in the final, but it was nothing exceptional and, in fact, their program had a somewhat weak ending. Even they knew it. Their dejection was evident to all as the television cameras zeroed in on the "kiss and cry" area of the arena, where the skaters sit, usually with their coaches, and wait for the marks to be posted. Nevertheless the Russians got high marks, and were in a comfortable first position within the group as Salé and Pelletier came onto the ice. The Canadians responded with a superb routine, filled with great skating and charisma, and received a thunderous ovation. I was sitting in the stands, waiting for the marks to be posted. One of my Canadian IOC colleagues, Charmaine Crooks, was ecstatic. "That was great!" she shouted. "It will be the gold for certain." I said, "Don't be too sure. This is a strange sport."

I remembered attending the World Figure Skating Championships the previous year in Vancouver. Competing against the same Russian pair, Salé and Pelletier had won the event. While I was delighted for them, I said to the person beside me, "Well, there goes the Olympic gold medal next year." "What do you mean?" I said that the ISU allows Canadians to win the occasional world championship, but never the Olympics. It had happened too often in the past for it to be a mere coincidence: to Brian Orser, Kurt Browning and Elvis Stojko. I was, sadly, convinced that there would be a repetition of this pattern in 2002.

The marks came up in Salt Lake City. The Russians remained in first place. Salé and Pelletier were second. They were stunned. The crowd was furious. The media were incensed. As the medals were presented, the Russians, with their body language, seemed almost to acknowledge that they did not deserve the gold medal. Salé and Pelletier bore the outcome with astonishing dignity.

However, these were the Olympics. We weren't at a world championship event in some far-off place where the audience, whether watching in person or on television, was marginal. Hundreds of millions of people from around the world had seen the obvious injustice. The sense of outrage did not fade away—it continued to grow. The pairs event was the first final in the skating events at the Games, so that as the crisis persisted, it threatened the integrity of the Games themselves. In addition to the public outcry, which might have eventually subsided, there was a more troubling disclosure. In the official report of the competition, the referee had noted that French judge Marie-Reine Le Gougne alleged she had been pressured to vote in favor of the Russian pair in awarding her ordinal rankings. Even faced with this disclosure, the ISU tried to ride out the storm and to stonewall any action. Its president, Ottavio Cinquanta of Italy, whose background was primarily in speed skating and for whom the vagaries of figure skating seemed almost as confusing as they were to the general public, could do nothing to stem the tide. At news conferences, he had a hard time responding to the probing questions of the media. As public relations exercises, his appearances were a disaster. He probably hoped that the matter would cool off, that the ISU could get out of Salt Lake City and, several months later, issue some pabulum-like statement to the effect that such things are always difficult and are matters of taste and opinion. The judges might get reprimanded, but the results would stand.

This was not good enough. My role in the matter was to speak with the new IOC president, Jacques Rogge, who was officiating at his first Olympic Games following his election in 2001. I explained that the result had been outrageous and that he, as IOC president, had to find a solution. His initial reaction was that judging was a technical matter and one that was the responsibility of the ISU. Technically, he was perfectly correct and I was quick to acknowledge that. However, I said, that was no longer the problem. It was not sufficient for us on the IOC to understand that the result of the competition had been affected by misconduct on the part of the ISU officials. The public at large would not bother to make the distinction between the despicable actions of a French figure skating judge and the Olympic movement itself. This was not just another ISU competition, but the Olympics. Millions of people now thought that the Olympics were tainted. They did not care about the niceties of international federation jurisdiction in matters of judging. It was our Olympic brand that was being trashed, not the ISU's. Ninety-nine out of a hundred spectators knew nothing about the ISU and could not have cared less. What they had seen were two athletes screwed out of their Olympic gold medals and this was an Olympic problem. Rogge would have to do something. And he would have to do it very soon, before the Games as a whole were irrevocably tarnished. That meant he could not allow the ISU to get out of town before the matter was resolved. I advised him that there was a precedent arising out of the Barcelona Olympics in 1992, and that it would provide the only practical solution to the mess that we now faced.

In the solo event in synchronized swimming, a judge had entered an obviously wrong score on the electronic scoring control for a figure performed by the then-reigning world champion, Sylvie Fréchette, another Canadian. The judge immediately recognized her error and tried to change the mark, which was permissible provided that the officials operating the central control panel realized the desire to change and cleared the previous score. Unfortunately, no one from the IF was paying attention, and the judge could not change the score on the scoring control. She tried to attract the attention of the referee, who could not, because of language difficulties, understand what the judge wanted. There were no flash cards in place, despite a rule that there should be in case of just such a problem, so that the judge could indicate the correct score. Because the referee did not understand that the judge was trying to change the score, she allowed the recorded scores of the five judges, including the incorrect score, to be displayed. This had a major consequence for the result—the difference between a gold and a silver medal for Fréchette.

This was bad enough. But it got worse. The chief referee, Judith McGowan, was from the United States, whose athlete, Kristen Babb-Sprague, was now the gold medalist. The American chief referee was called upon to deal with the situation. Instead of declaring that she was in a clear position of conflict of interest, she decided to "investigate" the matter, with no witnesses and no written record of what was said. She allowed the incorrect score to remain in place and refused to take any steps to have it changed to what the judge had intended to enter. To add fuel to the fire, in response to the Canadian protest, McGowan reviewed the decision she herself had made and concluded that it was correct. When a further appeal was made to the jury of appeal, it was McGowan who presented the case. No Canadians were allowed to present evidence. Not surprisingly with that procedure, the decision was maintained, and Fréchette was awarded the silver medal.

I had been only vaguely aware of the drama at the time. I had seen the Canadian *chef de mission*, Ken Read, at the track and field events later on the day of the competition and asked how things were going with the Canadian Olympic team. He answered that all was going well, but that there was a problem with synchronized swimming and that there would be an appeal proceeding later that evening. I asked if he needed help and he said that would not be necessary. The next I heard of the matter was when I returned home to Montreal after the Games, where I discovered the real problem and learned, much to my astonishment, that the local media regarded me as the villain for not having made sure that this did not happen to a Montreal athlete. It was, I suppose, nice that they thought I had such powers of persuasion, but not at all nice that the whole mess was now regarded as my fault. So I called up the Canadian synchronized swimming people and asked them to tell me what had happened. It was only then that I realized how flagrant the conduct of the entire matter had been.

I agreed that something had to be done. Sports officials are supposed to act correctly in order to keep sport from getting a bad reputation. It is not like so-called professional wrestling events, where the referee is so obviously part of the entertainment. We had to obtain justice for Fréchette, which amounted to the gold medal that she had earned but had lost because of improper conduct by the officials. I spoke to Samaranch and explained the situation. Typically, he washed his hands of it and said that the IOC would consider acting only if FINA (the diving IF) made a request to the IOC. Because this was a characteristic response from him, frankly I had not expected more. I told him that if we could not find some negotiated settlement, then I would help the Canadian Olympic Association present a case before the Court of Arbitration for Sport (CAS), involving both the IOC and FINA. He said he would be willing to try to convince FINA to act but would not do any more. I said that would be helpful, but that I wanted him to be on notice that the IOC would be involved in any proceedings before CAS, since it was the IOC that had awarded the medals and the Olympics were its event.

The Court of Arbitration for Sport was created in the early 1980s to provide an independent and specialized tribunal for the resolution of sports-related disputes. As sport has become more important in society, the number of disputes that arise has also increased. The great majority of these can be settled within the framework of sport, by having rules that are clear and mechanisms established by the sporting bodies to make sure that the parties have a chance to present their case to impartial arbiters for decision. The most difficult problems arose when these rules were not properly applied and the justice that should have been rendered was not. Suppose that an athlete was disqualified for a doping offense but had not been given a hearing. There would be no point in appealing to the organization that had already denied him justice. His only recourse would be to the ordinary courts, the last bastion in any country to ensure that rights are protected and enforced. The problem was that the ordinary courts had little experience and less knowledge of sport and their decisions were not always sound. The IOC decided to create an independent mechanism for resolving such matters by establishing the CAS, to which parties could agree to bring their disputes. A panel of experienced sport officials was created by the IOC, the IFs, the national Olympic committees (NOCs) and, importantly, by Olympic athletes as well, to act as arbitrators. CAS has developed a solid reputation and has been recognized as an arbitral body that is independent and whose decisions are accorded deference by other courts. Most IFs and NOCs now include recourse to CAS in their rules, as does the IOC. The existence of CAS will not prevent someone from taking things further and going to an ordinary court. But, unless CAS has breached some fundamental principle of natural justice, the ordinary court is very likely to say that the athlete has had a fair hearing and that it will not substitute its judgment for that of CAS.

An acceptable settlement is often much better than a good case. If we were to persuade FINA to act in the Fréchette debacle, we would have to help find a way that would allow FINA to acknowledge the injustice of the horrendous series of decisions that had been taken by it and its officials, while at the same time leaving it some face. The solution we decided upon was to seek the award of a second gold medal to Fréchette, but not to insist on withdrawing the gold medal awarded to Babb-Sprague. After all, it was not her fault that the officials had been playing their own little games. The American athlete had done her best and competed fairly, and it would be unnecessarily embarrassing for her to return a medal that she felt she was entitled to.

This strategy proved to be the key to our eventual success. After several months of work and negotiation, FINA agreed to submit a request to the IOC that a second medal be awarded. But this was only after we had threatened to reveal to the public, in excruciating detail, the conflict of interest and resolute denial of natural justice. The IOC acted as quickly as possible thereafter, and I was delighted to present the medal to Fréchette at a special ceremony in Montreal. Unfortunately, this was not until December 6, 1993, some sixteen months after she should have taken her place on the Olympic podium as an Olympic champion for all the world to see—a moment that was denied her because of the misconduct of officials who should have known better.

I described this to Jacques Rogge as the only possible solution to the Salt Lake City crisis. The Russian athletes had done nothing wrong. They had done the best they could in the competition and had seemed to sense—as athletes can—that on the big day, they had come up short. It was the ISU officials who had undermined the legitimacy of the result through their own conniving. The ISU had to be brought in and told to fix the problem. Rogge could give them the Fréchette solution as the best available in the circumstances, but they had to be told that the matter was to be resolved in hours, not months. A complicating factor was a well-meaning legal appeal that the Canadian team was in the process of organizing to contest the decision. My view was that this was playing right into the hands of the ISU, which would have been delighted to have the whole matter tied up in procedural red tape, to be resolved (against the appellants) at some later stage, well after the Games and out of the spotlight. Hence the pressure to do something at once that would cut across delaying tactics.

To his credit, Rogge did just that and, under enormous pressure, the ISU, belatedly, did the right thing. The ISU officials recommended to the IOC that it award a second set of gold medals to Salé and Pelletier, which the IOC was delighted to do. Apart from being the best solution to a situation of their own making, it was a decision almost universally applauded, except by officials of the countries involved, specifically Russia and France. I always thought that their petulantly expressed disapproval—including to Rogge, who voiced some palliative sympathy but did not change the result—was purposely designed as a diversion to draw attention away from their own tawdry conduct. I never sensed that the Russian athletes, pawns on the other side of the devious bargain, were at all unhappy with the award of the second medals.

The ISU later suspended Le Gougne, the French judge, and Didier Gailhaguet, the president of the French skating federation, for four years, a period that will include the next Winter Olympics in Turin in 2006. The French skating federation has nevertheless re-elected Gailhaguet as president, even following this suspension. That, I suppose, speaks volumes about the prevailing attitudes in the sport. Le Gougne has variously recanted her allegations and tried to explain her conduct, but has not been taken too seriously. Her evidence at the time of the Games was too damaging. Because the deals were all made covertly, those of us on the outside can never be entirely certain what the trade-off would have been for the French, but one of the consistent suspicions was that votes for the Russians in the pairs would be offset by votes for the French in the ice dancing.

• • •

In the days of the cold war, many of the same tensions that marked politics carried over to sport. Some observers likened the Olympics to a substitute for war. I was constantly furious that the media tried to turn this observation into an argument that the Olympics were, somehow, less than they should be and that they were, accordingly, an international failure. My response to this was that it sounded as if the media would prefer war so that young men and women could be sent to be killed and ordinary people could become casualties of civilian bombing. If sport did nothing else but act as a substitute for war, that, in my books, was an overwhelmingly powerful argument in its favor.

However, the political polarization did have an influence on some sports. Gymnastics is a perfect example. The former Soviet regime had a virtual stranglehold on the international gymnastics federation, the FIG. In addition, the Eastern European countries had more of a tradition in the sport than the Western countries, so it was not completely unnatural for them to be more active in the FIG. Apart from the Japanese, the Eastern bloc countries were dominant in the sport and controlled almost all aspects of it, including the management of the FIG itself and decisions about how the scoring would be determined.

This resulted in a bizarre occurrence during the 1976 Olympics in Montreal: the awarding of a 10—a perfect mark—to a gymnast. The background to this was unusual. The Montreal Organizing Committee for the Games was preparing the venue for the Olympic gymnastics events, which were to be held in the famous Montreal Forum, then home of the legendary Montreal Canadiens ice hockey club. All technical arrangements for each Olympic sport must be approved by the IF governing that sport. So the Montreal Organizing Committee was in constant contact with the FIG regarding the Olympic competitions. One of the questions related to the electronic scoreboards that would be placed throughout the gymnastics venue so that spectators could see the marks as they were awarded. Montreal asked how many digits should be included on the scoreboards. Marks in gymnastics are given in hundredths, so there obviously had to be two places to the right of the decimal point. Did the FIG want to have two digits to the left as well? No, that would not be necessary. Montreal said that it did not matter to them, and that it would be no more expensive for them to get scoreboards that would show a 10. The FIG said it never gave a perfect mark; that would imply that the routine could never be improved upon, which it would never admit. Montreal asked again if the FIG was sure. The FIG was sure and instructed Montreal not to have scoreboards that could show a 10. So, the scoreboards with only three digits were installed.

The Soviets had a strong team in gymnastics, but they had not taken into account the appearance of a new phenomenon within the gymnastics world. In Romania, there were two female gymnasts who were beginning to show signs that they would dominate the individual events: Nadia Comaneci and Teodora Ungureanu (later to be supplanted by Ecaterina Szabo). By the time of the Games, it had become clear that they would likely eclipse the Soviet star of the Munich Games, the elfin Olga Korbut. Indeed, their performances might well be strong enough for the Romanians to win the team competition, even though they did not have quite the same depth as the Soviet team. To the Soviets, this was unthinkable. Fortunately for the Soviets, their bloc had effective control of the FIG, and they were able to devise a strategy to avoid the embarrassment of losing the team event without overtly unfair marking of the Romanian gymnasts or patently obvious over-scoring of the Soviets.

In all judgment sports, where marks are a combination of technical components and artistic presentation, a baseline mark is established early in the competition using the results of the competitors recognized as the weakest. All of the subsequent, and better, competitors are then marked higher. The Soviet bloc agreed that it would start the marking of athletes at the bottom of the competition slightly higher than normal. By the time the best athletes were competing, the marks were well over 9 and the Soviets were in the high 9s. When it came to the uneven parallel bars, there was no alternative to show the obvious difference between the Soviets and Comaneci but to give her a 10, even though the difference in performance was greater than the difference in the marks. But, of course, they could go no higher and could hardly be publicly faulted for not giving her more than a perfect mark.

I was present, as secretary of the Canadian Olympic Association, when the mark was awarded, and I remember thinking (not then knowing the background) that the Montreal organizers must seem inept because the 10 had to appear on the scoreboards as 1.00. It took the crowd a few seconds to understand what they were really seeing, before they went wild with excitement. However, the Soviet strategy was effective in the end, where half the marks from the individual events were carried forward into the team competition: the Soviet team came first with 466 total points to the Romanian silver medal total of 462.35. The Soviets had managed to tweak the results just enough to be sure they won the event. Comaneci, of course, won the individual all-round competition.

• • •

Many of the other sports in which judging is so critical have had their problems, but their leaders seem to have come to an understanding that good judging makes for better sport, not worse. One notable exception remains boxing, in which the Association Internationale de Boxe

Amateur (AIBA) has resolutely been unwilling to control its officials. Part of the problem was in the selection of the officials, who were not necessarily the best, but who were given the Olympic assignment as a reward for long service in the sport. They were often so old that their vision and reflexes were not good enough to make the many instant judgments required in a fast-moving sport. Knockouts are rare in Olympic boxing, due to the headgear, size of gloves and the fact that the bouts are only three rounds. That is why a prearranged result could be achieved by collusion among the judges.

Probably the most flagrant example of this occurred during the 1988 Seoul Olympics where, in the light middleweight class, Roy Jones Jr. of the United States was deprived of a win in favor of a Korean boxer, Park Si-hun, who had clearly been outclassed. Later, after the dismantling of the Berlin Wall, evidence emerged from the records of the East German secret police (Stazi) that bribes had been paid to boxing judges. They certainly had not been paid to ensure that the American would win. The jury of appeal established by the IF for each major competition routinely upheld the judges officiating at the bout, so the injustice became a matter of Olympic history. The outrage was so thoroughly felt that even the IF responded with a gesture that it thought would calm the waters, but that in fact simply demonstrated how corrupt the judging had been and how impotent the leadership of the sport was in dealing with the corruption. The AIBA named Jones the best boxer in the Olympic tournament and presented him with an award! Boxing was incompetent as well as corrupt.

Much lip service is paid by the boxing IF to the need for improvement in judging, but no discernible progress is being made. Real change will require a thorough commitment from the entire federation and its leadership to eradicate the corruption and to use officials that are capable and impartial. A new method of scoring has recently been implemented. Boxing leaders, thick as their skin may be, eventually came to the conclusion that some change would have to be implemented and, after years of cautious experimentation, moved toward a new system. Each judge now has an electronic touch pad and must register each landed blow within a second or two. However, no significant improvement has resulted from this. Incompetence and bias can confound any judging system and, as anyone knows, the cyber-world adage "garbage in, garbage out" is as current as ever.

The inclusion of boxing on the Olympic program has always been problematic, mainly due to concern about the serious brain injuries that can result from blows to the heads of the athletes. It is probably still on the program because it is a sport that many small and developing countries practice and the universality of the Olympics is one of the main objectives of the Olympic movement. I think the health and safety aspects have, more or less, been dealt with and that the risks are within reasonable bounds. The real problem now is integrity.

My solution would be to remove boxing from the Olympic program until it can demonstrate that its officials have solved the problem of biased judging. The sport is another that has shown its judges to be less concerned with fairness than they are with their own interests. And the sport's leaders seem dedicated mainly to staying in power rather than dealing with the problems that everyone in the world, save the boxing supremos, recognizes.

*   *   *

Every sport must remain vigilant about its officiating. That includes the anchor sport of the Olympic Games, athletics (track and field). Officials in that sport have been guilty of manipulating results, including the outrageous alteration of the results of the long jump competition at the 1987 World Championships in Rome, so that an Italian jumper, Giovanni Evangelisti, would be awarded a bronze medal. Italian officials had deliberately mismeasured his result by more than half a meter; an alert journalist, who knew instinctively that the jump was not as long as the recorded result, ferreted out the truth and exposed the means of faking the result.

I had an interesting occasion to see somewhat the same activity during the track and field events at Seoul in 1988. Coincidentally enough, it involved Ben Johnson, during the semifinal of the 100 meters, when I had no idea of the role that I would be called upon to play in connection with his testing positive for drugs after the final. My wife, Julie, and I had climbed up to the top row of the Olympic stadium to join my Canadian colleague, Jim Worrall, and his wife, Birgitte. We wanted to get a different perspective on the events from the normal IOC section of the stands.

The semifinal was called and Johnson was in the first heat. His arch-rival, Carl Lewis, was in the second. The runners got into the blocks; the starting gun was fired and off they went, only to be called back by a second shot, indicating a false start. It had been called against Johnson. I had said, at once, that there was no false start. The starter had simply not believed how quickly Johnson had started and, I surmised, had second-guessed the mechanical device that would normally have signaled a false start. The starting blocks contain pressure plates; if there is an increase in pressure that indicates a runner has reacted before the firing of the starting gun, a signal is given through the earphones worn by the starter, who then indicates that a false start has occurred. Apart from lightning-like reflexes, Johnson had a very unusual starting method. Where most sprinters emerge from the blocks low and essentially off balance, Johnson appeared first almost to stand up and then to run forward. This gave him a very fast start, and he would almost always maintain that lead throughout a race.

The buildup to the 100 meters had been highly publicized and the battle lines drawn in both the media and the respective athletes' camps. There was no love lost between the two main protagonists. Johnson had beaten Lewis the previous year at the World Championships, setting a world record of 9.83 seconds in the process, and Lewis, the 1984 Olympic champion (Johnson had been third), was looking to defend his Olympic title. They had worked their way through the preliminary rounds of the event and were now getting to where things really mattered. The first four in each semifinal would move on to the final.

I said to Julie that it looked to me as though the officials were trying to take Johnson's start, his best feature, away from him, which would give an advantage to Lewis, who usually finished more strongly than the others. "What are you going to do about it?" she countered. "What am *I* going to do about it? What can I do about it?" "Go and talk to them," she said, pointing down to the international federation officials at the track level, all decked out in their official blazers. "I can't go down there," I said. She gave me an elbow under the heart that would have felled an ox and repeated, "Go down there and do something." So, rather than risk cardiac arrest, down I went, without much expectation that anything could be done, especially since the event had, by now, already been run and Johnson had qualified for the final.

Fortunately, I knew some of the on-duty officials from the IAAF, the international track and field federation. (At the time, the full name was the International Amateur Athletic Federation, but with the increasing professionalism in the sport, it is now the same initials but the International Association of Athletics Federations.) Arthur Takacs, for example, had been involved in the organization of the Montreal Games in 1976. He was on the IAAF executive and was also a technical official at the Seoul Games. Samaranch had hired him as a general technical expert on matters Olympic to consult for the IOC. There was no doubt that Takacs had a great wealth of information on sport. However, I always thought it was more likely that Samaranch had wanted someone on his own payroll inside the tent of his arch-nuisance, Primo Nebiolo—the IAAF president from 1981 until his death in 1999—who could report on Nebiolo's endless fulminations and machinations.

When I reached the track level, my IOC vice-presidential accreditation enabled me to get into the restricted area. I did not think there was much point in beating around the bush, especially when I was about to take issue with a technical decision the IAAF had made, so I opened the conversation by saying, "Arthur, this is not fair. You are taking away the start from Johnson to give Lewis an advantage in the final." He asked me what I meant. I said, "You know and I know that there was no false start in the semifinal. Your starter overrode his electronic monitors. You are trying to make sure that Johnson does not get his best start." "No, no," he said, "that is not possible. These matters are recorded electronically and the starters do not exercise any judgment like that." "Fine," I said, "show me the tape (the printed record of the start and the pressures on each starting block) and, if it confirms what you say, I will go away happy."

He went off and was gone for several minutes. When he came back, he did not have the tape with him. It had been inconclusive, he said. That was all I needed to confirm my suspicions. I said that I hoped something like this would not happen in the final, or I would make sure that the tape of the semis and the finals would be requested for examination. I was never able to conclude whether this was a deliberate attempt to determine the outcome of the race or merely incompetence, but the effect was the same. I seemed to have made my point. The start in the final was fair and Johnson enjoyed, however briefly, his stunning victory and a new world record of 9.79 (even though he eased up at the end of the race) before the revelation of his positive test for steroids that brought his world crashing down upon him.

●   ●   ●

Transparency is a concept that is currently popular. It is a useful notion, provided that it does not degenerate into mere mantra. I do believe that transparency should apply to judging in sport. All sports officials should be willing to take personal responsibility for their judgment when acting as judges or referees, just as every athlete does in the course of participation. If the officials' conduct proves to be incompetent or biased, each sport must have a mechanism to ensure that the offending individuals are removed from the competition. In addition, the officials should not be allowed to be anonymous. Their actions should be open to scrutiny by the players and public alike.

Following the judging scandal in Salt Lake City, the ISU moved—it says boldly—to adopt a new scoring system designed to avoid any duplication of that flawed competition. But, instead of increased accountability for the judges, the ISU has apparently decided that its judges are so compromised by the internal politics of the sport that the only way a "fair" result can be obtained for the athletes is if the judges are anonymous. So they will have larger judging panels, growing from nine or eleven, and they will drop the two highs and lows. Not all scores will be counted and no judge will know whether his or her score will be taken into account in the eventual mark for the competitor. That way, they say, they can judge fairly, without anyone knowing who gave what mark. So there will be no possibility of recrimination. What a sorry admission of the depths to which the sport has sunk and its unwillingness to clean up its own mess.

There are serious consequences for sport if the public loses confidence in the integrity of sports officials. It's completely demoralizing to see years of diligent effort and preparation trivialized—indeed, made all but meaningless—by judges or referees who make decisions on the basis of personal agendas, advancement within the committee structure of the sport, or chauvinism. Imagine the parents of an eight-year-old child who is thinking about starting figure skating. Imagine them watching what happened in Salt Lake City. They know the years of training and sacrifice that lie ahead for their daughter or son. They have seen what happened to others who followed the same path. Are they now likely to suggest some other sport—or, even worse for sport, some other activity instead—to spare their child from having his or her dreams shattered, not because of failure to achieve the performance for which the child trained, but because of something entirely unrelated to their own efforts? I bet there are parents right now who are wondering about precisely that. I cannot blame them.

This creates a new challenge for all sports officials and the governance of sport. The officials have to commit to the real principles underlying all sport, and they have to be uncompromising in the application of those principles. Officials are responsible for developing their aspect of the sport, encouraging participation, training competent judges and referees, organizing fair competitions and ensuring impartial application of the rules. Sports must convince the public that not only do they subscribe to these principles, but they will practice what they preach. Just as in society in general, they must detect those who cheat and sanction them. No one is forced to take part in sport. But anyone who docs must accept the governing rules. Anyone who doesn't should be kicked out. There is no middle ground. Athletes who compete in accordance with the rules—and that is the vast majority—must be protected against cheaters. And I do not just mean cheaters on the field of play. I mean the officials who purport to govern the sport. The rules are not to be applied to make it easy or excusable for cheaters to prosper. It is as simple as that.

03 Performance Cheats: Doping

It was September 1988 at the Seoul Olympics. Julie and I made our way to Juan Antonio Samaranch's presidential suite at the Shilla Hotel, where we were entertaining members of the Coca-Cola board of directors. I had to be there as the chair of our marketing efforts, and Coca-Cola was one of our most enthusiastic supporters. We arrived, just on time, and were met by a clearly agitated Samaranch. "Have you heard the news?" he asked. "What news?" I replied. "Is terrible," he continued. "What is it?" I said. "Has someone died?" "Is worse," he said. "For God's sake, what is it?" I asked again. He took me into his bedroom and closed the door. "Ben Johnson," he said. "He has tested positive." Only the day before, Johnson had run the most exciting 100-meter final in history, winning in an astonishing 9.79 seconds, well ahead of his fellow competitors. The analysis of the backup "B" urine sample was now under way and the International Olympic Committee's Medical Commission would meet that evening to deal with the matter. It was, or so it seemed at the time, a very long lunch, especially with many of the American Coca-Cola directors and their spouses congratulating us on Johnson's win and several of them saying how happy they were that our Canadian had beaten Lewis, who was not well liked. We smiled and thanked them, while dying inside, and could hardly wait to escape.

As soon as we got back to my room, I called Carol Anne Letheren, the Canadian *chef de mission*. She, along with Johnson's coach, Charlie Francis, and other team officials, left the team headquarters in the Olympic Village immediately to come to my room. A notice had been slipped under Letheren's door late the previous evening, advising of the positive result of the "A" sample, stating that the "B" sample would be analyzed that morning and inviting Johnson or his representatives to be present during the process. This had now begun and the Canadian team had someone on hand to observe. "What was the substance?" I asked. No one was sure, but it was apparently an anabolic steroid; some unofficial indication had been given that it might be stanozolol. "Charlie," I asked the coach. "Is he on anything?" The reply was less than comforting. "Stanozolol? Stanozolol? I would never give anyone stanozolol on race day. It tightens them up. I want my runners loose." Hardly reassuring! It may have been an indication that there had been a lack of communication between the members of the Johnson entourage. Johnson's doctor, Jamie Astaphan, later to be stripped of his medical credentials in Canada, may not have been fully in the loop.

"Well, then," I asked, "what is our position on this? Do we challenge the scientific results of the test?" That was a non-starter. The IOC-accredited laboratories were first-rate, and if they found something, it was a virtual certainty that the substance was both present and properly identified.

"What about the sample-taking process?" I asked. There was no comfort there. Johnson and his two accompanying personnel had signed the forms that indicated they were satisfied with the process. "You are not giving me any bullets to shoot," I said. "How do you account for the presence of the steroid in his system?" The theories began flying thick and fast: Johnson had been given a spiked drink at some reception he attended a few days before the event. Alternatively, it was hypothesized that something had been put in his drink between the time he stripped off his sweat suit at the beginning of the race and the time he got everything back at the end of the race. The gear would have been out of his possession for a maximum of, perhaps, twenty minutes. The other theory was that he had been given something while he was waiting to produce a sample, which had taken an hour or more after the race, during the time he was in the doping control station.

I was appropriately skeptical of these far-fetched theories, but, for lack of anything better, they had to be explored. Another theory was that an unidentified person in the doping control station had given Johnson a spiked drink, but there had been a security officer present and there was even disagreement on the description of the mysterious spiker. My view was that the scenario was so unlikely that it barely warranted consideration, and I told the delegation that there was very little chance that this explanation would be successful.

I also said I wanted to talk with Johnson himself before I would be ready to accompany them to the meeting of the IOC Medical Commission. The athletics team leader called the Olympic Village and arranged for Johnson to be brought to the hotel. Julie went to the lobby to meet him and shielded him from the media as he made his way to the elevator. She put him in the corner of the elevator and was tall enough to keep him almost hidden. Once he had reached the room, I took Johnson through to the bathroom, the only private space available, and asked him personally if he was on anything. He said he was not and did not know what was going on. I said that I could not go before the IOC Medical Commission and represent him if I knew he was guilty. He assured me he was not. I told him that things did not look good. Doping was a strict liability offense, meaning that he was responsible for ensuring that he did not ingest any prohibited substance. It was no defense to say that the steroid was taken unknowingly.

There was a dinner for the IOC executive board that evening before the IOC Medical Commission meeting. I told Samaranch that the Canadian delegation had asked me to represent Johnson at the meeting and that I had agreed to do so. He said to me, "Be careful. This is very dangerous. You have to be careful of your reputation." I told him I understood that, but the athlete had no one else to speak for him in such an environment and I thought he was entitled to the best defense available in the circumstances. Too often, I said, athletes were subjected to administrative proceedings in which they had no experience and it was not always clear that their interests were properly represented. If the hearing was properly conducted and Johnson had every opportunity to raise everything relevant to his defense, I would be satisfied with whatever the outcome might be.

It came as no great surprise that the IOC Medical Commission recommended disqualification of Johnson. I appeared with the delegation and put forward the arguments that had been devised. The commission listened to the arguments. The end became all too apparent when Manfred Donike, the head of the doping sub-commission, asked me if I would be interested in the "scientific results of the tests." Any lawyer with experience in court knows that such a question means you are about to be dead in the water. I said that I was not sure I would understand them (since I could not say I had no interest) but that our team medical officer might. Donike read off a series of figures and expressions that I did not understand. I turned to the team doctor and whispered, "What have we just heard?" He was as white as my shirt. He said that we had just heard that not only had Johnson tested positive for stanozolol, but that his results indicated that he was a longtime user.

There was, of course, no satisfactory response that we could make, and the results are history. The next morning, the IOC executive board accepted the recommendation of the medical commission, disqualified Johnson, requested the return of his medal, and Johnson left Seoul in disgrace. A day or so later, the gold medal went to another athlete: Carl Lewis, who had been disqualified for drug use at the U.S. Olympic trials in the 100 meters but exonerated by the U.S. Olympic Committee because his use of drugs was "inadvertent."

Perhaps someday, when the definitive history of doping in sport—and, I hope, its eradication—is written, the Ben Johnson disqualification will be one of the key dates. This was a definitive statement by the IOC that it would not cover up cheating, even by one of the leading athletes, who had set a world record in the premier event of the most important sport in the Olympic Games. Stanozolol was a prohibited substance; when it was used by the Olympic champion, he was stripped of that honor and disgraced for cheating. This drew attention, as never before, to the problem of drug use in sport. It did not, by any means, stop such use, but it served notice that the problem was far greater than sports officials had yet acknowledged.

• • •

To understand the problem of drug use in sport (referred to as "doping" in most of the world), you first have to understand something of the nature of competitive sport. Athletes are not satisfied with just doing their best in the competitions they enter. They want to win. They have deliberately placed themselves on the line, to be measured against other similarly motivated athletes. Each individual searches for the competitive edge that will increase the chances of winning. The tolerances in high performance have become marginal indeed, especially at the world level, so tenths, hundredths and even thousandths of seconds make the difference between finishing first or second or lower. The difference can also be measured in millimeters or grams.

The search for an edge has led to improvements in training and technique and better equipment. If there was one real problem in this search for a major advantage, it was that all these elements were available to all the other competitors, so the relative performances were not affected. Long before sport was organized to the degree it now is, athletes were experimenting with drugs that might improve performance. Drugs as dangerous as strychnine—which, if used in small, nonlethal doses, was a strong stimulant—were perceived as performance-enhancing. Thomas Hicks won the 1904 Olympic marathon with the help of doses of strychnine, brandy and raw egg. Dangerous as this practice may have been, there were no rules to prevent it, other than common sense and a perspective that sport was not important enough to die for.

When I was competing as a swimmer in the 1950s and 1960s, performance-enhancing drugs were not in widespread use, although by the time of the 1956 Olympics in Melbourne, it was common knowledge that U.S. track and field athletes had begun to experiment with testosterone. Soon, anabolic steroids such as Dianabol were developed. It is also clear now that the Soviets had used similar drugs for some time. Again, there was no rule to prevent such use, and athletes operated on the premise that what was not prohibited was permitted. This was quite proper in the legal sense if not the ethical one. Athletes were, therefore, free about telling their friends of their discoveries and so the use expanded.

By 1960, some concerns were being expressed within the IOC about the possible dangers to the health of the athletes using these substances. It was well known that stimulants, such as amphetamines, were widely used in cycling. The need to do something was underlined by the death of a Danish cyclist during the Rome Olympics that same year, the death being attributed at least in part to the use of stimulants. Momentum began to grow for a way to control such drugs and, by the time of the Grenoble Winter Olympics in 1968, the IOC had formed a medical commission for that purpose and had commenced drug testing.

The commission was chaired by Prince Alexandre de Merode of Belgium. Merode was not a physician, and as such, was a neutral chair. I always thought that he did the best he could in difficult circumstances, while knowledge was slowly accumulated and drug use expanded. If he had a failing, it was an inability to convey a personal and urgent commitment to the fight against doping. Also, he did not get much serious help from any of the three IOC presidents during his active tenure in that position, other than the occasional speech. There was no money available within the IOC until well into the 1980s under Samaranch, and even then there were other, more demanding priorities. There was no concerted effort to accelerate the fight.

When the IOC Medical Commission began its work, it was very much an exploration of uncharted waters. There is no doubt that the initial concerns were related almost entirely to the health of the athletes. At least anecdotally, it appeared that some athletes were taking industrial quantities of the drugs and the side effects were not all known. As evidence of certain uses became available, various substances—such as stimulants, different anabolic steroids and beta blockers—were declared prohibited either absolutely or in quantities above stated thresholds. Since there was no therapeutic justification whatsoever for anabolic steroids, any presence was a doping offense.

The use of caffeine and other stimulants was not considered to be doping if the amounts were below certain limits. However, the circumstances were examined if the amounts exceeded the minimum, and doping tests were deemed positive if the amounts exceeded a stated higher limit. To say that the scientific basis of all the decisions to list certain substances and not others was sound would be a vast overstatement. Caffeine, for example, has been removed from the list, effective in 2004, as the scientific data regarding its use have developed. What the commission did was to begin the process that would have a profound effect on sport over the next thirty-five years, and which continues today.

Prohibiting the use of certain drugs had immediate consequences. In the first place, it drove almost all the research in the field of performance-enhancing drugs underground and did the same with respect to the use of such drugs by athletes. Second, it was all very well to prohibit the use of the drugs, but quite another matter to be able to prove that they had been used. If the IOC was going to take away an Olympic medal because of drug use, it had to be able to present scientifically reliable evidence that the drug had, in fact, been used. This has always been the main, but far from the only, shoal on which rapid progress in anti-doping has foundered. It was a classic game of catch-up. The authorities had first to discover what was being used, develop some sense of the danger involved, and then develop a test to identify whether or not it had, in fact, been used by a particular athlete. The first element was made more difficult by the clandestine use of the drug; the second was hard to determine because of a lack of medical evidence based on studies of athletes or the population at large; and the third required money to fund the necessary research.

One of the most difficult aspects of drug use in sport has been to get a grasp on what the nature of the problem is and how it should be defined. This has proved to be almost as difficult as finding the distinction between amateur and professional athletes, something that confounded the Olympic movement for decades. I suspect, looking back, that one of the fundamental mistakes made by the IOC in the doping field was to leave the leadership in the hands of scientists rather than generalists.

The issue should have been seen as a series of ethical considerations, combined with concern for the health of athletes, that would provide a framework for the anti-doping rules and their enforcement; instead, it became solely a scientific question that was eventually controlled by a small group of biochemists—those who made up the IOC Medical Commission and, later, those who sat on a sub-commission on doping and biochemical matters. Many of the members headed up laboratories with specialized expertise and they operated in a clubby manner, determining which labs would be accredited as official IOC laboratories, giving them an effective monopoly with respect to testing within the Olympic movement.

The prohibited substances and prohibited methods of performance enhancement were determined by the IOC Medical Commission, on the advice of the sub-commission. The list grew like Topsy, with no generally agreed-upon criteria for why a particular substance was included while another was not. Quite often the decision was merely a function of a particular research interest—such as beta-2 agonists and glucocortico steroids—of one of the members of the commission. The banned substances included stimulants, grew to include steroids, and expanded to other, more esoteric products such as growth hormones and diuretics.

Detection was achieved by testing urine samples, using a method of gas mass spectrometry that permitted quite reliable analysis of even minute quantities of a banned substance. When they were first added to the prohibited list, many of the substances could not be detected, and there was much discussion about whether they should be included. Some scientists were reluctant to add something that could not be detected, because they felt that this was little more than an invitation to use the substance and that not mentioning it might prevent wider use. Others thought that such products should nevertheless be named, to warn against their use, even if such use could not, at the time, be detected.

No one could agree on what definition of doping could be applied. From a scientific perspective, the mere presence of the substance in the body of an athlete constituted the offense. This had some resonance with those required to administer the system and created a concept of strict liability, which did not require any proof of intention to dope, and left the burden of explanation to the athlete, who had to demonstrate how the substance got there. Artificial substances, such as anabolic steroids, were relatively simple matters to deal with. It was another story with those substances that the body produced itself, in some quantities, as a natural process. For example, testosterone is a natural substance produced by the body in certain quantities. Here the problem became how to determine what might be natural (in which case, there could be no doping offense) and what might have been unnatural—additional quantities, added over and above the normal levels.

The scientists, in an effort to lean over backwards and not to be criticized by their peers, established essentially arbitrary levels or ratios. For example, it was decided that the T/E ratio, the ratio of testosterone to epitestosterone, would be set at 6 to 1, despite the fact that there was no empirical evidence of such a level ever being achieved naturally. Knuckles would be virtually dragging on the ground at that level, but at least there was felt to be no way to challenge such a ratio. Limits of this nature have allowed people to play with the ratio, keeping it below 6 to 1, but likely far greater than any natural process could ever produce. It is a simple matter to ingest testosterone and then check to see what ratio has been produced and to experiment right up to the limit. In today's sport, you do not need much of an advantage to win by a fraction of a second.

So everyone muddled along, with no clear view of exactly what they were talking about when it came to doping, and the scientists retained the controlling hand. They decided what might, or might not, be performance enhancing; what the limits, if any, would be; what the sanctions should be; who would do the testing; how the results would be reported; and how the list would be developed. It was a sincere effort, but depended solely on scientific measurement to determine whether or not there was doping. There was no consideration of the humanistic or ethical dimension. I think this lack of an ethical basis was responsible for the early attitude of decision-making bodies faced with the job of enforcing the rules. They seemed to look for every possible reason not to find that an offense had occurred. Because they had no background to explain, in sport terms, why athletes should not dope, they ended up seeming to protect the cheaters at the expense of the athletes who competed fairly.

● ● ●

From the time the IOC Medical Commission was established and testing began, enforcement of the rules was left with the sports organizations. The acknowledged leader was the IOC, with one or two international federations also being active in the field as well, including athletics, through the IAAF (which at the time stood for International Amateur Athletic Federation) and cycling, through the UCI (the International Cycling Union, known by its French acronym). Almost none of the federations had programs of "no-notice" out-of-competition testing. Most agreed—some, such as weightlifting, under considerable pressure, mainly from the IOC—to have testing at their major events, including world championships.

These in-competition tests were useful for only certain drugs, such as stimulants or beta blockers, that are taken at the time of competition. They were manifestly ineffective for drugs taken during training periods that, although no longer detectable in the athletes at the time of competition, nevertheless provided a residual benefit. It was obvious to anyone who thought about the problem for a moment that a serious gap was still available to cheaters and those who helped the cheaters, but few international federations did anything to fill that gap. The undeniable message was that they did not, obviously, care about the problem.

The amateur field has gotten no help over the years from professional sports. There are hundreds of professional leagues around the world in which sport is provided as entertainment. Those athletes are before the public almost daily and the media are provided with constant publicity material, not unlike the Hollywood hype machine. By comparison, amateur sports labor in obscurity. The athletes train for months and years and may be seen only once a year at world championships or every four years at the Olympics. The owners of professional teams are in business. They pay large amounts to their athletes and they want the athletes to be available for the full schedule. That is often very demanding, and in many cases, too demanding. In the final analysis, owners do not care what the athletes do, or have to do, to meet such demands. What is important is that they be on the field on game days. If they need drugs to do so, so be it. They have to play even when hurt, and if they need painkillers or other substances, then they are expected to take them. Even where there is professed support for drug-free sport, such as in baseball, the testing programs are illusory. If there is a positive test, the sanctions are minimal, perhaps a mere warning not to do it again; the owners do not want an expensive player to be suspended for a meaningful period of time. The message is all too clear and the amateur athletes are influenced by it.

Nor have the courts been of much assistance. In professional sports, remuneration depends on results. If athletes use prohibited drugs to improve their performances and thereby achieve better results than they might otherwise have enjoyed, they commit an economic crime, in addition to the sport offense. They steal, in effect, from their fellow competitors, whose own results are thereby lowered. There have been cases in the European labor courts, especially in Belgium, where athletes have argued successfully that, even though they have cheated and stolen from their fellow competitors, they have a right to work and cannot be denied this right. Stripped to its essentials, the argument put forward on behalf of such athletes is that, even though I have been unmasked as a cheater and have stolen money that should have gone to my competitors, you cannot deprive me of my right to earn a living. Not a very convincing argument, you say to yourself. Surely no court in the world would accept such drivel? Wrong. The courts upheld the athletes' right to work and overturned the sport sanctions.

I know more about the North American professional leagues than I do about others, so I will concentrate on them. Their anti-doping activities range from complete denial that there is any problem to policies that purport to be vigorously in favor of drug-free sport. As part of my activities as president of the World Anti-Doping Agency (WADA), I wrote to the commissioners of the principal leagues and organizations in the spring of 2003, asking them to consider adopting the new World Anti-Doping Code, which the World Conference on Doping in Sport had just unanimously approved in Copenhagen as the basis for the fight against doping in sport. The National Hockey League (NHL) refused to reply to my letters. The Professional Golfers' Association (PGA) Tour simply said that there was no problem of drug use in golf. The National Football League (NFL), the National Basketball Association (NBA) and Major League Baseball (MLB) replied, but said that they were completely satisfied with their own commitment to drug-free sport and that they had effective programs in place to ensure compliance with their rules. They would be willing to meet with us, but they also pointed out that such matters were a question of agreement between the leagues and the respective players' associations.

We should acknowledge a few preliminary facts. First, these organizations are for-profit businesses. Second, they are largely entertainment businesses. Third, there are large amounts of money at stake, for both the players and the owners. Finally, there are huge public relations strategies at play, in which the media and the public are fed highly sophisticated communications on almost a daily basis. The only issue arising from drug use that affects these businesses is off-the-field activities that may damage the image of the leagues, such as domestic or other violence, or the publicized usage of social or recreational drugs by the athletes. Daryl Strawberry's umpteenth visit to rehab to kick his cocaine habit does little to enhance the reputation of major-league baseball, especially in the eyes of a dad taking his son to the game and having to explain such extraordinary conduct in a supposed hero. That is where the bulk of the anti-doping thrust in these businesses is directed, not at performance enhancers. The line I often use with the media is where the father's at a game with his son, saying, "My boy, someday, if you fill your body with enough dangerous chemicals and lie convincingly enough about it, you may make it to the major leagues."

Take MLB, for example. A few years ago, St. Louis star Mark McGwire publicly admitted that he used andro, a steroid compound, to build up his strength, which he applied to hitting a record number of home runs. He said there was nothing in MLB's drug policy that prevented this, even though, had he been an Olympic athlete, he would have been summarily disqualified. I made several public comments to the effect that I could not understand how the national sport of the United States could reconcile its responsibility to the youth of the nation with a message like that. I was strongly criticized by MLB officials for drawing attention to such use and it was suggested that I should keep such opinions to myself.

What was the effect of McGwire's disclosure? By the next year, usage of andro had multiplied exponentially and was being taken by young athletes on an unprecedented basis. Even McGwire recognized the consequences and, to his credit, urged young people not to use it. MLB offered up the lame explanation that mere use of andro did not result in home runs, that much more was involved in hitting a fast-moving baseball out of the park than strength. That is true only in part. The fact of the matter is that a lot of the fly balls that would have stayed in the park a few years back were leaving it now, when players have forearms the size of my legs.

Under pressure from the U.S. Congress, following the death of a young player in 2003 that was linked to drug use, MLB reluctantly agreed to include more drug tests. But its proposed testing program was a joke. First of all, it warned the players that they were going to be tested. Then they limited tests to those for steroids, ignoring all the other drugs used. To make sure the results would not be too high, they did not test out of competition, but only in-competition. If a player tested positive, he would be retested, presumably once the drugs had cleared his system. If the second test proved to be negative, that would cancel the first test and the slate would be clean. This is worse than a joke. It is a travesty. It amounts to almost complete abandonment of responsibility with respect to the integrity of the sport—the national sport—and the health of the participating athletes. Moreover, it is an insult to the intelligence of the public.

The technique adopted of making drug testing and anti-doping policy a matter of collective bargaining between the leagues and the players' associations is, in my respectful view, designed to ensure that progress, if any, will be glacial. MLB is in a position to say that the sport will be governed by certain rules that are designed to enhance the sport, protect the health of players and serve as an example to all. No one is forced to play in MLB, but, if someone does, then he accepts such rules. There is nothing complicated about that. But, to make this a part of the struggle between labor and management—where it gets combined and confused with other issues—is to all but guarantee that progress will be difficult. The players bear their own responsibility here, as well. They should, if properly led and advised, be insisting on a clear and effective drug-control policy, which would include no-notice out-of-competition testing and meaningful sanctions against cheaters. They should be able to understand that this is in their own, and the game's, best interests as well. They too have abandoned their responsibilities in this misguided tug-of-war with the owners of Major League Baseball.

MLB is not alone in this approach. Although, to be fair, the NFL has made some improvements to its own policies, its program is far short of effective. Suspensions for drug use currently last for four games and there is talk within the players' association that this may be perceived as too serious. The message is all wrong. The NBA is much the same. The social drugs that may cause players to behave poorly off the field are the main targets of its drug policies.

Basketball, like ice hockey, is a sport in which athletes from the professional leagues are permitted to participate in the Olympics. Once a player indicates that he is willing to be considered for inclusion on his country's Olympic team, he becomes subject to the anti-doping rules applicable to all Olympic athletes. The problem, of course, is that until such an announcement, he is not and there is a genuine concern that he may have been able to benefit from the laxer rules of the NBA and carry forward some advantage over athletes who have been subjected to stricter rules. This is also the case with the Women's National Basketball Association (WNBA), and women are no less subject to the risks of performance-enhancing drugs than are men.

The day I received a reply to my letter to the PGA Tour, advising me that there was no drug problem in golf, there was a statement in the media by Nick Price, one of golf's leading players, to precisely the opposite effect. There was indeed a problem in golf that had been noted among the players. This detracts from the game that is known for its integrity and for the strictness of observance of the rules by the players themselves. If they say there is a drug use problem, then there is. The PGA Tour, and the related golf organizations around the world, should be taking active steps to ensure that golf does not degenerate into the lowest-common-denominator approach that has characterized other sports. Denial of a problem is the worst possible means of preventing it.

In January 2004, President George W. Bush incorporated a message against drug use in sport into his State of the Union Address. It was the first time that the issue had been elevated to that level of U.S. administrative attention. It happened partly as a result of the ridiculous response of the professional sports (especially baseball); partly as a result of constant criticism, including my own, of the lack of U.S. leadership in the fight against doping in sport. It was also partly because of the lack of commitment that the U.S. Olympic Committee and USA Track & Field (USATF), track's national governing body, have shown in the anti-doping battle, including the cases of shot putter C.J. Hunter and sprinter Jerome Young, who tested positive to doping before the Sydney Games.

The emergence of the designer drug THG (tetrahydrogestrinone) across professional and Olympic sports undoubtedly contributed to raising this issue at the presidential level. Some media have suggested that the presidential attention may have been attracted only to draw attention away from the Iraq initiative or that it might add to the 2004 presidential campaign. I don't much care what the motivation may have been, so long as there is serious follow-through. It seems to me that drug use affects far more American youth than the Iraq war and that this is a helpful presidential position on an issue that could have profound effect on generations of Americans.

Only weeks after the Bush speech, indictments were announced against two operators of a San Francisco laboratory that had been producing illegal steroids, and against a personal trainer and a coach accused of distributing the drugs. The indictments were noteworthy for two reasons, first because they were announced by the Attorney General of the United States, not some local district attorney in San Francisco, and second because the first indictments were directed at the suppliers of the drugs, not the athletes who used them, a message that the government views their role as at least as important as that of the drug users. The U.S. process is less than swift and the stakes are high, so expensive lawyers will be looking for every possible way, procedural and other, to delay the final determination of the proceedings. But the message has been delivered quite strongly—distribution of illegal drugs will lead to criminal prosecution.

• • •

Ironically, it was a statement by Samaranch in the context of cycling that would lead to a significant change in the Olympic movement's approach to doping in sport. Samaranch was equivocal, at best, on the subject; although he made the right public utterances, usually in speeches written for him by others, his own reactions were quite different. He always thought the IOC Medical Commission was dangerous. "These people," he would say, "all they live for is to find a positive sample." I would say to him that this was their job, but he was unmoved. He agreed with Primo Nebiolo, president of the IAAF—the athletics international federation, or IF—to hold off the announcement of a late positive test at the 1984 Los Angeles Olympics, so that the Games would not end with a bad image. The medical commission had received minimal cooperation from the Los Angeles Olympic Organizing Committee, and the records of several tests were removed from the IOC's storage place (the organizing committee refused to provide the IOC with a safe) immediately after the Games, before they could be acted upon. This led to the perception that the IOC was soft on drugs and that it did not want to find positive cases at the Games, but it was the L.A. organizing committee that had removed the evidence before it could be acted on by the IOC.

In 1988 in Seoul, Samaranch and Nebiolo pushed their way to the front of the line to make the presentation of the 100-meter gold medal to Ben Johnson, refusing to allow Jim Worrall, the senior IOC member in Canada, to present the medal to a Canadian winner. It was interesting to see their backpedaling after the disclosure of Johnson's positive test for stanozolol. The later medal presentation was made virtually in private, under the stands at the Olympic stadium.

The other aspect of the world perception of the IOC in relation to doping was that it had little remaining credibility, even with respect to the Olympic Games. The Los Angeles legacy, the rumor that the IOC had deliberately suppressed some known positive results, still persisted, and the more recent scandal of the Russian use of bromontan that was uncovered during the 1996 Games in Atlanta simply reinforced the idea that the IOC talked a lot but did nothing to ensure that its own Games were clean. When the Russians appealed the disqualifications, the defense put forward by the IOC was so weak as to invite the conclusion that it did not really want to win the appeals before the Court of Arbitration for Sport, or CAS.

Samaranch's attitude on doping would lead to a crisis that was still in the process of resolution when the Salt Lake City scandal broke. It came to a head during the 1998 Tour de France, when the French police discovered doping substances and equipment in the possession of one of the teams

(Festina) and began arresting team officials and athletes. Samaranch was watching this on television in his room at the Lausanne Palace Hotel, in the company of a reporter from one of the large Spanish daily newspapers who had been invited to share a day in the life of the IOC president. As he watched the television coverage, Samaranch said that prohibited drugs, whether performance enhancing or not, should be limited to those that were dangerous to health and that the current list was too long. The reporter could hardly believe his ears and, since the day was on the record, he published this revelation the next day. It immediately caused a huge furor and the suspicions about the IOC were revived and expanded, to the point that the organization was losing all its credibility in the fight against doping in sport. The issue would not go away, so, in August, Samaranch was forced to call an emergency meeting of the IOC executive board to try to find some way to diminish the tide of criticism directed against him and the IOC.

At my initiative, the IOC had been making some progress in creating a medical code, a document that had been referred to in the Olympic Charter for many years but did not really exist. It was, more accurately, the written musings of a succession of medical commissions and sub-commissions that would have been impossible for anyone to enforce properly. By 1996, the IOC was beginning to allow appeals from some of its decisions to the Court of Arbitration for Sport. I had been concerned that once the final decisions moved from the IOC Medical Commission to an independent arbiter, the IOC might well find itself without a legal basis for its actions, such as disqualification of athletes. Faced with the Tour de France problem, we agreed that we should concentrate on a code that addressed doping only and leave the broader medical questions to another time.

The mythical IOC Medical Code, therefore, became the very real IOC Anti-Doping Code and the focus narrowed. We decided that this code would be presented to the IFs in November 1998 and that they would be asked to adopt it into their own rules. The IOC code, although complete in most respects, was necessarily limited to application at the Olympic Games, and the IFs needed to adapt it to their own events. Having seen the cyclists being dragged off to jail during the Tour de France, their attention had at last been attracted to the fact that the same treatment might apply to them, so we had a greater receptivity than ever before.

My suggestion during the emergency executive board meeting was that the IOC should create an independent anti-doping agency that would not be controlled by the IOC, nor any other stakeholder within the Olympic movement. This would be the only way to defuse the suspicion and criticism directed at the IOC. We already had, I said, an example of the type of mechanism that was required, with the International Council of Arbitration for Sport, the governance structure for the CAS. The international council consisted of equal numbers of representatives from the IOC, the IFs, the national Olympic committees (NOCs) and athletes. No single stakeholder controlled it and there was no complaint that the CAS itself had any bias in favor of the IOC. The Swiss courts had already given official recognition to the CAS as an independent tribunal, to whose decisions the state courts would be willing to accord deference. We could do the same with respect to an independent anti-doping agency. This met with approval.

We decided that we should organize a World Conference on Doping in Sport in Lausanne the following February (1999), to which we would invite not only representatives of the Olympic movement, but also governments and international agencies involved in drug enforcement. In preparation for that event, we would get the IFs to commit to adoption of the IOC Anti-Doping Code, which would evolve into the Olympic Movement Anti-Doping Code to make it more inclusive and to give the IFs the impression that they were not signing on to something the IOC had imposed on them. I was responsible for the theme of the conference dealing with the independent anti-doping agency and chaired a working group that was to prepare the presentation for the conference.

The problem of doping was obviously somewhat more complex than the routine sport-related disputes referred to the CAS, since the stakeholders were necessarily more extensive than the four groups that made up the International Council for Arbitration for Sport (IOC, IFs, NOCs and the athletes). I envisioned two further groups that should be equally represented on the eventual governance structure: governments; and an assortment of sponsors, event organizers and the pharmaceutical industry. To make sure that participants understood the degree of commitment required for the fight against doping in sport, I indicated that an initial capital commitment of US$25 million would be required. That was the presentation I was to make in February 1999.

Little did we know what the Olympic landscape would look like at the time of the conference. It was held only seven or eight weeks after the Salt Lake City revelations had turned the Olympic world upside down, and right in the middle of a firestorm of intensely negative press heaped on the IOC generally and on Samaranch in particular. So much negative press was raining down on us that there was even some doubt that we should proceed with the conference, but the negative effects of abandoning it would have been far worse than going ahead, even knowing that most of the media attention would be focused not on our efforts to improve anti-doping efforts but on the many failings of the IOC.

That part was certainly true. Hardly a single speaker missed the chance to comment on the perfidy and corruption of the IOC and its general unworthiness. We had little alternative but to submit to the criticism and try to keep some attention on the problem at hand. Even in that regard we were widely criticized by governments and athletes as being insincere, while most of the IFs kept their heads down lest attention be drawn to the fact that, apart from the two weeks of the Olympic Games every four years, they exercise control over their sports and the athletes in them. There was some consensus on the idea of a two-year ban for first serious doping offenses. The principal objection was the possibility of civil courts overturning such sentences and thereby exposing the sports authorities to expensive lawsuits in courts that had little experience in such matters.

When the time came for me to explain the structure of the proposed international anti-doping agency, the government appetite for criticizing the IOC had not yet been sated. About forty governments were present, and they all declared the model to be completely unacceptable, unthinkable. They would not even consider participating unless they had at least 50 percent control. Perhaps because he had been so beaten down by the avalanche of negative press over Salt Lake City, Samaranch saw this as a disaster and a failure of the conference.

I said that it was just the opposite—in fact, it could not be better. What did I mean, he wanted to know. I said, "We already know that the Olympic movement is incapable of controlling the use of drugs in sport on its own. We do not have the legal or the financial means to do so and, frankly, there is little enthusiasm for the struggle itself among many of the IFs. If we bring the governments to the table as full partners, we will have all the necessary means at our disposal, and we can lay off half the costs of the initiative on them." This revived him somewhat and he sent me off to meet with the government representatives. The meeting was short. I said, "I understand that you have irreconcilable disagreements with the model I put forth." "Yes," they said. "You insist that you have 50 percent control?" I questioned. "We do," they answered. "You've got it," I replied. "What?" they exclaimed. "We agree," I said. They could hardly believe their ears.

Now there were two matters that we had to deal with. First, we had to negotiate the terms of the creation of the agency quickly, not with the usual speed of negotiations involving governments. We needed to be up and running before 2000, the year of the Sydney Games. This was an important enough issue to the Olympic movement, I told them, that we would go ahead on our own if they could not make this commitment and they would be left to explain to their publics why it was that they were unable to act on a matter to which they had been attaching such importance. They agreed to a fast track and, to their credit, did manage to get organized in time to permit the IOC to create the resulting organization, the World Anti-Doping Agency, by November of 1999.

The second was that, if governments were to insist on 50 percent of the control of the agency, they would have to assume 50 percent of the costs. After all, I said, we do not need you to tell us how to spend our money. This was, to no one's surprise, more difficult, as anyone who has tried to get money from governments will understand. Even though the amounts involved came to well under US$10 million per year, spread among two hundred governments, they asked if the IOC would carry all the expenses (their portion and our portion) for the first two years, so they would have time to get "organized." In the interests of having them on board, we agreed, naively thinking that they would actually use the period to get organized.

Samaranch's next problem was who would take charge of the World Anti-Doping Agency (WADA). At a meeting in Athens in September 1999, even while the structure of the WADA was still being finalized, he asked me to do it. I was still handling the marketing and television portfolio and had barely recovered from the stress of the Salt Lake City inquiry. I asked him, "Jesus, Juan Antonio, why me?" He said he could not appoint Merode, since the IOC Medical Commission chair's current credibility in the fight against doping in sport was non-existent and, if he were to appoint the vice-chair of the commission, Jacques Rogge, also from Belgium, "I will cause a civil war." So I said OK, I would do it, at least until it had been properly set up and was operating, and that is how I became the inaugural president of the WADA. Apart from the extra work it would involve, I was not all that unhappy, because I had long thought that doping in sport was the next big problem we would have to deal with and I had confidence in my ability to get the job done without compromising any of the issues that needed to be addressed. It was also of some comfort to know that the marketing and television matters were already under control until 2008.

•   •   •

The World Anti-Doping Agency is a unique organization. It is a private foundation that was created by the IOC under Swiss civil law. It is a separate legal entity and has what is called a foundation board that governs its affairs, not unlike a corporate board of directors. None of that is particularly exciting, but what is fundamentally different is its governance structure, which consists, as I had negotiated, of equal numbers of representatives named by the sports movement

74

and those named by governments. The Olympic movement is represented by four members that are named by the IOC; four Olympic athletes; a total of four representatives from the Olympic sports federations (three summer and one winter); four representatives from among the national Olympic committees; one representative of the General Association of International Sports Federations; and one from the International Paralympic Committee (yes, doping also exists among disabled athletes). The governments have divided their representatives on a continental basis, five from Europe, four from Asia, four from the Americas, three from Africa and two from Oceania. WADA's mission, as an independent agency, is to coordinate and monitor the fight against doping in sport on a worldwide basis.

With such a diverse membership and therefore differing levels of knowledge and expertise, the early stages of organization were complex. Among governments, there was considerable concern that WADA was just another emanation of the IOC and, for a considerable time following the conference in Lausanne, there was residual objection to the agency, which led to meetings among governments, ongoing criticism of the IOC and vocal doubts about the new organization that was to be created. There was even a meeting in Sydney in late November 1999 after WADA had been established.

Much of the opposition was by the United States, whose spokesperson was General Barry McCaffrey, director of the Office of National Drug Control Policy in the Executive Office of the President. He was vehemently opposed to the IOC, had made public statements outrageously critical of Samaranch as its president, and we had exchanged some sharp correspondence and combative comments through the media. Efforts to meet during the summer had been unsuccessful. So there I was, president of WADA, and one of the countries we most needed to be engaged in the fight against doping in sport was apparently totally opposed to the organization and, in all likelihood, to me.

There was no point in trying to avoid the problem, so it was finally arranged that I would go to Washington to meet McCaffrey on December 1, 1999. I was given a soup-and-sandwich lunch in the Wardroom of the White House and then we went to McCaffrey's office in the Old Executive Office Building across the street (it has since been renamed the Eisenhower Executive Office Building). I had the opportunity to see Richard Nixon's office there, since he apparently hated the White House, and was shown the door that had been bricked in behind his desk—so that no one could come in from the connected office—and the place where the infamous tape recordings were made.

When we got to McCaffrey's office, a dozen or more people were there and his staff had prepared a list of requirements that the United States insisted upon. There were about twenty items and we went through them one by one. Most of them were quite sensible and I was able to say either that we were already carrying them out or that we could do so. One or two were, I thought, impracticable, such as storing all collected urine samples forever, but I said that we could certainly study the possibilities of establishing a Fort Urine somewhere, including the possible scientific obstacles (how long the integrity of samples could be guaranteed), the legal problems arising from no statute of limitations, and the costs.

It did not take long to get to the end of the list. McCaffrey seemed surprised at the outcome and I said that when sensible people sat down to consider the issues in the fight against doping in sport, they were quite likely to have much the same lists and arrive at much the same conclusions. All in all, it had been a good meeting. McCaffrey said that there "might" be some media waiting downstairs. I said that no one knew I was in Washington, so that was somewhat surprising. His staff members suddenly took a great interest in the design of the office ceiling. "Well," I said, "how do you want to play this?" McCaffrey replied, "Why don't we go downstairs and you tell them what we have decided and I will agree with everything you say." So we did, I did and he did. From that time on, McCaffrey was a firm supporter of WADA and played an active role in the early organization of its activities. We got on very well personally and although I understand the politics of regime change(s) in the United States, I was very sad to see him go from his position as director of the Office of the National Drug Control Policy.

The biggest problem WADA has is collecting money. The understanding, from the very beginning, was that the annual budgets would be funded equally by governments and the Olympic movement. The IOC manages the Olympic movement portion, drawing from the television revenues for the Games. Governments agreed on a continental allocation for their portion (whereby Europe would pay 47.5 percent, the Americas 30 percent, Asia 20 percent, Oceania 2 percent and Africa 0.5 percent). Within each continent, the governments were to determine an appropriate allocation. Europe has done so, as has Oceania and Africa. Asia does not, for a variety of historical and political reasons, have an established intergovernmental mechanism, so Japan has been carrying an extra burden of the costs. The Americas have been slow to find a solution, with the result that Latin American countries other than Cuba have never paid anything.

One of the main objectives of WADA is to try to get a harmonized approach to doping, across all sports and in all countries. Each sport had its own anti-doping rules and there was no consistency of application. Some sports had lifetime bans for the first doping offense, while others had four-year penalties, some two years, and others a range of sanctions that might be as little as a warning. Governments had a range of legislation, from specific sports laws to general regulation of certain drugs and even—in some cases, especially in developing countries— no legislation at all. We developed the idea of establishing a World Anti-Doping Code that could be adopted by all sports authorities and be enacted by governments, so that sports and governments would all be reading off the same page. The idea was easy to conceive, but the practical diffi- culties of achieving the objective were awesome. The first step was to make sure that WADA itself supported the idea, since without encouragement from the stakeholders repre- sented on WADA, the idea would be stillborn.

With something as complex as the WADA Code, and the huge set of stakeholders, there was a very high risk that some might suggest we study the matter further. To short-circuit this possible tactic, we fixed a date for a World Conference on Doping in Sport in Copenhagen in early March 2003 for the purpose of considering and adopting the code. My role was to chair the conference, which involved a certain risk. If the conference were to be a success, it would have been as the result of the careful preparations. If it were to fail, it would be my fault. Still, it was worth the gamble, especially if we wanted to have a new code in place by the time of the 2004 Olympic Games in Athens.

The purpose of the conference was for all the parties to agree on the concept of the code and for them to commit to make it part of their own legislation or rules. We had a careful staging of the discussion and a show of solidarity for the participants, with the entire executive committee of WADA at the head table. We invited Jacques Rogge, Samaranch's successor as president of the IOC, to give one of the opening speeches, which he did, expressing strong support for doping-free sport and for the new code. He continued his support throughout the conference and was accompanied by the four IOC vice-presidents. He also made it clear that the IOC would be adopting the code at its forthcoming session in Prague.

François Carrard, the IOC director general, acted as secretary of the conference, keeping the participants on track and drafting the various resolutions. He had worked with me on the original Lausanne declaration following the 1999 world conference and had managed the negotiations with governments on behalf of the IOC that led to the constitution of WADA. There is no one in the world I would rather have had at my side in order to maximize our chances for success. Outside counsel Richard Young, an experienced sports lawyer from the United States, went over all the main areas, explaining things with endless patience and good cheer, in such a non-threatening manner that no one could take offense.

Apart from winning acceptance for the code as the basis for the fight against doping in sport, a major aim of the conference was to get the participants to approve a declaration that would later be signed by governments. It was important for government representatives at the conference to provide a morally binding declaration of their political will. It has been said that there are two things one should never be seen being made: sausages and legislation. Negotiating the terms of the documents was particularly challenging. While the objectives were clear, the non-WADA representatives on each drafting team seemed committed to incorporating as little substance as possible.

The conference resolution was reasonably simple, with the main challenge being to keep out of it matters that were restricted to governments only, while still making it clear that governments were part of the conference consensus. As to the declaration to be made by the participating governments, the government representatives wanted as many loopholes as possible, even though the ministers wanted to show commitment, and we were trying to make it as watertight as possible. Carrard was at his best in these situations, cajoling, scolding, chiding, and finding a way to move forward. Eventually we settled on the language and prepared copies of both documents to be distributed at the beginning of the final session.

The governments would, following the conference, determine the appropriate manner in which to agree among themselves as to how this could be accomplished. The mechanism chosen was to develop an international convention, under the umbrella of the United Nations Educational, Scientific, and Cultural Organization (UNESCO), that would be approved in 2005 and be effective in time for the Winter Games in Turin in 2006. While there was some grumbling on the part of the sports authorities as to why the governments needed the extra time, in the end they recognized that it is much more complicated for governments to enact legislation than it is for sports organizations to do the same thing.

I confess to having had little sympathy for any suggestion that the sports movement should not be required to act until governments had acted. After all, the whole point was to deal with doping in sport, which was the sports movement's primary responsibility, not the governments'. I felt the same about complaints that professional sports were not subject to the same rules and that amateur sports should not be required to act unless professional sports did the same.

Only two things remained for the final day. One was for the conference as a whole to agree with the terms of the resolution and declaration. Carrard read the documents to the conference. The governments had agreed on the terms of their declaration, which was their decision and not one that

Pierre Frédy, Baron de Coubertin, renovator of
the modern Olympic Games.

De Coubertin's early draft of the IOC rules.

Spyridon Louis, a twenty-four-year-old Greek shepherd, and winner of the marathon at the first modern Olympic Games in Athens, 1896. His gold medal was a highlight for the host country, which had originated and named this long-distance event.

Spyridon Louis meets Adolph Hitler at the 1936 Berlin Summer Games.

Jesse Owens, four-time gold medallist at the 1936 Berlin Summer Games, running the 200 meters.

The first Winter Olympic Games were held in 1924 in Chamonix, France.

The start of Dick Pound's illustrious Olympic career was as an athlete. Pound was a member of Canada's Olympic swim team and competed at the Summer Games in Rome in 1960.

At the 1960 Rome Games, Pound was a double Olympic finalist, finishing fourth in the 400 meter medley relay and sixth in the 100 meter freestyle. He went on to win four medals—a gold, a bronze, and two silvers—at the 1962 Commonwealth Games in Australia.

Roberto Andrei

The Canadian Olympic Swim Team, Rome 1960.
Front (left to right): Judy McHale, Sara Barber, Irene McDonald, Margaret Iwasaki, Mary Stewart.
Back (left to right): John Faulkner (coach), Steve Rabinovitch, Bob Wheaton, Dick Pound, Cameron Grout, Ernie Meissner, Dick Jack (manager).

Avery Brundage, IOC President (1952-1972), visits Canadian Olympic Association head-quarters in Montreal during Dick Pound's early years as COA Secretary, circa 1970.

Left to right: COA Executive Director, Lee Crowell; Avery Brundage; Patricia Ramage, COA skiing representative; Dick Pound, circa 1970.

The darkest chapter in Olympic history, the 1972 Munich Summer Olympics. In his final days as IOC President, Avery Brundage addresses the crowd at the memorial service for 11 members of the Israeli team who were taken hostage and killed by terrorists from the Black September organization during the Games.

Left to right: Lord Killanin, Dick Pound, and Berthold Beitz at an Executive Board Meeting in Lausanne, 1983. Lord Killanin succeeded Avery Brundage as IOC President in 1972.

Left to right: Jean-Claude Killy, Olympic champion and president of the Albertville Organizing Committee; Dick Pound; Josep Miquel Abad, CEO of the Barcelona Organizing Committee. The signing ceremony in Lausanne, circa 1988, that brought the IOC's official sponsorship program, The Olympic Program (TOP), into effect for the 1992 Games. TOP became the most successful international sports sponsorship program in history, with revenues of over $700 million for 2004.

had to be ratified by the conference, but if the sport representatives had not been satisfied by the level of government commitments, they might not approve the conference resolution, so both documents were carefully studied. There were a few minor suggestions that were incorporated into the final resolution. The second remaining item was that WADA had now to enact the code so that the other documents would refer to an actual document. We adjourned the conference for an hour while the WADA foundation board retired to consider the code. It was, predictably, not a long meeting and the code was adopted unanimously. Since it was an historic meeting and document, I had arranged for the preparation of copies that would later be bound and had signature pages for each of the board members and our senior staff to sign for posterity.

We then reconvened the conference to announce that the first World Anti-Doping Code in history had been adopted. Carrard read the amended resolution that incorporated the suggestions made earlier. Then I asked whether the conference was in favor of adopting the resolution. The customary fashion of indicating approval on such occasions was by applause, which was forthcoming. I then took my final risk of the conference. I asked if there was any person or organization that was opposed to the resolution. There had been some international federations—notably cycling and football—that had made many complaints about the code during the consultation process, and I did not want to have to deal with them later on the basis that they had not approved the resolution. I waited to see what the former complainers might say, but they did not indicate any opposition, so I declared that the resolution had been unanimously adopted. There was a signing ceremony and a photo op for the governments present that had authority to sign the declaration. After a brief closing ceremony, it was all behind us.

. . .

It may take years to measure the success of the Copenhagen conference. It was a remarkable achievement in many respects. In less than two years, WADA had managed to prepare an anti-doping code—one that will eventually be applied across all sports and all countries—that created a single list of prohibited substances and methods; a standard set of sanctions; standards of best practices; and a process for amending the list on an annual basis; and also put the resolution of any related disputes firmly in the hands of one body, the Court of Arbitration for Sport. It had managed a process that led to the acceptance of the code by the entire sports movement and participating governments. It confirmed WADA as the principal coordinating body in the fight against doping in sport and underlined its independence from any of the stakeholders. My own view was that if, before the conference, I had written on the back of an envelope everything I hoped to accomplish, I would have checked off every single item on the list.

Now we all need to continue to encourage sports bodies to adopt and, more importantly, apply the code. We have to find ways to coordinate testing activities so that an athlete is not tested five times in one week and then not for a year. This means we have to know where the athletes are located and will have to train IFs and their national federations and NOCs to provide the necessary information on their whereabouts. We will receive all results from accredited laboratories and follow up on the management of those results, so that we can account for every anomalous laboratory result and make sure that possible positive cases are not swept under the rug or that appropriate sanctions are imposed when there is a positive test.

As far as I was concerned within the Olympic movement, once the IOC adopted the code, the rest of the dominoes would fall almost as a matter of course. Implicit in the IOC's adoption was the fact that only sports that applied the code would be allowed to be or remain on the Olympic program. It would be almost impossible for a sport to say that it would no longer be part of the Olympics because it was not willing to endorse and apply a universally accepted anti-doping code. I was also certain that the IOC would adopt the code, not just because it was the right thing to do, but also because President Rogge was determined that it would do so. His support for the anti-doping agenda was the reason I had agreed to stay on as the head of WADA after the IOC presidential elections in 2001.

The code is now mandatory for the Olympic movement, but there has been no real uptake yet by professional sports. Recent developments in the United States such as the 2004 State of the Union address, the prosecutions, and the mounting public and political pressures on the professional leagues to address the problem in a meaningful way may change that, but our idea was that we should get the Olympic movement house in order before trying to tackle professional sports.

As a newly defeated candidate in the 2001 IOC presidential race, with strong and well-known opinions on most Olympic issues, I had thought the right thing was to resign from all my positions so that the new president would have a free hand in putting together his own team, which included the representatives of the IOC on WADA. I confess, in addition, to being acutely annoyed at finishing behind Un Yong Kim, who had been all but expelled from the IOC after an inquiry into inducements that were offered to and requested by IOC members by bidders for the 2002 Salt Lake City Games, and I had a temporary lack of enthusiasm for doing anything for an organization that had assessed our relative contributions accordingly. When Rogge kindly asked me if I would continue with WADA, I said I would only do so if he were 100 percent behind the fight against doping in sport. He said he was, so I carried on and he has been completely supportive ever since. We have occasional differences of opinion, such as whether the IOC should pay its share of contributions even if governments do not, and how far the IOC should go in pressuring governments to pay their contributions, but I appreciate that he is the president of the IOC and that I am the president of WADA and that we do have different mandates and different perspectives.

Part of my role with WADA is to raise the level of public perception of the importance of doping-free sport and the need to deal with those who cheat. That means I have to be in the face of anyone or any organization that is not fully committed to this. I can say things more directly than someone who has to try to balance other issues as well as doping and who has, therefore, to be more diplomatic or circumspect. I do not, for example, regard doping in sport as a matter of diplomacy. It is cheating. It may be dangerous cheating, depending on the substance or method involved. It is destructive of the essential ethical values in sport. It needs to be prevented and, if it cannot be prevented, then it must be detected and swift measures taken to ensure that the athletes and officials involved in such practices are removed from the sport. This does not require nuance. It requires firm and consistent action. There is more doping activity now than there would have been if the sports leaders in the 1970s, '80s and '90s had been less diplomatic and more proactive. I do not propose to add to that dubious diplomatic history.

I do not think it is any accident that U.S. President Bush included a statement in his 2004 State of the Union Address about the use of performance-enhancing drugs in sport. And I hope for two results: that it will serve as a call to genuine action within the United States, and that the U.S. leadership will encourage other countries to follow suit.

The THG scandal that has led to the criminal prosecutions in the United States is a sad demonstration of the lengths to which some are prepared to go in order to cheat. What happened here is that scientists, doctors, coaches and trainers, plus athletes with whom they were in contact, deliberately set out to develop, distribute and use a new performance-enhancing drug that would not be identified in the normal testing process. It is an approach that is completely antithetical to everything that sport stands for and involves sophisticated manipulation of molecules of known steroids. Cheating became a sordid business, entered into for profit on one side and corruption of sport on the other.

Discouraging as it may seem, we may also have to confront the possibility of genetic manipulation within sport. Scientists are now able to produce increased muscle mass in laboratory animals. The experiments have been designed to try to find cures for such disabling diseases as muscular dystrophy, by altering the genetic makeup of the muscle cells, and the prospects of better treatment of such conditions are quite exciting. But the same scientists acknowledge that a significant portion of the questions they receive about their work come from persons interested in the possible application of it for performance enhancement in sport. This, while it may be a few years in the future, is a very disturbing prospect for those who maintain a humanistic view of sport and it will require concerted action to make certain that the ethical and regulatory framework for gene transfer technology limits it to therapeutic applications and that tests be designed to identify any application that is nontherapeutic.

The sports movement let the use of drugs get out of hand by not acting quickly enough or firmly enough at the beginning. It must not make the same mistake with genetic manipulation.

One way or another, however, as long as I have any connection with WADA or the Olympic movement, my approach to cheaters will be that they may run, for a while, but they can no longer hide.

04 The Flame Flickers: Politics and Terror

The biggest worry for organizers of modern Olympic Games, including, in particular, Athens in 2004, is the threat of terrorism. It is a consuming challenge that occupies every waking moment—and probably many sleeping moments as well—of the hosts. They have to anticipate every form of attack, from within the country and from outside, devise a preventive mechanism and develop responses to any emergencies that may arise if the preventive measures fail. It is an awesome responsibility, especially in a world that faces increasing activities of this nature, and success is measured only by what does not happen.

Athens has been spending hundreds of millions of dollars to ensure that nothing goes wrong, and much Greek political capital will go into persuading other governments that it has the situation under control. All of its capital will then go into delivering on that promise. The Olympic perimeter will be the most heavily secured in Olympic history and every modern technique and equipment will be concentrated on the key sites. In favor of a successful outcome is the fact that it is much easier to protect a certain place for a certain time than to protect the world at large all the time. But no fortress is impregnable and no target absolutely safe, especially from persons who may not be concerned with later escape. So fingers will be crossed until the Games are over and everyone has got safely home.

In a perverse manner, becoming a target of boycotts or terrorists is a vindication of an institution's importance. If the Olympic Games were not considered as something to which attention could be drawn on a world scale, no one would bother with them. If they were not universal, no one would care who came and who stayed away—or why. There were many Israeli targets for Palestinian terrorists in 1972, but they picked the Munich Olympics and the Israeli team because they knew that they would attract attention all over the world.

•   •   •

From the outset, the Olympic Games were conceived as an event that should be separate from political considerations. They were to be contests between individuals, coming from different countries, but not competitions between countries. The founders had an instinctive recognition that states as such should not become involved in the new venture, even though they would be needed to create the infrastructure for sport and for the Games, whenever and wherever they were to be held. Pierre de Coubertin, in particular—reflecting France's constant fear of its larger, more aggressive, neighbor—would not have wanted his conception of the Games to descend into another forum in which Germany would triumph over France. The memories of the latest Franco-Prussian War were all too strong. Over time, the nationalistic aspects of the Games and the increased coverage of them by the media led to medal counts, country rankings, and even the declaration of winners of the Games, but the Olympic catechism regards the Games as a collection of individuals competing against other individuals.

Only five official Olympic Games of the modern era had been held before the First World War—Athens, Paris, St. Louis, London and Stockholm. They were generally uneventful and did not attract much political attention outside the host countries. No one was picketing or trying to use the Games for political purposes. It was clear that, by 1912 in Stockholm, the Games were likely to survive and that they were becoming recognized as an important sports festival. The interruption caused by the First World War proved not to be fatal. The 1916 Games planned for Berlin were canceled, but resumed at the first opportunity, in 1920, less than eighteen months after the end of hostilities.

These Games were held in Belgium's capital city, Antwerp, and the losers of the war—Germany, Austria, Bulgaria, Hungary and Turkey—were not invited. This was not a boycott as such, since it was not the idea of the losers to refuse to participate in order to draw attention to some complaint with the host country or the Games themselves. More interesting was the fact that in 1917, during the late stages of the war, the Russian Revolution had occurred and the shaky empire of the czar had collapsed into the Bolshevik Communist regime that would grow into the Union of Soviet Socialist Republics (USSR). Sport was considered too bourgeois for the Communists and they had no desire to participate in the Olympics. The attitude might have constituted a boycott, but the plain truth seems to be that they simply did not care for the idea of sport, nor, for that matter, much contact at all with the decadent West. It was a very inward-looking society.

By 1924 in Paris, the number of participating countries had reached forty-four and in Amsterdam in 1928, Germany was once again allowed to take part. Los Angeles was very far away from Europe and the effects of the Depression kept participation in 1932 low, despite a good organization and excellent performances by the athletes. Only a year earlier, blissfully unaware of what political turmoil lay ahead, the International Olympic Committee had chosen Berlin as the host city for 1936.

As Adolf Hitler and the Nazi party increased their hold on Germany, the persecution of Jewish people and others began to become apparent, and there were calls for a boycott of the Games. Most of the pressure for a boycott came from the sports community, often at the request of Jewish groups. In many countries, including the United States, the boycott question was hotly debated and spread to other groups. The U.S. decision to participate was made by the narrowest of margins and only because the votes of the executive of the Olympic committee were weighted to count for more than ordinary votes, like some voting shares in the stock market. The Olympic officials had convinced themselves that they could trust the promises that Germany would have Jewish athletes on their team. They were not the only leaders who were fooled by German promises made during the mid-1930s. Three years after the Berlin Games, the world was at war once again and the Games of 1940 (originally scheduled for Tokyo) and 1944 (scheduled for London) did not take place.

It fell to London to stage the Games in 1948, following the war; as if by custom, the losers, Germany and Japan, were excluded. Although the Soviet Union did not take part, some of the countries under its new postwar domination did, including Czechoslovakia, Finland, Hungary and Poland. It was at the Helsinki Games in 1952 that the Soviets propounded their unique sense of Olympic security. Their demand for heightened security was not due to concerns about external attacks on their teams so much as their fear that their athletes might wish to defect. Their idea of security was to keep their athletes in, rather than to keep others out. They insisted on a separate Olympic Village for their athletes. It was a paranoia that they would maintain throughout their Olympic involvement, although they were quickly weaned from their demands for a separate village. They insisted on having their own ship in the Montreal harbor during the 1976 Games and were in the process of demanding the same in Los Angeles before they decided to boycott.

Suspicion ran in both directions. It was widely believed that the ship in Montreal contained a sophisticated laboratory to monitor drug dosages for the Eastern bloc athletes; no inspections were permitted. The Soviets' security paranoia led to extremely close discipline in their areas of the Olympic villages, and their athletes were forbidden from interacting with other athletes. The constant presence of so-called minders, who were likely Soviet political officers, reinforced these edicts.

Boycotts began to become more fashionable by 1956, when two separate events occurred that were used as the basis for Olympic-related protest. The Suez Canal had been taken over by British, French and Israeli forces, which led Egypt, Lebanon and Iraq to withdraw from the Games. And after the Soviets invaded Hungary, three countries—the Netherlands, Spain and Switzerland—boycotted to protest the presence of the Soviet Union. Almost unnoticed was the withdrawal of the People's Republic of China at the last minute, protesting the presence of Taiwan. The Rome Games in 1960 carried forward the Chinese problem, and Taiwan (whose official name was the Republic of China) was forced to participate under the name of Formosa, which it did, but, at the opening ceremony, its team marched in behind a sign that said FORMOSA, behind which was another sign that said UNDER PROTEST.

Fortunately, a solution has been found for this problem and Taiwan's participation has now been settled.

●　　●　　●

Without doubt, the low point in twentieth-century Olympic history was the terrorist attack on the Israeli team at the Munich Olympics in 1972. The story has been well documented elsewhere, so I do not need to enter into all the details. At the time, I was the secretary of the Canadian Olympic Association (COA) and had been appointed assistant *chef de mission* of the Canadian team. Early in the morning of September 5, equestrian team manager Denis Whitaker announced that he was heading out for his usual morning run. Those on duty in the team headquarters in the Olympic Village took no particular notice until he returned moments later. That prompted some irreverent banter about the length of his workout. "No, no," he said. "There's some guy out there in the next building with a gun, telling everyone to get back inside."

Whitaker was a much-decorated war hero and not one to overreact, so this did attract the attention of staff members, who went to the windows to look where he had indicated. They could not tell much, but we knew that the Israeli Olympic team was in the building next to ours. Thus began our exposure to the darkest chapter in Olympic history.

Earlier that morning, terrorists of the Black September organization had scaled the fence surrounding the Olympic Village—not a difficult operation, since athletes out past their team curfews routinely crept back into the village by climbing over the fence—and had broken into the quarters of the Israeli team, taken hostages and killed one or two resisters. A siege had begun that would end that evening with the death of all the hostages and five of the terrorists during a failed rescue attempt at the Munich airport.

During the day, we had no real sense of what was going on, other than that the crisis involved the Israeli team and armed terrorists, who were holed up in their quarters. We were further hampered by the fact that all the broadcasts—radio and television—were in German, so we got whatever news there was filtered through interpreters of varying proficiency. Apart from that, as is the case in the midst of all crises, there is a plethora of wrong information, disinformation, rumor, repetition and speculation. The scheduled Olympic events went on during the day, despite the confusion, and we eventually learned that negotiations had resulted in an agreement that the terrorists, together with their hostages, would leave the village under safe escort and be transported to the airport, where plans had been made to fly them to some sanctuary.

The negotiations with the terrorists had been conducted in part by Walther Tröger, the mayor of the Olympic Village, who would eventually become one of my IOC colleagues. The talks were very difficult, not only because of the terrorists' demands but also because of the reluctance of the German authorities to negotiate, under any circumstances, with terrorists on German territory. There was the added legacy of the relationship between Germany and Jews and the city of Munich itself, where the most famous of the Nazi rallies had been held. We were in the dark and had no idea how things would turn out. When we heard, we were as shocked as everyone else. Virtually all the athletes were afraid that the old farts, as we irreverently referred to the IOC executive, would cancel the Games.

The Germans were faced with a real dilemma. They feared being seen as weak in the face of terrorism at a time when hostage taking was on the increase, led in part by the Baader-Meinhof Gang following their breakout from a Berlin prison in 1970. On the other hand, they did not want to do anything that might put Israeli hostages in even greater danger. It was only with the greatest of reluctance that the political authorities allowed negotiations to proceed; it was with even greater reluctance that they allowed arrangements to be made to fly the terrorists out of Germany. In the end, they authorized a tactical rescue operation at the airport, complete with sharpshooters. It failed, with the tragic results we all know. "They're gone. They're all gone." The anguished statement of ABC TV's Jim Mackay expressed both the horror and the futility of further words. Within the Olympic world, the shock was comparable to that to be experienced by the rest of the world on September 11, twenty-nine years later.

Everyone was stunned and devastated. This was not supposed to happen at the Olympic Games. There had been no Hollywood ending, with a Cinderella rescue. No one knew what the old and unpredictable men of the IOC would do. Israel wanted the Games canceled. The Germans wanted them to continue. There was overwhelming consensus among the athletes and team leaders that the Games should continue and that terrorism should not be permitted to achieve its goal of destroying something as important as this international gathering. To allow that to occur would only encourage similar behavior. We all waited anxiously to see what would be the outcome of the meeting.

I was asked to speak with the Canadian media, and expressed our shock but also the hope that the Games would be allowed to continue. I said we were, like everyone, shocked and saddened by what had happened and that we extended our deepest sympathy to those who had suffered and to those who had been killed. I thought the Games should go on, that the world could not allow itself to be brought to a standstill by terrorists and that I believed—and I did—that the Israeli athletes would have wanted the same thing. Finally the word came out. The Games would go on, but there would be a day of mourning and a memorial service at the Olympic Stadium in remembrance of the slain Israelis. It was a moving ceremony, marred only by IOC president Avery Brundage's completely inappropriate linkage of the massacre with the exclusion of Rhodesia (now Zimbabwe) from the Games because of its apartheid-like political regime.

Munich changed the landscape of Olympic security. What had previously been a comfortable exercise in control of movement and access to the athletes' village now became a deadly serious responsibility. Security forces in the tens of thousands, "mag-and-bag" searches, photo IDs, car checks, vetting of employees, and other such precautions are commonplace today. There seem to be many who can be persuaded by political and other leaders that the indiscriminate killing of civilians and themselves is a path to some imagined glory.

The Olympics remain an appetizing target, so great care must be taken to provide a secure environment. In 1976, Montreal had the first major responsibility to ensure that Brundage's prophecy that Munich would be the last Olympic Games was proven wrong, although the Austrians did a fine job in Innsbruck earlier in the year at the smaller Winter Games. The Montreal security was tight, but not oppressive, and the Games were celebrated with good humor and a sense of fun. Even the weather cooperated. The African boycott—linked to New Zealand rugby ties to apartheid South Africa—was more annoying than disruptive to those who attended the Montreal Games.

•   •   •

It is easier to provide a secure environment in closed societies or dictatorships. Juan Antonio Samaranch always said that, from this perspective, it was better for the Games to be held in such countries because we would have nothing to worry about. "Leesten, Deek," he said to me at one point, "for us, it is much better to go to these countries. There will never be security problems." This is a rather cynical view and it overlooks many of the disagreeable features of such countries. But, as it related to the preparations for the 1980 Games in Moscow, security was a matter that could safely be left to the Soviet hosts, and international Olympic officials could focus all their security worries on the Games that would follow in Los Angeles in 1984.

We ended up with more than our share of concerns about Moscow after the Soviet Union invaded Afghanistan in late December of 1979, barely six months before the Games. It will take many years to properly assess the strategic considerations that led the Soviets into their Afghanistan adventure. The country lies on the border of the Soviet Union, and the Islamic countries had always been a matter of great concern to the Soviets. Today's altered state of the former Soviet Union underlines the importance of the relationships and it comes as little surprise that many of the difficulties that Russia is now experiencing are centered in that part of the world, including, but by no means limited to, Chechnya. At the time, the Soviet-backed puppet ruler seemed to be on the verge of destabilizing the country. The Soviets did not hesitate to move in to prop up the regime, just as they had in central Europe, in Czechoslovakia and Hungary, when they felt their interests to be threatened. How a Soviet-occupied Afghanistan could conceivably be a matter of vital interest to the United States is also a matter historians may take years to unravel.

What did matter, however, was that a weak U.S. president, Jimmy Carter, had been taken by surprise with the

Soviet move. The U.S. intelligence of the day in that part of the world seems to have been no better than it is now. Carter was hurt that Soviet premier Leonid Brezhnev had lied to him about Afghanistan. It is worrying to think that the president of the United States in that era was surprised with anything that came from a government for which mendacity was a way of life.

Carter had been frustrated by the Iranian hostage scene in Tehran, unable to do anything to end the degrading captivity of Americans in their own embassy. He was running for re-election in 1980 and his marks for foreign policy were abysmal. He seized on the latest Soviet adventure as some kind of final crossing of the diplomatic Rubicon and, to bolster his electoral chances, decided on the "bold" policy initiative that the United States would boycott the Moscow Games that summer unless the Soviets were to get out of Afghanistan in thirty days. The demand itself showed precious little understanding of either Soviet foreign policy or military reality. The foreign-policy interests for the Soviets far outweighed the importance of the Games and it is far easier to get into a country such as Afghanistan than it is to get out in one piece.

Quite predictably, the Soviets ignored the demand that they leave. The United States set about trying to cause the Games to be canceled, postponed or moved. It used every bit of diplomatic muscle, sometimes not very diplomatically applied, to achieve this objective. The U.S. government had great difficulty in persuading its own Olympic committee, the USOC, to agree, and resorted to placing enormous pressure on its officers, members and athletes to force the USOC to bow to Carter's demand. Many other countries followed suit and the occasion was filled with much bitterness in a good number of them, including Britain, Australia and Canada. Through all of this, it was apparent that the political authorities of the world (including the United States) had no intention of going to war over the Soviet adventure. No one's vital interests were threatened. The Olympic boycott attracted a great deal of media attention and allowed politicians to sound firm and resolute, while doing nothing more than preventing their athletes from going to the Games.

To give some idea of the real political flavor, Canada cut down Aeroflot flights from four to three per week and canceled a ballet tour. At the same time, it sold more wheat to the Soviet Union in 1980 than ever before. Such was the ferocity of the response to the invasion of Afghanistan. When Canadian athletes dared to complain that the response seemed uneven, the agriculture minister of the day, Eugene Whelan, was heard to say, "Fuck the athletes. The farmers are more important."

In the United States, there were complaints from the business community that they would suffer from any further sanctions than the Olympic boycott. The USOC held out until Carter was forced to declare that the proposed boycott was a matter of national security, a characterization so far from the truth as to be laughable. In the end, the USOC decided that it had a patriotic duty to respect the wishes of the president, even though it disagreed with his actions. The whole exercise demonstrated to the Soviets that they were all but unhampered in any pre-emptive move they might wish to take in that part of the world, short, perhaps, of an outright oil grab in the Middle East. There would be harsh words and much blustering from the Western allies, but no action.

I was, at the time, president of Canada's National Olympic Committee, or NOC, and I said that the IOC should understand that the NOCs would be put under serious pressure by their governments and that while the IOC should definitely resist the U.S. pressure, it should understand that as a matter of practicality, many of the NOCs would not be able to run counter to the dictates of their governments. Sure enough, I was unable to persuade either our government or even our Olympic committee, whose national federations depended on government financial support, to vote in favor of participation. I could understand that our government would not want to offend the United States (unlike a later decision to avoid the intervention in Iraq) on an issue that seemed to matter to it, even though this fell well short of a national security issue. Even the government knew that the matter was less than really serious, as its own actions confirmed, and it was unwilling to resort to legislation to prevent participation. But Canadians have an ingrained view that what the government wants must be correct and it was a matter of huge personal disappointment to me that the COA voted, by an even greater margin than the USOC, to boycott the Games.

Our corporate community was more American in opposition to going to Moscow than even the U.S. business community. Members of our Olympic committee were outraged that I had spoken, as president, against a boycott. I had, in a moment of weakness, agreed to support the nomination of Denis Whitaker as *chef de mission* of the Canadian team in Moscow, following the death of the former Hungarian fencer Imre Szabo, the original choice. At the annual meeting of the COA, where the decision was taken, Whitaker came up to me after the meeting and said, "That was a great speech, Dick." I thought he was being serious, so I said, "Thanks, but I am afraid that it did not work out." I was wrong. He was furious. "You, you, criticized the government," he sputtered. I had. I had pointed out the fact that, apart from demanding a boycott of the Games in Moscow, the government had done nothing about the Soviet actions. "Of course I did," I replied, "and quite properly." "You are a disgrace," he said. "You should resign." It had been the end of a long struggle, in which I had managed to hold off the inevitable until the last minute, but had failed. "Denis," I said, "fuck off."

It was interesting that, after the Games and after people had had time to cool off, that many came to me and said that I had been right to oppose the boycott and that the position of the Canadian government, among others, had been totally hypocritical about the Olympic boycott. Even more annoying to me was that in Moscow on the eve of the Olympics I ran into some of the sport officials who had voted to keep our athletes from attending the Moscow Games. When I said that I was surprised to see them there, they replied, somewhat sheepishly, that they felt they had to be there to support their sports. My estimation for their sense of principle dropped to rock bottom.

I had had a personal problem with attending the Moscow Games. I was a member of the IOC, which had come out in strong support of continuing to hold the Games in Moscow. I agreed completely with that position. I was, however, the president of the Canadian Olympic Association, which had, more or less over my dead body, decided not to participate in the Games, largely as a result of the decision of the Canadian government. Canada was also in the process of running Calgary as a candidate for the 1988 Olympic Winter Games, which would be voted on the following year, and its chances would not be helped at all as a result of a boycott of the Moscow Games. I wrestled with this dilemma for weeks, before making my decision to attend the IOC session prior to the Games, but, since Canadian athletes had been prevented from participating in the Games, to leave Moscow after the IOC session and before the Games began. I could hardly bring myself to watch the Games on television, even as news items, since neither Canada nor the United States covered the Games as a sports event. NBC and CBC provided only minimal news coverage of the Games.

The Moscow boycott was as cynical a use of government power as I have ever experienced and did no credit to the leaders of many of the Western democracies. Nor, I should say, to the media of these countries, who jumped on the issue with all the self-restraint of a sailor on shore leave. It was a classic case of a triumph of form over substance. The sleight of hand had the desired effect of drawing attention away from the real issue of powerlessness in the face of the Soviets.

●　●　●

I have considered the matter of Olympic boycotts on many occasions. The political objective of a boycott—a concerted action directed against a target—is to inflict some damage on the intended target of the boycott. Olympic boycotts have precisely the opposite effect. It is as if the political leaders are saying to the target that they are willing to inflict punishment upon themselves, through innocent Olympic athletes, who will be denied the opportunity to participate, in order to punish the target country. So, in 1956, Spain punished its athletes to show the Soviet Union that it did not care for the invasion of Hungary. What did the Soviet Union care about such a stupid gesture? It was enraged about the Moscow boycott, partly because it did not under-stand why anyone would care about its protection of an obviously vital interest, and partly because the boycott ruined the coming-out party that everyone had hoped for in 1974 when the Games were awarded to Moscow. But it was also helped by the Olympic movement, which refused to mix politics with sport.

Moscow should be forever grateful for the IOC's resolve in the face of tremendous pressure from the most powerful country in the world. The IOC, rallying around the IFs and the NOCs, took on the United States and its many allies and stood up to the extraordinary efforts to destroy the Games, which included pressures that were almost unbearable on individual citizens in many countries, such as the United States, Britain, Australia and Canada.

The bottom line on Olympic boycotts is that the politicians who call for them do nothing more than eviscerate their own citizens, to no useful purpose. My view is that such boycotts are political failures; that the governments who order them appear inept; that ineptness is the most terrible political sin; and that no politician wishes to appear to be inept. That is why political boycotts of the Olympics do not work. They are an ineffective tool in this context and the proponents are shown to be ineffective. After Moscow, this lesson became increasingly apparent and the Soviet attempt to get revenge by boycotting the Los Angeles Games in 1984 was not successful, the minor boycott by Cuba and North Korea in 1988 even less so. By 1992, there was a sizable stake through the heart of political boycotts of Olympic events.

The Moscow Games were a joyless occasion, but they did take place and the Olympic movement showed surprising resilience in the face of massive political and media pressure. To some extent, it was fortunate that the next Games were Winter Games, in Sarajevo—if not fully within, at least close to the Soviet sphere. These were the last years before the horror was unleashed in Yugoslavia, but the Games were charming and a delight for the Yugoslavians. Brezhnev had died in November 1982 and been replaced by Yuri Andropov, former chief of the KGB. Relations regarding the Games in Los Angeles had thawed to the point that the senior IOC member in the Soviet Union, Konstantin Andrianov (who looked remarkably like Nikita Khrushchev), was, in early

1984, actually upbeat about the forthcoming Games in Los Angeles. Unfortunately, Andropov died in February during the Sarajevo Winter Games and was replaced by Konstantin Chernenko. That aging apparatchik was under the domination of Andrei Gromyko, who hated the United States and immediately set out to ensure that the Soviets would boycott Los Angeles, both on general principles and in retaliation for the U.S.-led Moscow boycott four years earlier.

The pretext was not, of course, any retaliation. That would be un-Olympic. No, once again, it was a matter of security. The Soviets were afraid their athletes might not be secure from attack in America. Granted, the largest collection of crazies in the world can be found in and around Los Angeles, but there was never a security risk of any credibility. The Soviets triumphantly held up a T-shirt that said KILL A SOVIET TODAY as evidence of such a plot. It was nonsense, of course, and was probably a shirt commissioned by them for propaganda purposes. The U.S. State Department did little to ease the situation and the collective rhetoric was full-scale cold war. Ronald Reagan was the president and Gromyko (nobody paid the slightest attention to Chernenko) the arch-enemy. There was no compromise in sight.

Samaranch became justifiably worried that the situation was headed for a showdown and convened meetings in Lausanne with the Soviet national Olympic committee, the Los Angeles Olympic Organizing Committee and the IOC executive board, to try to find a solution. The Soviet NOC president was Marat Gramov—another apparatchik, but younger than Chernenko—who had orders from the Kremlin and was not going to deviate from them one iota. I remember saying that I was so sure there was no security threat that affected the Soviet team that I and my family would be more than willing to live with the Soviet team in the Olympic Village. This got no reaction from Gramov, since it was never the real issue. But it did get one when I mentioned it to my wife—she almost killed me!

• • •

Artfully timed to coincide with the arrival of the Olympic flame in the United States on May 8, 1984, the Soviets announced that they would not be participating in Los Angeles. They also announced that this was a principled decision, applying only to the Soviet Union, and that they would, as faithful Olympic members, not be using any influence to persuade other countries to follow suit. Nothing could have been further from the truth. A battle then ensued to see how many countries they could recruit to join their boycott, and the Americans finally woke up to the fact that their Games could be seriously jeopardized and began to mount their own countercampaign.

The IOC, under Samaranch by this time, responded much quicker than it had four years earlier and used its own network in support of the Games. He had gone to Washington to visit Reagan, too late to cool some of the hard-line positions taken under his leadership, and, at the end of May, sought a meeting with Chernenko and the Soviet leadership. Having been Spanish ambassador in Moscow before becoming IOC president, he knew at once upon his arrival that his mission was doomed. He could tell, from the protocol level and the type of state-owned guest house to which he was assigned, that he would not be successful. He was not permitted to meet the real leaders and, when he reported to the IOC executive board in Paris in June (celebrating the ninetieth anniversary of the founding of the IOC), he said that he had failed.

There were, however, some bright spots. The Soviets were having much more trouble in rallying support for their boycott than they had expected. The pretext was transparent and barely credible. Many countries that had endured severe pressures to come to Moscow in support of the 1980 Games felt that they had done enough for the Soviet Union and that the Soviets were not playing fair with the Olympic movement, which had come to its rescue in that hour of need. The countries that had been forced to boycott in 1980 did not want to miss yet another Games. The Soviets were stung when Yugoslavia, host of the 1984 Winter Games, said it would attend Los Angeles, but they were really stunned when Romania, a formal member of the Warsaw Pact, announced its intention to participate.

The Soviets lost much international political face for being unable to hold their own political union in place. The People's Republic of China also broke the Communist solidarity by agreeing to participate. It was all too clear that none of the Soviet allies were happy about not being allowed to compete in Los Angeles, an attitude that was to become much more important four years later in relation to the Seoul Games.

If the Soviet Union sought to punish the Americans with its boycott of their Games, the results can only be assessed as a dismal failure of political policy. First, the Soviets were always difficult and truculent guests and the American public was just as happy to have them stay at home. Second, the absence of the Soviets and their allies meant there would be more medals for the Americans, which suited them just fine as well.

For the IOC, the Los Angeles boycott added to its experience with international politics, building on the Montreal and Moscow chapters. In both of those, the IOC had been slow to intervene and ended up paying the price. It responded swiftly to the early signs of the Soviet boycott and earned political points for trying to head off the crisis. When that fell short, the IOC immediately activated its own network of political and quasi-political contacts to lobby against the boycott and played an important part in the combined efforts that minimized the impact of the Soviet initiative to a mere fourteen countries, less than a quarter of the number that had boycotted Moscow. Since life goes on and the Soviets were an important part of the Olympic equation, Samaranch made his first official visit to Moscow, early in the fall of 1984, to begin the healing process. At a special session, held in Lausanne at the end of 1984, the IOC decided against any punishment of the boycotting countries. The situation was quite different from the last-minute pullouts in 1976. The Soviets had announced up front that they would not be accepting the invitation or attending because of the "security" concerns.

Deciding not to punish the boycotters may sound noble, but the plain fact of the matter was that there was no legal basis to sanction a national Olympic committee that decided, for its own reasons, not to take part in the Games. The IOC did, however, change its own protocols to depoliticize the location of the Games. Up to and including the Los Angeles Games, invitations had been sent by the organizing committees, so that for example, the invitation to participate in Los Angeles had come from the Los Angeles organizing committee. If a country wished to play political games, it could say that it was refusing an invitation emanating from the United States. Our response to that was to say that, from now on, the invitations would be sent by the IOC. The IOC also decided that henceforth the invitations would go out a year ahead, with a date specified for the acceptance, so that there would be no last-minute surprises.

Changing the sender was sensible and reflected the underlying reality in any event because the Games belong to the IOC and not to the particular host country. A significant aspect of receiving an invitation from the IOC was that it removed the possibility of claiming some political objection to the host country as an excuse for not accepting. We also made it clear that the IOC considered it a primary role of the national Olympic committee in each country to ensure the participation of its athletes in the Olympic Games. Obviously, you cannot force any country to take part and there may be some occasions when natural disasters or emergencies occur that effectively prevent it from attending, but, if you sign on to the Olympic movement, there is a reasonable expectation that this includes support of the main event, the Olympic Games. Otherwise, what is the point of having a national Olympic committee?

• • •

Ahead of us lay an even more formidable challenge, with all the potential of a disaster—Games in Seoul on the Korean peninsula, a tinderbox fraught with political and military issues that could explode at a moment's notice. What has been generally described as the Korean War, which broke out in 1950 and led to an armistice in 1953, has never been conclusively resolved. An uneasy truce has been maintained since then and the harshness of the political rhetoric has kept the world on tenterhooks, with major commitments of the superpowers to their client states: the United States to South Korea, and the Soviets and Chinese to North Korea.

The leadership of North Korea was regarded as extremely volatile and unpredictable (and still is) and many attempts were made to destabilize the South, including assassinations, plane bombings and massive troop movements on the part of an army that had become the third or fourth largest in the world. Seoul was only some 50 kilometers from the line of military demarcation. If ever security at the Games had become an overwhelming issue, this was the time. The Soviets were still belligerent about their boycott of Los

Angeles and had not been mollified by Samaranch's early visit following the Games. They could be counted upon to protest at every possible opportunity against Games in Korea, and the North would do the same. South Korea had been ecstatic about winning the race to host the 1988 Games, especially over its defeat of Japan, its traditional enemy. The South Koreans were equally belligerent about holding on to their prize and matched verbal sally with verbal sally, all of which were conducted with the vehemence and hatred that can spring only from a divided country.

Although we had little doubt that Seoul could organize the Games from a financial and technical perspective, the big question was whether they would get the chance to do so if the political and security problems could not be solved. I have always thought this was Samaranch's finest hour and am certain that had the IOC followed its traditional practice of waiting for the political authorities to find a solution, the Games would never have taken place.

The Soviets and the Chinese were very helpful in making it clear to the North that they would not look kindly on any adventure initiated by the North. North Korea had been suspected of being involved in detonating a bomb at Seoul's Kimpo airport shortly before the Asian Games in 1986 and had been linked with other similar activities. (The Asian Games, modeled after the Olympics, are held every four years, midway between summer Olympic Games.) The security problem all but disappeared, as a practical matter, when the Soviet Union—not then knowing how close it was to extinction—opened a consular office in Seoul to handle Olympic and other matters. It was the first official step leading to diplomatic recognition of a government in direct conflict with that of its own client state. It would have been diplomatic suicide for the North to have done anything that might put the Soviet personnel in Seoul at risk. The opening of the consulate also helped to improve relations that had deteriorated since the Soviet shooting down of Korean Air Lines Flight 007 on August 31, 1983.

In the end, only a handful of countries did not participate in Seoul and, of these, only Cuba and North Korea were countries of any sporting or political importance. This was the second time in a row for Cuba, but the Soviet Union had cut way back on its financial support of Cuba, and its new banker—despite its own desperate economic conditions—was North Korea. Castro could not risk losing his last-chance financial sponsor, so his athletes again paid the price and watched from the sidelines.

There has been no serious threat of a political boycott of the Games since 1988. The challenge in 1992 was to come from the United Nations regarding the hostilities in Yugoslavia, and the difference in significance was not so much the size of the target, which was small, but the fact that the member states were being called upon by an international governmental organization to respond to the actions of another state by denying access to its nationals. That cut across the ability of citizens to travel to the Games and put Spain, for example, in the difficult position of trying to reconcile its obligations to the IOC (free access to the country for purposes of the Games) and its international obligations as a member state in response to a resolution of the UN Security Council (Resolution 757). We found a way to let individuals participate at the Games without using the name of their country or its flag, and got, if not approval, at least an informal no-action response from the UN. No one had much appetite for trying to boycott the United States in 1996, or Sydney in 2000. The IOC management of the boycott agenda may finally have driven a stake through the heart of Olympic boycotts.

• • •

Security at each of those Games remained a major issue and continues to this day. South Korea and its allies were on full alert for 1988. The Koreans started to demonstrate their readiness as early as the Asian Games in 1986, when part of the opening ceremony involved military helicopters and tactical soldiers who demonstrated their skills, descending ropes, fully armed, with no safety nets in case of a fall. A particularly impressive demonstration was the paratrooper squad that jumped from a couple of helicopters several thousand feet above the stadium. The plan was for them to land in the stadium as part of the ceremony. That would have been impressive enough, but that was not all they had in mind. They landed, each a few seconds after the other, not just in the stadium, but in line, and all in the same lane of the track! On several occasions in Seoul leading up to the Games, I saw SWAT teams rehearsing entry into skyscrapers by rappelling down the buildings to enter windows high above the street. The message to anyone planning a security breach was clear: their best team was in the field and was fully prepared for any contingency.

Barcelona sent the same message. There was massive security in place, including a tank stationed outside the IOC hotel. Additional security was provided to protect the many chartered ships in the harbor that were used as floating hotels during the Games, as well as the heads of state and royalty who attended the Games, including François Mitterrand, John Major, Fidel Castro and, although not yet head of state, but the most poignant of all, Nelson Mandela, there to see the first South African athletes participate in thirty-two years. Perimeters around the Olympic sites were all but impermeable without proper Olympic and photo-ID accreditation. The same was true in Atlanta and no incidents occurred in any of the Olympic facilities. The single bomb that exploded was the work of an individual with no political agenda and it was detonated in an area under the control of the Atlanta police force. It may be unfair to blame them for a random act such as that, but there was a level of bad attitude, incompetence and intransigence in the Atlanta police, who were in the middle of contract negotiations, that will always make me wonder if they were focused on their jobs of making the Olympic city safe—or just being obstructive.

Sydney had the natural advantage of its location on an island continent, which made the external threat much less than other countries would face. That did not do away with the need for careful planning, but the host country already had a highly effective control of its frontiers, which meant that the bulk of the effort could be directed at local threats. Despite the events of September 11, 2001, and the raising of security awareness within the United States to unprecedented levels, there was never too much concern that the Salt Lake City Games would be particularly vulnerable. The geography worked in its favor, as did the relative homogeneity of its population and, as is common with Winter Games, the climate. There was, nevertheless, a tremendously visible security apparatus, much provided by the military, with so much duplication that I eventually concluded that they were using the operation as a training program. All's well that ends well, I suppose, and I am sure the Monday-morning quarterbacks would still be second-guessing everyone had something gone wrong.

It is different with Greece. The most serious uncertainty, one that hangs over the Athens Games like the sword of Damocles, is the matter of security. The escalating rhythm of terrorism has attracted more attention throughout the world than ever before. No country is immune from it. The Western countries got their most compelling demonstration of this in 2001, but there have been other examples on a regular basis that keep the specter fresh in everyone's mind. Greece is located in a particularly volatile region of the world. It has had its own terrorist organizations, which it has been curiously and notoriously slow to root out and bring to justice. Only world pressure arising out of the Olympic Games has caused some concerted action to occur. Without that pressure, it is unlikely that what should have been done years ago would yet have been done. Greece is located near the Middle East, which is known to be a center of terrorist activities, and there is no guarantee that her neighbors will be unwilling to export their activities. On top of all this will be the usual international terrorist suspects, who would welcome the opportunity to disrupt such a visible, worldwide peaceful gathering.

This combination of infelicitous circumstances has led to an unprecedented security effort that will make Athens all but an armed camp. While the final configurations will have to wait until the eve of the Games, when the risk assessments are updated, it is certain that the security apparatus will far exceed the 1988 concerns about an unpredictable North Korea; the highly visible Barcelona security designed to discourage the Basque ETA terrorists; the surly Atlanta police; and the post-9/11 police and military security in Salt Lake City.

There is not much the IOC itself can do about security, other than to seek such assurances as it can from the government of the host country that security must be a priority. This is due diligence, but no government can possibly be unaware of the risks and of its responsibility in the circumstances. It must ensure that it has, or creates, the international networks that will allow quick and effective exchange of information on terrorist movements and techniques. Above all, the host country must avoid falling into some false sense of national pride that it, alone, has all the experience and knowledge to deal with terrorism. That is a prescription for disaster. It is reassuring that the Greeks have not fallen into that trap. They hired the chief of security from the Sydney Games, Peter Ryan, have collaborated with the European security and intelligence networks, and have invited the FBI to review the plans. I think we can be assured that the security will be state-of-the-art, but we will have to accept the risk that no strategy is foolproof and that making a plan is one thing and executing it effectively in response to a threat is quite another. A certain Olympic legacy, however, for any host country is a significant upgrade in its knowledge and experience in matters of national security.

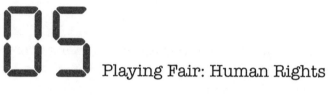# 05 Playing Fair: Human Rights

From its very beginning, the Olympic movement has embraced two elements: ethics and internationalism. The internationalism dimension was new for sport, but relatively straightforward, since it was a matter of extending the horizon of competition to include countries and not simply domestic activity. The ethical foundation was the combination of sport and culture into what has become known as Olympism, built on what were regarded as universal principles of fair play and the absence, indeed the prohibition, of discrimination. The articulation of these values has evolved over time, as society has expanded to include forms of political governance that did not exist when the Olympic Games were revived, as women became more emancipated, and as sport expanded to the working classes and gradually became regarded not as a privilege but something bordering on a basic human right.

One of the principal objectives of the modern Olympic movement is a commitment to universality and the concept of human dignity, including freedom from all forms of discrimination, whether based on race, religion, color or gender. As with the human condition generally, it is far easier to write the words than it is to live them, however deeply and genuinely they may be felt. The International Olympic Committee has had its share of difficulty in applying these concepts, but, on the whole, has one of the best records of any organization in the world of practicing what it preaches.

● ● ●

The South African apartheid regime was an example of a degrading and often brutal disregard of fundamental human rights. After apartheid became law in 1948, purported justifications for this system of white supremacy were puerile and unconvincing, but apart from condemning the entire concept, the international community seemed powerless to do anything about it. Over time, pitifully ineffective steps were taken to draw attention to the situation. South Africa was excluded from the Commonwealth after many years of wrangling. Universities and other concerned groups took steps to rid their investment portfolios of the stock of any companies that had significant business interests in South Africa. Human rights activists railed against apartheid. One of the world's greatest leaders in the struggle for racial equality, Mahatma Gandhi, honed his passive resistance tactics in pre-apartheid South Africa before leaving the country to return to Indià in 1915; others, such as Nelson Mandela, were imprisoned for decades for daring to take action once apartheid was law.

It fell to a group of largely conservative, predominantly white males, members of the IOC, to eventually take a step that had a definitive impact on South Africa, reaching into the very fabric of that country, drawing home to it the degree of outrage experienced by the outside world. South Africa was expelled by the IOC from the Olympic movement in 1970. The government-censored media in South Africa consistently misrepresented apartheid and the sanctions to its own people. The Olympic sanction could not be adequately explained by the government, and this ate away at the domestic resolve to continue with the apartheid regime. To be fair, it was not a state of enlightenment that came easily to the IOC, which was dragged, kicking and screaming, to the point of action, but the organization acted nevertheless.

Much of the reluctance stemmed from the fact that exclusion of a country from the Olympic movement would be perceived as a political, rather than a sporting, action and the IOC was founded on the premise that sport and politics had to be kept separate. The high priest of this catechism, as matters began to draw to a head, was the redoubtable Avery Brundage, a self-made millionaire and former U.S. Olympic athlete, president of the IOC from 1952 until his retirement twenty years later. Brundage made many important contributions to the Olympic movement, some of which I discuss elsewhere, but he was slow to understand that while sport should, indeed, be run by the sports community, inevitable political issues surrounded it and had to be assimilated.

As it happened, the Olympic Games in which I participated in Rome in 1960 would be the last for South Africa for more than thirty years. Civil rights leaders, most of whom were political activists or politicians, began a campaign to exclude South Africa from the Games, using the most powerful weapon at their disposal, the threat of a boycott. They enlisted support from within Africa and added to it the weight of other like-minded countries, some of which acted on principle and others from a political self-interest to strengthen their influence in Africa for trade and political support in other forums. The IOC, initially, tried to push the problem in the direction of the South African National Olympic Committee (SANOC) and extracted a promise that no non-white athlete would be barred from participation in the Games. Despite this assurance from SANOC, it was obvious that the government would not be willing to go far enough and, by the beginning of 1964, it was clear to the IOC that the invitation to South Africa to participate in the Tokyo Games later that year would have to be withdrawn.

The same pressures continued with respect to the Mexico City Games in 1968. The IOC sent a commission to South Africa in 1967, chaired by Michael Morris, the Lord Killanin of Ireland, who would succeed Brundage as IOC president in 1972. The government reiterated its position that there would be no integrated sport in South Africa, even if it was required to send a single team to the Games. The IOC waffled, but, in the end, decided to withdraw the invitation to the Mexico Games as well. It was not until 1970, at its session in Amsterdam, that the IOC finally revoked its recognition of SANOC and thereby brought to an end South Africa's right to participate in the Games.

But now South Africa was isolated, and more individual sports federations—particularly those involved in the Olympic sports—joined earlier federations such as soccer's Fédération Internationale de Football Association (FIFA) and the International Weightlifting Federation (IWF) in excluding the country from their competitions. What was worse, for the South African government, was that its public became aware of, and had to live with, the stigma of becoming an international pariah. For a country that was sports-mad, this was a significant burden. The government had no response, other than to lobby, federation by federation, for continued recognition, and it had some success with sports such as rugby and tennis. The Olympic world had, however, closed its doors.

With South Africa out of play, the next focus became countries with policies that, while perhaps not precisely apartheid, were nevertheless the practical equivalent of such regimes. The target selected for this purpose was Rhodesia (now Zimbabwe) whose government, under Ian Smith, had unilaterally withdrawn from the Commonwealth in 1965 to prevent black majority rule. It was clear to the IOC that trouble was looming and, at the last moment, to avert a boycott, the invitation to Rhodesia to participate in the 1972 Games was withdrawn. Brundage, in his final days as IOC president, was furious, as was clear at the Munich Games when he brought Rhodesia into his statement at the memorial service for the slain Israeli team members. This was universally condemned and Brundage left office under a cloud of criticism that effectively undermined a lifetime of well-intentioned work in the Olympic movement.

The IOC, under his successor, Lord Killanin, sent a commission to Rhodesia in 1974 and, in a report drafted by my colleague James Worrall, observed that there was, as everyone suspected, a two-tiered sport system, in which the rights and privileges of the white participants were radically different from those available to the black participants. Recognition of the Rhodesian National Olympic Committee was withdrawn in 1975 and was only reinstated (in 1980) after Rhodesia had morphed into the legally independent nation of Zimbabwe.

The bar was raised even further as the 1976 Games in Montreal approached. This time the idea of the political gurus was to exclude countries that had any sporting contacts with South Africa. The designated target was to be New Zealand, whose rugby team (ironically, in the circumstances, named the All Blacks) had participated in a rugby tour in South Africa. So had many other countries, including the United States, but there was no desire to tangle with the U.S. The activists, led by Abraham Ordia of Nigeria and Jean-Claude Ganga of the Supreme Council for Sport in Africa, threatened a boycott if New Zealand were to be allowed to participate in the Games. This was a crisis that developed late in the period leading up to the Games and, in my view, was one that was badly mishandled by the IOC. Had Killanin's successor, Juan Antonio Samaranch, been president of the IOC in Montreal, I am convinced that the boycott would never have occurred. But he would not be elected until 1980, in the midst of yet another political crisis, and it fell to Killanin to manage the process.

Neither Killanin, an affable Irishman who was not adept at politics, nor his imperious director, Monique Berlioux, liked Ordia and Ganga (later a member of the IOC who was disgraced in the Salt Lake City bidding scandal of 1999). They regarded the pair as opportunistic troublemakers. As the boycott rhetoric escalated, and Ordia and Ganga realized that the problem might well get out of hand, they sought a meeting with Killanin, to see if a solution could be found. Samaranch would have given them an audience, in fact would likely have initiated such a meeting, but they could not break through the wall of Berlioux and Killanin.

Many of the African teams were already in Montreal. By this time, the problem had come to the attention of the political leaders in Africa, who cared not a whit about the Games, but who perceived political advantage in pronouncing a boycott. More than twenty countries ordered their teams to withdraw the day before the opening ceremony of the Games. It was very sad to see athletes such as the world-record holder in the 1,500 meters, Filbert Bayi of Tanzania, become pawns in the greater game, leaving the Olympic Village in tears, their Olympic dreams shattered. Ordia and Ganga knew perfectly well that rugby was not an Olympic sport and that the New Zealand Olympic Committee had no power whatsoever to prevent rugby teams from New Zealand from competing wherever they wanted, including South Africa. Samaranch would have arranged for the New Zealand Olympic Committee to issue some sort of statement supporting the Olympic principles and undertaking to raise the matter with the New Zealand government and the rugby association upon its return from Montreal. This would certainly have defused the crisis and the Africans would have made their point. Both sides miscalculated and both paid the price. The same issue did not arise at subsequent Games, despite continued contact with South Africa in some non-Olympic sports, so perhaps both learned from their mistakes.

As the effects of sporting isolation were felt, year after year, in South Africa, some progress was gradually being made to consider how the apartheid apparatus might be adjusted, at least in sport. It was frustrating, both inside South Africa and in the sporting world, that this progress was so slow. Following the expulsion of South Africa, little further attention seemed to be paid to the country, even by the African leaders, in relation to sport. It was as if all that mattered was to expel the country.

The larger question of genuine reform was, apparently, to be left to the international community to solve and there was precious little resolve to do so. Minor economic sanctions were applied sporadically, but the major relationships were left intact. There was some rationalization about not breaking up major relationships on the basis that doing so might provide a toehold for communism in a country with a strong strategic position at the tip of Africa, but by and large politicians around the world were reluctant to absorb any significant economic pain to bring about a solution to an issue that was regarded, essentially, as an African problem. This was certainly partly true, as whatever the solution might be, it would have to be satisfactory to the African governments as a whole or it would not work. Sport was the meat in that particular sandwich and the solution to the sport problem was perceived as one that must follow the politics.

It was, perhaps, naive on my part, but I began to think that maybe sport should assume some leadership in finding a solution to the apartheid problem. I thought South Africa was seeking a way out of the box in which it had placed itself and that there might be some way to make progress on the larger scene other than to wait for the whole problem to be solved. I thought sport should become more proactive in the process. I first mentioned the idea publicly at a session of the Canadian Olympic Academy in Halifax in 1987, simply saying that sport should consider becoming more proactive and imaginative in its approach. The academy is a leadership development program of the Canadian Olympic Association and it was an off-the-record situation, in which ideas relating to the Olympic movement could be explored and discussed. I thought this was an issue that deserved some ventilation and consideration.

Also attending the session, as a guest, was Sam Ramsamy, a South African in exile in England who was running a non-official South African Non-Racial Olympic Committee (SANROC) from London. It had no status within the Olympic movement, but was a lobbying effort to promote, without much success, nonracial sport in South Africa. For reasons that were never clear to me, Ramsamy concluded that my observation signaled some kind of retreat from the IOC position. And despite a clear understanding that the meeting was a forum for exploration of ideas that was not public, he circulated a letter to African IOC members and others claiming that I was, in some way, supporting apartheid. To give Ramsamy the benefit of every possible doubt, since he never discussed the matter with me before launching his assault (nor has he acknowl-edged that he was unjustified in doing what he did), it was a most unfortunate failure to understand what I had actually said, not to mention a serious breach of protocol. I had to send my own letter to all the IOC members explaining that I was not supporting apartheid and that the IOC was not retreat-ing from its position. But, of course, the first impression is always stronger and it had come from someone who was African, so my denial was undoubtedly discounted by many of the recipients.

I was always interested in trying to see what could be done to find a solution to the apartheid issue. At the IOC session in Rome in 1982, I had a meeting with Samaranch, who by then was president of the IOC. When I arrived in the room, he was finishing a meeting with Ganga, who, by that time, had decided that he would like to become an IOC member. Given his involvement with the Montreal boy-cott, I was not at all in favor, and made this quite clear to anyone I spoke with, including Samaranch. On this occa-sion, I again took the bull by the horns and said that, as leaders respectively of the Olympic movement and African sport, I thought they were missing an opportunity to show that sport could find solutions to a difficult problem that had, to date, baffled the political leaders.

Why did they not focus on ways to use sport to show the way? Interracial sport was practiced in many countries, with great success. These models might be a way to make some progress in South Africa as well and might even point the way to a larger solution. It was clear that the status quo of waiting for the glacial progress of the political authorities was not likely to be advantageous. I cannot say that they both leapt high in the air and clicked their heels with excitement at this suggestion, but I do not believe they had previously given any serious thought to taking the offensive in search of a solution. They, like almost everyone else, seemed content to wallow in the apparently overwhelming difficulties. It may, however, have planted a seed that bore fruit ten years later.

During my early years as an IOC member, the IOC resisted requests from South Africa to send another commission of inquiry to examine the state of sport. Reginald Honey, the country's IOC member, was already seventy-four years old when I swam in the Games at Rome in 1960. He was still there when I became an IOC member in 1978, having stayed long past the time he would have wanted to retire, but his membership on the IOC was one of the last links of South Africa with the Olympic movement. He was not expelled at the time that South Africa was, based on the philosophy that IOC members were not delegates of their country to the IOC, but, rather, were representatives of the IOC in that country.

He was constantly urging the IOC to take another look at South Africa. I remember, at the 1980 IOC session in Moscow, some ten years after the expulsion of South Africa, he was trying to attract the attention of Lord Killanin, who made every effort not to notice him and was about to close the meeting. I was clearly in Killanin's line of vision and raised my hand. "Mr. Pound," he said. "Mr. President," I said, "I think Mr. Honey is trying to attract your attention." He was then stuck and had to give the floor to Honey, who made his request once again, to no avail. The matter would be studied and, when the time was ripe, the IOC would establish another commission. It would be another decade, and another president, who would also delay until the time was right.

By late 1990, it was clear that there was potential change afoot in South Africa. Mandela was out of prison and publicly leading the previously banned African National Congress (ANC). F.W. de Klerk was nearing the end of his own mandate. National elections were in the offing and provided there was no tampering, there was little doubt that Mandela and the ANC would win. Mandela was putting together a political consensus among the other potential rivals as to the forthcoming governance of South Africa, such as Thabo Mbeki, who was to succeed him as president in 1999. Samaranch was following the developments closely and decided that the time had come for the IOC to send another commission to South Africa. The essential difference was that he was on the verge of empowering the commission to negotiate, not just to observe the conditions in South Africa, and to see if it might be possible to agree on terms for the country's return to the Olympic movement. The main players in this were the two leaders, de Klerk and Mandela, one in office and the other such a powerful moral force in South Africa that it would have been unthinkable to conclude any agreement without his active support. Both leaders must be given credit for the solution and, indeed, the Nobel selectors did exactly that when they jointly awarded them the 1993 Peace Prize, following the formal transition of power from the white minority in South Africa.

The IOC announcement in 1991 that it would readmit South Africa to the Olympic family was a major breakthrough in a conundrum that had defeated all previous political efforts to find a solution. It was such an important step forward that U.S. president George Bush waited to see what the media and public reaction would be to the IOC's decision before lifting the U.S. sanctions against South Africa. Just as had been the case with the problem of Games in South Korea and the problem of the two Chinas, the Olympic movement found an acceptable solution to a political impasse that had resisted all professional diplomatic efforts.

Thus, for the first time since 1960, South African athletes participated in the 1992 Olympics in Barcelona.

Nelson Mandela was an honored guest. The team was racially mixed, although a considerable majority of its members were white, reflecting the history of better opportunities offered to them for training and coaching. Development programs have been instituted to try to narrow the gap and future teams may show a balance that is more reflective of the population as a whole. There is still much work to be done in South Africa to recover from the many years of apartheid, and many risks affect the continued stability of the country, but the institutions and laws that suppressed the black majority have finally been abolished and a process of national reconciliation, instituted by Mandela, continues.

•   •   •

The Olympic movement can take justifiable pride in its record of fighting racial discrimination. The way was not smooth and there were occasional setbacks, but, on the whole, it has set an example that is more worthy of admiration than condemnation. It has had the interests of athletes at heart and has not wavered from that objective. There is a tendency in the world to expect too much from a small organization such as the IOC. It has, in the military sense that is often applied to international politics, no divisions. In that sense, it has little political power, although it has influence that cannot be entirely discounted. It reminds me of the position I have as chancellor of McGill University and, as I have heard explained, of other people in my position: that I have no power, but I have considerable influence, though only with those who do not realize that I have no power. The frustrations that many have regarding abuses of human rights are profound and when the inequities cannot be solved as quickly as one would hope, people turn to a convenient target and blame the target for failings that cannot reasonably be attributed to it. Such is often the fate of the IOC.

Some of this frustration was exhibited in relation to the barbarous treatment of athletes in one of the more brutal regimes in the world, Iraq. In late 2001 I began to get e-mails and telephone calls from the media about reports of torture of Iraqi athletes by the son of Saddam Hussein, Uday, who was president of the Iraqi national Olympic committee (NOC). I had no personal knowledge of any such acts. The media were insistent that there were reports of such acts and wanted to know what the IOC was going to do about them. My view was that, although I had no knowledge of them, the fact that there were accusations was sufficiently serious that I thought the IOC should investigate, and I undertook to raise the matter with IOC president Jacques Rogge. If there were any truth to the rumors and allegations, such conduct—especially by someone acting as president of the NOC—was so disgusting and so antithetical to the values of the Olympic movement that it could not be countenanced.

I did raise the matter with Rogge because it was important. It was, however, particularly complicated by the fact that the IOC is a small organization of volunteers that has no power to bring about regime change in Iraq. I nevertheless thought that, at the very least, the IOC should interview the athletes who had reported the torture and see if they were credible, and, if they were, to pursue the matter further. I am enough of a lawyer to know that the credibility of a witness must be assessed or tested, especially where there are strong political and other views or objectives involved. I remember being criticized in some media for not accepting, untested, any of the allegations, as though the allegations were gospel. I had, indeed, been careful to make it clear that, pending investigation, they were merely allegations. On the other hand, I pressed for proper investigation of the allegations, because, if true, they were so serious that Uday Hussein should be removed as president of the NOC and, possibly, the NOC itself should be suspended.

Again, the ability of the IOC to act was limited at best. In an international context, there are matters of internal governance that must be accepted as facts of life, however disagreeable they may be. That is an internationally accepted protocol, whereby states are not entitled to enter into matters of domestic policy in other nations. It is rare indeed when such incursions are made, as witnessed by the U.S. intervention in Iraq to bring about a regime change. For the IOC, as an international sport organization, it would be very difficult to gain the access to the country, and to the individuals in the country, that would enable it to conclude that the outrageous events had actually occurred. Without compelling evidence, it would be impossible for the IOC to insist on a change of NOC leadership or, more drastically, a suspension of the NOC and the resulting ineligibility of all Iraqi athletes to participate in the Games.

The standards of a responsible, albeit concerned, international organization such as the IOC had to be higher than those of the media, who bore no responsibility for the expression of irresponsible opinions. Rumor and suspicion are one thing: evidence is quite another. Moral certainty that something is drastically wrong is not enough to justify an action. It is more than enough to require action towards verification, but there is no one I know, from any culture in the world, who would agree that a penalty can be imposed solely on the basis of suspicion. Indeed, many of my IOC colleagues have altogether too much personal experience with the suppression of rights on the basis of mere suspicion to be comfortable with such a system.

I want to be clear that I was under no illusion about whether Uday Hussein was a disgusting and perverted individual who did not deserve to be president of his country's NOC. There was little doubt as to how he got there in the first place: daddy's rank had its privileges. Daddy's example was well short of instructive. But, as is the case with doping in sport, you need evidence and you need to notify an accused of the case against him and provide the opportunity to respond. This is not because you have the slightest doubt that he is guilty, but because any accused is entitled to a basic presumption of innocence and the right to a fair and impartial hearing. Did I, at the time, believe that Uday Hussein probably tortured athletes? Without doubt. Everything I had heard and read about him suggested that he was loathsome and depraved. But did I have any evidence that would allow me, were I a decision maker, to demand his resignation, suspend his NOC or prevent Iraqi athletes from participating in the Olympic Games? No. So I urged the IOC to make the necessary inquiries and to make it clear that the allegations were sufficiently serious that the IOC was willing, indeed morally compelled, to make inquiries.

Even the fact that the IOC was considering the issue was preferable to doing nothing and, more important, to be suspected of not caring. What might come of any investigation was doubtful. A mere inquiry would, of course, bring nothing but an angry denial. An IOC delegation to the country would be under careful state control and access to impartial witnesses severely restricted. There would be little, if any, leverage available to an organization such as the IOC. Prior to the U.S.-led military action, there was little enthusiasm by any sporting body for an investigatory visit by the IOC.

Uday and his brother Qusay are now dead. There has been no outpouring of sympathy for them and it is probably safe to say that none was warranted. A new NOC has been established, and efforts have been made to enable Iraqi athletes to participate in the Athens Games without fear of recrimination and torture. Part of the practical problem is that Iraq was not able to participate in the international qualifying events for the Olympics, but the IOC has been flexible enough to find a solution on other occasions and there is no reason to believe that this will be an exception.

• • •

The IOC has been able to find a solution, in sport, to the difficult problem of the so-called two Chinas, something that the finest diplomatic and political brains have not. The problem is well known: following the Second World War, the former government of China withdrew from the mainland in the face of the growing political importance of the Communists and established itself in Taiwan. From there, it purported to exercise control over the newly established People's Republic of China (PRC), despite the all-too-obvious fact that this could not have been further from the truth. In fact, it bordered occasionally on the surreal. I remember once, during a visit to Taiwan, reading in a local newspaper of the criticism launched in the national assembly at the minister responsible for mines for his failure to prevent some disaster in a mine on the mainland.

Internationally, countries were faced with a choice of recognizing either the PRC or Taiwan, but not both. In Olympic terms, the PRC would not participate if Taiwan participated. It was a difficult situation, especially since the PRC was the most populous country in the world. After years of unsuccessful attempts to find a solution, in 1979, the president of the IOC, Lord Killanin, who much preferred the PRC to Taiwan, brought the matter to a mail-in vote of the IOC members, who decided to expel Taiwan as the political price of bringing the PRC into the Olympic fold. This led the IOC member in Taiwan, Henry Hsu, to commence a legal action against the IOC. Killanin was furious and, at the 1980 session in Moscow, was determined to have Hsu expelled. I talked him out of it and, in the process, said that I thought Hsu might well be successful in his action. Since it was his last session as president, Killanin let the matter drop and it was left to Samaranch, his successor, to see if he could find a solution.

Samaranch was much better suited to the process than Killanin, and it was not long before he had found an answer that, if not fully satisfactory to both sides, was at least sufficiently acceptable that it could be adopted. Both national Olympic committees would be fully recognized by the IOC. The PRC would have the Chinese Olympic Committee and Taiwan the Chinese Taipei Olympic Committee. The PRC could use its national flag and anthem, while Taiwan would have a specially designed Olympic flag and anthem. It was not necessary to face world political issues head-on and the PRC could take some diplomatic cover behind the fact that there were other NOCs in areas that were under the political control of countries who, in turn, had their own NOCs, including Puerto Rico, the Netherlands Antilles and some of the British colonies such as Bermuda. It was a difficult decision for the Taiwanese, who resisted with great stubbornness and came close to refusing to agree. I remember writing to Hsu, saying that he should do whatever was necessary for Taiwan to stay in, because, if ever it was excluded, it would never get back in, so this was the last chance.

The legal actions were dropped and action against Hsu was no longer a consideration. The only residue of the episode is that the oath taken by new IOC members includes an undertaking to regard decisions of the IOC as binding and not subject to appeal, which I always refer to as the "Hsu amendment." My only other active role in this matter was to persuade Samaranch to co-opt a new member in Taiwan when Hsu was ready to retire, to ensure that there would be someone inside the IOC to make sure the elements of the solution would not be forgotten. The flexibility of the IOC has made it possible to achieve a *modus vivendi* that is beyond the reach of the professional politicians. It reminds me of an expression used by Sir Arthur Gold, a former chair of the British Olympic Association, (who may well have borrowed it from someone else): "Remember, the *Titanic* was built by experts and the Ark by an amateur."

*   *   *

There is much evil in the world. On occasion, it seems people expect the IOC to solve all of the world's problems, using its lever of the Olympic Games. Why did we allow Uganda, when led by the outrageous Idi Amin Dada, to participate? The answer is both complicated and simple. On a purely political basis, what would be the justification for excluding a country that is recognized by the world diplomatic community, and is a member of the United Nations and other international and regional political bodies? All of these political and diplomatic niceties do not reflect any approval of the domestic policies that the country may pursue. Indeed, continued membership and recognition may be the best way to influence change within the country.

Sanctions are not always the best course, because the full brunt of any such action falls on the very class that has the least to do with the policies that are found to be offensive—in our case, young athletes. Where we have acted to expel or suspend a country, we have made no judgment regarding the country as such, but acted where the athletes have been subject to discrimination. In South Africa, it was apartheid that discriminated against non-white athletes; much the same was true in Rhodesia; in Afghanistan, an Olympic committee had been hijacked by the Taliban regime. In these cases, the discrimination was directed specifically at sport, which prevented sport organizations from acting independently, and the political authorities made it clear that they were unwilling to change, so the sport sanctions were imposed. In the larger political context it is sometimes possible to get a rogue nation to learn to behave (somewhat) more sociably.

It is often difficult to maintain a balance. I would not have wanted Amin at the Games, but I would be hard-pressed to say that no Ugandan athlete should be allowed to participate just because Amin was an unprincipled dictator. Many of these issues land on our doorstep because people are frustrated with the limits of traditional diplomacy, where, just as within the Olympic movement, there is a view that inclusion, even reluctant inclusion, is better than isolation. On a different level, it is not unlike the special interest groups in Olympic host countries. They expect the Olympics to cure poverty, advance education, beat inflation, solve regional disparities and a plethora of other ills, all without costing them anything.

Typical of this situation was the internal strife in Toronto regarding the 1996 Olympic Games bid. Special interest groups drew attention away from the focus of winning the Games by protracted arguments over such issues as wheelchair access ramps and day care centers in the Olympic facilities, producing hot debate and divided votes in city council that sent mixed messages to the IOC about Toronto's commitment to the Games. Atlanta, which had far more substantive problems than Toronto and internal tensions that made Toronto's look like a joke, managed to keep its eye on the main objective—to win the Games—and try to deal with the problems after it was successful. The access ramps and day care centers could easily have been dealt with once the prize had been secured.

• • •

One of the legacies of the original conception of the Olympic Games, framed by gentlemen of the Victorian era who defined sport in the idealistic sense of activity practiced by the gentleman amateur, was that there was no place in this concept for women. It took until 1928 for women to be allowed to compete in track and field, but, since then, the IOC has pursued the advancement of women within the Olympic movement, both on and off the field of play. At the 2004 Athens Games, 44 percent of athletes competing will be women, up from just 20 percent in Moscow in 1980 and 38 percent in Sydney in 2000. IOC president Jacques Rogge predicted that within a decade of the Athens Games, "there will be 50 percent women participating at the Olympics." The IOC has advanced the competitive opportunities for women and has encouraged the development and advancement of female sports administrators, including members of the IOC. It was not until three years after I became a member of the IOC that the first two women members were co-opted, some eighty-seven years after the IOC was established.

The progress has been steady and is worthy of some recognition, but not sustained applause, since there is much more to be done and the pace of change has been well short of urgent. There is a desire to provide more balance in the IOC membership, although far more is said than is done. Even with its limited female membership, the IOC is well ahead of most international sports federations (IFs) and NOCs. It set guidelines designed to start raising the level of women's participation in the administration, phasing in over a period of time from an initial 10 percent level to 20 percent by 2005. IFs and NOCs regularly say that they are unable to attract "qualified" women to senior posts, but no one has ever discovered compelling evidence of a concerted effort to find and encourage women. If anything, the opposite is true.

Part of the problem arises from traditional stereotyping. At one of my first IOC sessions, at Moscow in 1980, the IOC, in its elderly all-male splendor, considered the matter of whether the marathon event for women should be added to the 1984 Los Angeles Olympic program. There was considerable discussion and a basic reluctance to proceed. One or two members offered the view that it should not be added because it would be too difficult for the "weaker" sex. Even though I was still the newest member of the IOC, who should probably have been seen but not heard, I felt that I had to intervene. I said that the IOC might decide either way on the question, but that if the decision were to be negative, under no circumstances should the IOC indicate that this was because it had decided women were not capable of running a marathon. Such a position would make us laughingstocks all over the world.

The event was added in time for the Games in Los Angeles and Joan Benoit made it all too clear that women could handle a marathon with no more distress than men when she won the gold medal on August 5, 1984. I have always nurtured an instinctive feeling that if the marathon were to be 60 kilometers instead of 42, women's times might well surpass the men's. I confess to never having engaged the services of physiologists who might confirm or reject the suspicion. Women athletes are just as well conditioned as their male counterparts and, apart from events that depend on size and strength, where men have a physical advantage, are no less able than men in any sporting activity. Murray Rose of Australia won the 400-meter freestyle in my Olympics (1960), with a brilliant tactical race, setting a new Olympic record in the process. The women's event was won in a time that was more than 32 seconds slower. Within twelve years, the women were snapping at his winning time in their own event and, by 1976, Rose would have had trouble making the final in the women's event. Today, teenage girls go through 400 meters, on the way to 800 meters, much faster than Rose could ever have contemplated swimming, without even being out of breath.

Apart from presenting the medals in the 100-meter freestyle (the closest I'll ever come to a gold medal in my old event), I like to draw attention to women's sport by presenting medals in women's events. All are exciting, but my favorite to date was the women's ice hockey in Salt Lake City in 2002. I had a certain nationalistic interest as well, since I hoped that Canada might win, but I have always supported women's ice hockey and have been tremendously impressed by the speed with which it has developed from not much more than organized shinny to extremely high quality. Frankly, it is easier to appreciate the skills and the plays in women's hockey than in men's, where there is always some goon smashing into the puck carrier. In any event, I had promised that if the Canadian women won the gold medal, I would be the one to present it. The final was particularly close, but the Canadians prevailed and I had the enormous pleasure of giving the medals, accompanied by the Latin two-cheek kiss, more a Quebec than a national tradition. I always brag that no one can match my record of kissing some twenty happy women in a row.

Although the percentage of women's events at the Olympics and the percentage of women athletes at the Games have continued to rise, there is clearly still active discrimination against women in areas of the world, such as the Middle East and parts of Asia and Africa, sometimes on the purported basis of religion. The IOC has been reluctant to act as firmly as it should to prevent or to relieve this discrimination, probably for fear of stirring up religious fervor and partly because it would almost certainly have meant suspending a significant number of NOCs. There can be no credible political or, even more importantly, religious basis for a dismissive or degrading treatment of women athletes or would-be athletes. The IOC should be active in using its moral suasion to deal with such obvious discrimination against women. Failure to do so would be an abrogation of its moral responsibility, asserted under the Olympic Charter. A champion is needed who will elevate the issue to the point where the IOC executive board will be forced to act and to engage other organizations and agencies in the struggle. When the discrimination is exposed to bright light, those who practice it or try to defend it are easily revealed as bigots or charlatans.

This chapter should end as it began: the Olympic movement must always be a living statement of respect for human dignity. If it delivers this quality, it succeeds; to the extent that it does not, it fails. As a member of the IOC, as a human being, I consider it a fundamental duty to be ever vigilant that sport be at the service of humanity. Throwing or kicking a ball, running, swimming and jumping are all important for their own sakes and the healthier people they produce, but, when elevated to organized competition, whether local, national or international, they have a higher calling. They should contribute to the advancement of society, the improvement of the human condition, the development of understanding and mutual respect and the building of a better and more peaceful world. If properly nurtured, supported and directed, sport can be an expression of goodwill unmatched by any other social initiative.

 Keeping Corporate Company:
Sponsorship

The International Olympic Committee lived from hand to mouth for the first sixty or seventy years of its existence and the criticism often directed at it—that it was a rich man's club—was entirely true. To be a member meant that you had to be able to pay all your own expenses to attend the meetings and the Olympic Games. There were no significant revenue sources for the Games themselves, other than the willingness of countries to assume virtually all the expenses of building facilities and paying for the organization of the competitions. Occasional contributions were received from companies in the host country and donations from public-spirited citizens, as had been the case with the original Games in Athens in 1896. Apart from intimations that television rights might become an important income stream, even as late as 1980 there was no concerted effort to develop private sector support of the Games.

To give great credit where credit is due, one of the first priorities that Juan Antonio Samaranch established when he became president of the IOC in 1980 was to generate some degree of financial independence for the Olympic movement. This has led, over a series of Games, to the IOC taking over television negotiations and increasing the proportion of the television rights fees shared by itself, the international sports federations (IFs) and the national Olympic committees (NOCs) through the IOC's umbrella sport development program, Olympic Solidarity.

The economic model of the Olympic movement at the time he became president was a prescription for disaster. Governments provided almost all financial resources and were not the slightest bit shy about tying such support to their own political agendas. The Berlin Games in 1936 have always been regarded as a major propaganda initiative for Nazi Germany. Rome and Tokyo used the Games to announce their re-entry into the world mainstream following the unsuccessful belligerence of Italy and Japan in the Second World War. Germany did the same with the 1972 Games in Munich. The Soviet Union proclaimed that awarding the Games to Moscow was a vindication of Soviet policy and the motto of the Games, SPORT, PEACE, PROGRESS, was designed to reassure its public and persuade the world of Soviet accomplishments.

Such private sector support as existed was derived almost entirely from television revenues, and of these, about 95 percent came from a single source, the United States. Only a dozen or so national Olympic committees had ever generated significant sponsorship revenues, foremost among which was the U.S. Olympic Committee (USOC), whose fundraising activities benefited from congressional support in the form of legislated protection of the Olympic rings and the word "Olympic" when used in a commercial context. In 1982, Samaranch established the IOC Commission for New Sources of Finance, with the mandate to explore possible new sources of funding for the Olympic movement. It was, at the outset, a rather naive commission, with very little commercial expertise aboard, but it was at least a signal that something had to change.

In and around the new commission hovered Horst Dassler, an inveterate sports politician who was responsible for part of the family-owned Adidas operations. Few figures in the international sports field have aroused more curiosity than Dassler. The only son among the five children of Adolph (Adi) Dassler, founder of Adidas, Horst had been sent to Adidas France to learn the family business. That enterprise was directed from the Bavarian town of Herzogenaurach, bizarrely divided into rival camps of Adi Dassler and his brother Rudolf (Rudi), masters of the Adidas and Puma brands, respectively, and bitter, implacable rivals.

Over the years, Adidas instituted a successful program of developing great sports shoes and then encouraging well-known athletes to use them, in return for unlimited supplies of clothing and equipment, plus whatever relatively minor cash payments may have been permissible under the IOC's amateur rules, which under Avery Brundage were enforced so rigorously that the ability to get cash payments was practically non-existent. Horst Dassler was a slight, soft-spoken and even somewhat shy person, who was helpful and supportive, but, at the same time, diffident. He was also young and ambitious. His first brush with the Olympics involved giving away Adidas shoes at the Olympic Village in Melbourne in 1956, and then he got more ambitious in 1960 in Rome and after.

Dassler listened and learned a great deal about the international sports scene and the networks that made it function. Little by little, he became fascinated by it and began to have some influence. It was not long before he was recognized as someone who could help make things happen in the sport world and he became addicted to this role. He developed a vast network of contacts in Africa, Eastern Europe, Asia and Latin America, where the Adidas organization had day-to-day contacts at the grassroots level of sport in the developing countries in particular. His support was a major factor in the election of Samaranch as IOC president in 1980 and Joao Havelange as president of the Fédération Internationale de Football Association (FIFA) in 1974. Both were elected to their positions without major support from mainstream Europe, where a significant number of the voting members were located. Rumors abound as to the possible role of money to assist the winning candidates on both occasions and the role of Dassler in such activities. To my knowledge no evidence has ever surfaced to support the rumors.

The Adidas network gave Dassler regular and personal contact with all sports leaders in almost every country, and the prospect of free or highly subsidized shoes, uniforms and equipment guaranteed him the full attention of sports officials whenever he wanted it. Through a family-owned corporate structure, ISL, Dassler had acquired the worldwide marketing rights of FIFA, the international federation governing soccer, notably those relating to FIFA's marquee event, the World Cup. He thought that a similar marketing arrangement might be possible for the IOC. It would not be as easy to develop such an international program for the IOC; FIFA was able to dictate terms to its member national federations, but the IOC did not control the NOCs. Indeed, the NOCs did not want the IOC to be engaged in marketing or sponsorship programs in their countries, correctly concluding that this would eat into their own potential revenues.

My first involvement in an IOC commission had been as secretary of the Canadian Olympic Association, when I was appointed, in 1974, to what was then called the Emblems

Commission. It was concerned with the protection of the Olympic rings—which Pierre de Coubertin had designed as the Olympic symbol—and the conditions under which they would be used by the IOC, the NOCs and the Olympic Games organizing committees. I had lobbied very hard, and successfully, to make sure that the IOC could not engage in any such marketing or sponsorship programs, in any country, without the consent of the NOC. Any form of sponsorship involved granting the sponsor the right to use the Olympic rings in conjunction with its own corporate name and imagery. It would be an uphill struggle for the IOC to put together such a program, but discussions commenced and it was decided to see what might be possible.

Companies that wanted to be Olympic sponsors had a particular problem, especially if they wanted to exercise sponsorship rights on an international basis. Coca-Cola is a good case in point. It was, at the time we began to consider possible international sponsorship, already a sponsor of the 1984 Los Angeles Olympics. To become a sponsor of the Games, it first had to negotiate a contract with the Los Angeles organizing committee. But then, in order to use those rights, even in the United States, it then had to negotiate a separate contract with the USOC. If it also wanted to exploit those rights in other countries, it had to go, one by one, to each of the NOCs and make separate arrangements with them. It was a convoluted and time-consuming process, inefficient to the point of being uneconomic.

Apart from a dozen or so of the major markets, most of the other countries had little economic value. The difficulties were compounded, since knowing that Coca-Cola had the Olympic rights in a particular country allowed the NOCs in other countries to go to the company's competitors and generate an auction for the rights that gave competitors a chance to diminish the value of Coca-Cola's sponsorship, and for very little expense. The same happened even in the host countries of the Games, where the NOCs could negotiate for sponsorship rights with competitors of the Games sponsors, as, for example, was the case in Montreal in 1976; and in Los Angeles in 1984 with Kodak and Fuji. Not only was the result a confusing commercial clutter, but it acted to depress the value of sponsorships and to inhibit companies from venturing into the field at all.

ISL developed a novel proposition for us to consider. What about a worldwide sponsorship program that would provide sponsors with advertising rights not only with respect to the Games, but also with every participating NOC? If this were to be combined with exclusivity within each product or service category, would the whole not have a value considerably in excess of the sum of its parts? Both Peter Ueberroth, president of the Los Angeles Olympic Organizing Committee, and Gary Hite, then responsible for the Olympic activities of Coca-Cola, approached me to see what I thought of the idea. I suppose they thought that, since I was now on the IOC executive board and responsible for television negotiations, I might have some influence on sponsorships as well as television. I believed in the concept, but was initially doubtful that they could organize anything on that scale. But if ISL was using the Adidas network and was willing to invest in the exploratory work to determine the financial and logistical parameters, it seemed to me to be a worthwhile endeavor. I said as much to Samaranch and he authorized Dassler to see what could be done. Monique Berlioux, the IOC director, was to be the IOC contact.

ISL put together a tentative program and there were some encouraging signs, especially from the access generated by the regular contacts Adidas personnel had with NOCs, that it might have some potential. Berlioux, however, was less than enthusiastic about any process that might reduce her control of the agenda and insisted that ISL was to go out, negotiate the contracts with potential sponsors, and then come to her for approval and such adjustments as she considered appropriate in each circumstance. It was a completely unworkable concept. The relationship between ISL and Berlioux deteriorated rapidly because ISL could see that a concept with potential was being thwarted by its client. I had not yet been drawn into the direct negotiations, but was kept informed of the progress and the problems.

Based on experience stretching back to before the Montreal Games, I had no faith whatsoever in Berlioux's ability to manage relationships with sponsors. That required an understanding of sponsor needs and the flexibility to manage those needs in conjunction with our own principles, something that could not be done by way of edicts from the autocratic IOC director. Berlioux and I had, by then, developed a healthy mutual dislike for each other. At a meeting of the IOC executive board in Calgary in early 1985, when Berlioux was reporting on developments, I made the point that we were getting reports based on versions of contracts that were out of date by one or two drafts, and insisted that we could not continue to proceed in such a manner. Samaranch, who was finally getting to the end of his rope with Berlioux, something that would come to a head a few months later, said, in the middle of the meeting, "Fine, Deek, you will be responsible for this now." "No, no," I said, "I don't want to do it. I just want the executive board to be properly informed when it is called upon to make decisions." "No," he said, "you do it."

That is how I got involved in the marketing portfolio. Stuck with something that I knew nothing about, I convened a meeting with the ISL representatives that same evening in Calgary, and asked for a situation report. They described the difficulties with Berlioux and said it was completely impossible for them to act as a consultant to the IOC if it meant trying to negotiate contracts with major international sponsors while having to go back to the sponsors with new demands issued by Berlioux. It destroyed any credibility they might have with potential sponsors and they could not even get a meeting with several of them under such circumstances. "What," I asked, "if you were able to go to them as the official agent of the IOC, the organizing committees of both the Summer and Winter Games and all the NOCs, backed up by written authorization?" They thought they had died and gone to heaven. They had not dared even to hint at such an arrangement to Berlioux, who would have rejected it out of hand.

I instructed them to design a program that would be presented on that basis and to come back to me within the next two weeks. Now that I had been put in charge, I said, we could make it happen, provided ISL was confident that it could get the NOCs, or at least a significant number of the most important ones, to agree. I would personally make the IOC and organizing committee portions of the puzzle work. And so The Olympic Program (TOP), the most successful international sports program in history, began to take shape. The revenues have gone from about $95 million for TOP to something in excess of $700 million for 2004.

One of the first problems I had to solve involved Dassler's suggestion that Coca-Cola become a shareholder in ISL. Dassler was trying to bring his allies into the financial tent to get commitment to the venture. I convinced Gary Hite that such a move by Coca-Cola would not be well perceived. I believed that all the sponsors should be at arm's length from the marketing agency. ISL proposed to "buy" each category of sponsorship from the NOC in each country, by guaranteeing the committee a specified sum of money. If

Coca-Cola were a partner in the agency, it would be seen as working to guarantee the lowest possible amount to each NOC, instead of an independently negotiated market-driven amount. That would do no good to Coca-Cola, especially as it was characterized as the archetypal U.S. company, even though it made more money outside the United States than it did at home. As a further reason, I said that I did not know enough about how ISL ran its soccer business and that Coca-Cola might wish to be careful about linking its reputation with that of ISL. As it turned out ten years later, my caution proved to have been well placed.

On the other side of the fence, I also made it clear to Dassler that I would not participate in the program unless it were understood and accepted that Adidas would not be included in any of the product categories in the program. This was a profound disappointment to Dassler, but he accepted that any such arrangement would ultimately be seen as a possible conflict of interest on his part. He reluctantly agreed to accept the limitation. It was essential that we get the program up and running in time for the 1988 Games in Calgary and Seoul, which were, by then, well into their preparations, so there were constant negotiations and discussions throughout the early part of 1985. I wanted to get the approval and go-ahead for TOP from the IOC session in the spring of 1985.

The U.S. lawyer who acted for ISL was Bernie Patrusky. Like Dassler, he was an inveterate cigar smoker. They seemed almost to have an ongoing contest between them as to who could find the biggest cigars. There was an amusing episode that arose out of Dassler's arrangements of meetings. A meeting would be scheduled between principals, but, before the actual meeting, there would often be a "pre-meeting" and, occasionally, depending upon the complexity of the issues and the varying interests of the parties, a "pre-pre-meeting." On one of the latter occasions, Dassler and Patrusky had locked themselves in a hotel bathroom to discuss some preliminary matter, fully armed with their cigars, and the discussion was animated enough and the smoking furious enough to set off the sprinkler system. They emerged in a great hurry, soaking wet, with the sodden remains of once-proud cigars.

In any event, we were ready for the executive board meeting and got the program approved, over the objections of Berthold Beitz, then the most influential member of the IOC's Finance Commission, fueled, no doubt, by Berlioux, who was not at all happy with having been removed from yet another position of influence and control within the IOC. Her departure from the IOC was soon to come—in fact, only days later at the same IOC session at which the TOP was given grudging approval.

There were the usual worries about being tainted by the dreaded commercialism and the expression of concern by risk-averse members who were worried about their personal financial liability in the event that the program was not a success. They did not seem to understand that they were not liable for the debts of the IOC under Swiss law, which governed such matters. We had also moved all the financial risk onto ISL, which provided the financial guarantees for the NOC buyouts. I dealt with all the questions and gave the most reassuring answers possible. It was enough to calm most of the doubts, and if it did not bring the session to its feet, cheering, we did get the approval. Our baby was born and we now had to be sure we made it work.

●　●　●

Because some of the sponsorship deals for the 1988 Games were already in place, the first edition of The Olympic Program was somewhat ad hoc. But later programs were more integrated and, over the years, TOP has become one of the most successful international marketing programs in the world, having a value of hundreds of millions of dollars. The proceeds are divided in half. Marketing rights are contributed by the Games organizers and the NOCs, and the revenue shares are designed to reflect these contributions. One-half goes to the organizing committees of the Games, of which roughly two-thirds are allocated to the larger Summer Games and one-third to the Winter Games. The other half is split 80 percent to the NOCs and 20 percent to the IOC for its own rights and the assistance given to organization of the program.

Of the NOC share, fully half goes to the USOC, a reflection of the importance of the U.S. market. The other NOCs share the balance and their portions generally reflect the relative importance of the markets in their countries. The U.S. share is, of course, resented enormously by the other NOCs and generates considerable ill will toward the United States. We have had a great deal of difficulty explaining that this is a marketing program that bears a relationship not to the importance of a country within the Olympic movement (in the form of the number of athletes who participate in the Games or the number of medals won), but only to the desirability of access to the various markets by commercial sponsors.

Most of our difficulties with the program arose out of the negotiations with the NOCs as to what their shares would be. We had to negotiate one by one with them and there were many jealousies to be reconciled as each NOC felt that it was far more important than any of its counterparts. The Soviet Union wanted as much as the United States, because it was as big politically and produced as many athletes, and Hungary claimed a larger share because it produced more athletes per capita, and so on. There was an element of redistribution of revenues, since only a handful of the NOCs had any sort of marketing programs, but we thought that all NOCs should get something from the program, even if it was a relatively token amount. Anything these NOCs got was essentially found money for them—and in U.S. dollars. It gave them access to funds that they would never have had without TOP. We negotiated some minimum amounts for each of the small NOCs such as Togo, Papua New Guinea and Mauritius, and allocated the balance on the basis of the relative values of the markets for the sponsors. Once everyone was equally unhappy, we knew we had it pretty well right.

In most cases, the TOP revenues exceeded anything the NOCs could have raised on their own and, in the final analysis, they knew that as well, so their professed reluctance to be herded into the program was largely theatrical posturing for negotiating purposes. We preserved the niceties and did not push the IOC into making the program compulsory, which would have been easy to accomplish by changing the Olympic Charter had we wanted to do so. It looked better to have a program agreed to by the NOCs than to have one forced on them by the IOC.

The organizing committees of the Games (OCOGs) were as much a problem as the NOCs. They always believed they were being screwed by TOP and were convinced that they could have sold each sponsorship category for much more than they got from TOP. In some respects, that was undoubtedly true, but OCOGs have a typically myopic view of the Olympic movement. They do not care a whit about anything other than their own Games. What had happened before their time and what might happen after was of not the slightest interest. The idea of an Olympic continuum was completely foreign to them. They did not accept the idea that other components of the Olympic movement would have a critical impact on the success of their Games, nor recognize that the TOP sponsors were opinion leaders in the marketplace and that their involvement with the Olympics made the other sponsorship categories reserved for the OCOGs that much more valuable. They invariably ended up resenting the TOP sponsors and did their best to make things difficult for them.

Whenever possible, they would try to sell sponsorships that encroached on the TOP categories. The most egregious example was what Sydney did to United Parcel Service (UPS) at the 2000 Games. The OCOG sold a category that was directly competitive with Olympic sponsor UPS to TNT, an Australian company, and simply refused to honor the TOP agreement, using pretexts, such as being unable to get the delivery envelopes ready in time, that were patently false as justifications for its behavior. The result was that UPS withdrew from TOP and we lost an excellent international sponsor in a category that would be hard to replace, one that was not replaced for 2004.

Other difficulties were the need to ensure that the sponsorship rights granted were exclusive, so that no competitors of the TOP sponsors could become Olympic sponsors anywhere in the world. This exclusivity was one of the main features of the program, since we were able to approach sponsors and say that not only would they be able to exercise their rights in every country of the world, but none of their competitors would be able to use an Olympic connection with their marketing activity. It was a significant value-added benefit for Olympic sponsors. The main international culprit in this regard was American Express. We had approached Amex as one of our first marketing calls when TOP was established in 1985. It turned us down, mainly, I think, because it thought we had no alternative in the credit card category and figured it could get a better price when we came crawling back. Instead, we took the audacious step of contacting Visa, which was a loose association of some sixteen thousand (at the time) banks. We reached an agreement, to the astonishment of Amex and, to some degree, ourselves.

The Olympic Program was a huge success for Visa and became one of the company's principal marketing thrusts. Amex was furious and tried on several occasions to ambush us and Visa with promotional and other programs, including a medallion program purportedly authorized by an organization with a name suspiciously similar to the IOC, to the point that legal actions were threatened and some taken. We unmasked several such initiatives and, each time, forced Amex to back off.

By 1992, I had personally ceased to use my American Express card for anything, but continued to carry it around with me and made it widely known that, if Amex undertook a single further ambush program, I would call a news conference and, in front of whatever media we could attract (which, if we stated the purpose of the conference, would have been extensive), I would publicly cut my card in half, saying that I could not countenance doing business with an organization that was associating itself improperly with the Olympics but was doing nothing whatsoever to support either the organization of the Games or the athletes who were training for them. Amex finally abandoned its campaign. Interestingly, after just a few years of the The Olympic Program, no Amex official who had been part of the initial rejection of the IOC offer was still employed by that company.

●　●　●

Anyone who has ever been part of a marketing sponsorship program is aware of yet a further difficulty, that of defining the category in which exclusivity is granted. The original categories included soft drinks, film, credit cards, typewriters, audio-video and messenger services. These have expanded in later programs to beverages, still imaging, document management, payment systems, wireless communications and so on. When we first started TOP, the categories were quite simple. We had Visa for credit cards, Coca-Cola for soft drinks, Kodak for film, and so forth. This was all well and good when the program was young, but businesses and appetites change and expand. Visa is not just credit cards anymore, but has evolved to payment systems generally. Kodak was, essentially, a chemical company that produced film, but film has all but disappeared and the category has become "still imaging." Coca-Cola now has all sorts of non-alcoholic beverages, not just soft drinks. John Hancock started as insurance, but the business has morphed into financial services and products. Even more troubling was the manner in which many businesses began to converge and it became harder and harder to identify the core category that had to be protected as activities began to overlap.

The computer category was an interesting story. We made an early presentation to the marketing department of IBM in Armonk, New York, in 1985, only to be dismissed, practically out of hand, by the company's marketing gurus. Their core business, we were told in no uncertain terms, was mainframe computers, a business-to-business operation, and nothing the Olympics had to offer was of the slightest interest to them. In vain, we urged them to consider that their business was changing, and how direct contact through the Olympics would be a wonderful platform for them. We were sneered out of the room. It was not until Lou Gerstner arrived at IBM in 1993 that we finally got back in the door. Having been with Amex, Gerstner recognized the opportunity that had been missed on the first round of Olympic marketing.

IBM became a sponsor for the 1996 Games and we made a two-Olympiad deal, both parties thinking that there could be a useful carryover from Games to Games. We had some idealized vision that the systems and solutions from one Games would be put into a package that could be plugged in at the next and be up and running perfectly at the flick of a switch. Neither of us realized the speed with which software would develop, making yesterday's solutions all but useless four years later, so the perceived advantages did not materialize. For our part, we did not anticipate the institutional difficulties of dealing with Big Blue—endless, agonizing meetings; huge bureaucracy; inflexibility; and an inability, bordering on the pathological, to admit either that it did not have an in-house solution to every need or that someone else could do it better and cheaper. After a disastrous failure of some of its systems in Atlanta, its response was to throw more and more people at the problems, with the result that its expenses were more, and it cost IBM and us more than we could possibly afford. We decided that the relationship would not be renewed after the Sydney Games in 2000, where, to IBM's credit, everything worked perfectly. At what cost to IBM, I dare not even guess.

By 1995, however, it had become clear to us that the ISL relationship was no longer satisfactory. Dassler had died and a series of ineffectual people was foisted on us. The new management, led by Christoph Malms, who was married to one of the Adi Dassler daughters, had, in my opinion, a completely unrealistic view of what was needed. ISL had taken on a series of financial commitments that seemed to us to be wildly extravagant and we decided that we should get out of the relationship.

In late 1995 in Karuizawa, Japan, I organized a meeting with Jean-Marie Weber, who had been one of Dassler's major advisers and became overall chair of ISL, during which I persuaded him that he was firing the IOC, not the reverse. The relationship was bad and this was, undoubtedly, the IOC's fault, I admitted, but continuing the partnership risked making ISL look bad at a time when it had so many other clients demanding attention. We had to find a way for ISL to announce that it was withdrawing from the IOC relationship but still providing some general advice for a transitional period. We would express our gratitude for the services rendered over the past ten years and generally make it clear that we would do our best to struggle along on our own.

By the time they figured out what had happened, it was too late. We had a harder time convincing Samaranch that this was the right thing to do, because he did not like change. We persisted, however, and it proved to have been an enlightened decision, because only a few years later, ISL's financial mismanagement caught up with it and it was forced into an acrimonious bankruptcy that was surrounded by allegations of fraud and other secret financial transactions. Several international federations, such as FIFA, had all their eggs in the ISL basket and were put in very difficult circumstances. ISL owed them millions, which they had little hope of collecting. The IOC was the only organization that had seen the signs of disintegration in time and had taken timely steps to disassociate itself from ISL.

Our ongoing strategy was to approach Laurent Scharapan, who had handled the NOC aspect of The Olympic Program for ISL, and Chris Welton, working at the time with the Atlanta OCOG under an uninspired marketing director (who had come from IBM), and to encourage them to establish their own company, Meridian Management. The IOC was willing to finance it, and it would become our

155

exclusive marketing agency. They could take on other clients if we agreed that this would not detract from the level of service we required. We got better service, for much less money that we had been paying the top-heavy ISL, and were soon providing much better service to our sponsors and the OCOGs than ever before.

The IOC maintained a 25 percent equity interest in Meridian, to help recover the costs of establishing the company, since Welton and Scharapan had no money, but the IOC had voting control, to ensure that IOC interests were protected. After I gave up the marketing portfolio in 2001, the IOC took the decision to buy full control of Meridian from Welton and Scharapan, which by then was an expensive proposition (to the tune of several million dollars) for the IOC. I have never been persuaded that this was a sensible step, but, as they say, those who are absent are always in the wrong. A regime change is a regime change, to the point where, although I inaugurated and ran the program for seventeen years, not a single request for a marketing comment or advice has come my way since July 2001.

I always considered it to be an advantage to have a buffer, however slight, between the IOC and the sponsors, as well as the NOCs and the OCOGs. If difficulties developed, we could point the finger at Meridian and say we would deal with the problem. If Meridian was getting flak from a sponsor or OCOG or NOC, it could blame the IOC, while working toward a solution. Since the interests were not fully congruent, temporary alliances could be established for the resolution of specific issues. Now that everyone knows Meridian is the full creature of the IOC, that convenient fiction—which was very useful on many occasions—has completely evaporated. Instead of remaining as a last resort to resolve problems, the IOC is now on the front line, not in the wings as the final arbiter, of any disputes. Only time will tell.

•   •   •

Marketing is a relationship business. Your sponsors have to know that you believe in the relationship, that you recognize their contributions as valuable to the Olympic movement and the Games, that you will support their promotional efforts and that, when necessary, you will fight for their rights. Much of my marketing time was spent in maintaining and strengthening our relationships. I met regularly with the CEOs and marketing vice-presidents, attended their internal workshops, made public statements about the value they provided to us and, quite often, defended their rights in front of my colleagues, who did not always understand the importance of the relationships.

The IOC members maintain a distressing tendency to believe that money grows on trees and that all they have to do is ask for more and it will fall into their hands. Marketing, in fact, is a tough business and it will generate value only if value is given in return. My insistence on giving value for value received undoubtedly did little to enhance my personal reputation among colleagues, although they seemed to appreciate the enhanced resources we enjoyed as a result of those efforts. But the sponsors appreciated the same efforts, and their confidence in my integrity was an important factor in maintaining their support.

In fact, there was an additional, and entirely unplanned, benefit from this when the Salt Lake City bidding scandal erupted in 1999. As the person responsible for leading the IOC's investigation into allegations that IOC members had accepted inappropriate benefits which swayed the choice of Salt Lake City as the site of the 2002 Games, I assured the sponsors that we would deal with the situation and clean up the mess. Because of our relationships through the marketing

157

portfolio, they believed me. They knew that I would not flinch from doing what was right, and they stuck with us through a difficult period (as outlined later). Without that relationship of confidence and trust, I am not sure that any of the North American–based sponsors would have remained.

One of my favorite TOP sponsors has been John Hancock. The executive who drove the sponsorship is David D'Alessandro, its CEO and the man still responsible, after the recent merger with Manulife, for the insurance and investment activities of the merged corporation in North America. He has always had a clear view of the value of a brand and recognized the fit between his brand and the Olympic brand. The marketing programs Hancock developed in conjunction with its Olympic sponsorship have always been both successful and very supportive of the Olympic message we hope to send. At the same time, D'Alessandro has been insistent that his Olympic partners do nothing that would tarnish his brand and, when the Salt Lake City scandal broke, he was very critical of the IOC for its role in it.

I could not have agreed more with his position and met him for lunch in New York to assure him that I would deal with it, but that, because of the peculiar nature of the IOC as an organization that met only once a year and consisted of volunteer members, we could not accomplish every-thing as quickly as might be the case with a corporate organization. In business, if something like the Salt Lake City scandal had occurred, the CEO and any others involved would be fired (probably with handsome settle-ments), the problem would be declared "solved," and life would continue. We could not act that quickly, I told him, but we would act and we would have the matter resolved before the end of the year.

His public criticism of us was not popular, especially with Samaranch, who thought it was terrible for a sponsor to criticize the IOC and its president in such circumstances. I disagreed. Our actions had tarnished our brand and those of our partners, and I thought it better to have this kind of pressure to make sure the IOC would deal firmly with the unacceptable behavior of its members. I was deathly afraid that the response might get watered down and that the IOC would be perceived as soft on its own shortcomings. That would have been the end of us. D'Alessandro stayed in our face throughout 1999.

Finally, once the offending members had resigned or been expelled, the IOC reforms had been adopted and Samaranch had made an appearance in the U.S. Congress, I made my last trip of the year to Boston just before Christmas to meet with D'Alessandro. "David," I said, "we have done everything I told you we would do, even though it took longer than you would have wished." He was very fair and agreed that we had. The big question was whether John Hancock would be willing to renew its TOP sponsorship following the Sydney Games. For me, it was an absolutely crucial moment, because if the sponsor that had been most critical of the IOC were to come back into the fold for the next four years, it would be the best evidence that the IOC had dealt with its problems. "Now that we have done all this, are you 'in' for 2004?" I asked. He thought for a moment and said, "I'm in, and, furthermore, I am not going to nickel-and-dime you to get the price down because of all the problems." That is my idea of a great partner. Demanding, as it should be when our conduct was unacceptable, supportive with tough love, and solid going forward. For me personally, it was the best moment in an otherwise Olympic Year from Hell.

• • •

I am always both perplexed and somewhat amused by the concerns that are expressed in the media about commercial support of the Olympic Games. This feature attracts more ink and electronic comment than almost any other aspect of the Games, often appearing in danger of overshadowing the Games themselves. This never seems to emerge as an issue in the context of any other sporting event, where sponsorship is an accepted and welcome fact of life. I take some heart from the concern, however, because where it is genuine, as opposed to mere carping about a successful undertaking, I treat it as a recognition that the Olympics are, indeed, special in the minds of the public at large. And we on the IOC are very conscious of this special nature of the Games. We do our best to preserve and enhance it.

Before reaching a snap judgment on commercial involvement, we should consider the alternatives. The financial pressures on governments today make it unrealistic to expect them to be able to underwrite all the costs of a high-end event such as the Games. Their responsibility is to ensure the basic infrastructure appropriate to the needs of their particular societies and to develop an accessible sport system that has a high performance component. That is a good reason for some countries not to aspire to hosting the Olympic Games too early in their development.

Where, then, does one look—to the athletes or participants themselves? This is a complete non-starter and, even if feasible (which it is not), would restrict sport to the wealthy, a backward social step that I do not even want to contemplate. We have come too far in making sport available to the whole of society to consider such regression. That leaves, if only by default, the private sector. I do not, however, regard this as a default consideration. I believe it is both right and proper that the private sector be actively involved in the Olympic movement and the Olympic

Games. Don't forget that the whole sports system all around the world is essentially a manifestation of volunteers in the private sector, not of governments. Far from avoiding such involvement, we actively seek it, but on certain terms and conditions that we believe to be important for the Games and, in the long run, for the private sector itself.

Generally speaking, the private sector participates in two ways. The first is by buying tickets to the Games and, to a lesser extent, souvenirs. The amounts involved will obviously vary from country to country and according to the size of the stadiums, as well as the economic conditions that prevail in the host country. The next level of private sector involvement in the Games comes from sponsors. There are some important ground rules that need to be understood about commercial sponsorship. The first is that sponsorship is not charity. It is a business decision that is expected to generate a return on investment. Sponsors have an obligation to invest their stockholders' money to generate a return. Corporations, their brands, their products and their services seek to associate themselves with the many evocative images and values of the Olympic movement. These Olympic images add value to their enterprises.

We, in the Olympic movement, have several obligations of our own. In relation to sponsors, we have the duty to give value if we want to receive value. I want happy sponsors, not those who are disappointed or for whom the Olympic sponsorship is neutral—just another media buy. I would happily forgo any money we might get from an unhappy sponsor. My view has always been to try to be sure we leave some extra value on the table and that we not extract the last dollar from any sponsor. I want Olympic sponsorship to deliver more than we promise and to generate a higher return for sponsors than they think they have paid for.

We have to protect the rights we grant, resorting to legal action if necessary, although I find that public exposure of ambushers or parasite marketers is generally more effective than lawsuits. We had an interesting example of this in Atlanta in 1996. Nike is a company that produces excellent products, but it had adopted an aggressive marketing posture, essentially a counterculture to real sports values. The company was running an ad campaign in Atlanta that used the tagline "You don't win silver, you lose gold." It was a completely inappropriate campaign at the time of the Games and we asked them to stop it. They refused, saying that it worked very well for them. We asked them to withdraw it, at least during the Olympics. They refused. "All right," I said, "then we are going to hold a press conference, to which we will invite the young American gymnasts who have just won the silver medal, and have them appear, with the appropriate amount of tears, to say they do not understand why a company like Nike is mocking their achievement and all their years of work." Nike relented and withdrew the campaign.

We did not leave it there, however, and did our best to convince Nike that it would be better for them to become mainstream and support the efforts of aspiring Olympic athletes, since they did have superb product lines. This paid an unexpected dividend less than three years later when, in the middle of the Salt Lake City crisis, the 2000 Games sponsor, Reebok, suddenly withdrew its sponsorship, for reasons unrelated to the crisis. We immediately got through to our Nike contacts and said there was an opportunity for them, if they could act quickly. We put together a full sponsorship deal for Sydney in forty-eight hours, working round the clock, and were able to make it public in the midst of the crisis, thus showing the ongoing value of the Olympics despite the current furor. Even the Australians were impressed with this ability to replace one of their sponsors so quickly and effectively. It also saved expensive and time-consuming litigation with Reebok, whose officials were equally stunned by the speed with which they became irrelevant.

● ● ●

We have an obligation to be sure that the Olympics remain the premier sporting event in the world. So far, I believe we have delivered on that obligation. There are many external validations of this, as can be seen from the huge long-term television and sponsorship agreements we have reached, some of which extended to Games whose locations had yet to be decided. We must, in marketing terms, continue to enhance and preserve the Olympic brand. In recent years, we have begun to think of the Olympics as a special form of franchise, in which the IOC is the franchisor and the host cities are the franchisees. It is up to us to define the basic parameters and standards we expect, and to see that these standards are met and even exceeded by our franchisees. Above all, we must be sure that no franchisee devalues the Olympic franchise.

In the relationships we have with sponsors, we accept that the level of investment entitles the sponsors to visibility—and lots of visibility. After all, the event could not occur without them. Not only that, but in the promotion of their sponsorships, our sponsors spend millions—hundreds of millions—of dollars enhancing our own franchise. Anyone who has seen the commercial messages at the time of the Games will recall how positive they were and what wonderful support they generated for everything we are trying to develop, in a way that we could never afford to do with our limited budget. This visibility is, however, controlled by the IOC. We have well-established guidelines regarding publicity and the appropriate use of the Olympic rings.

Unlike any other international sporting event, for example, the Games have a strict rule that there will be no advertising in the competition venues. Our sponsors, after some initial resistance, have come around to understanding that this feature is better for them in the long run, and that it underlines the special nature of the event they have helped to make possible. Even a company such as Coca-Cola, which believes in and specializes in presence marketing (it uses this in almost every other sponsorship), and which was always trying to find some way to create visibility for itself on the field of play, has acknowledged that the Olympic sponsorships should differ from the norm. The longer a company has been an Olympic sponsor, the more it becomes a partner with us in protecting the specialness of the Games.

We had a relationship with Mars Inc., the confectionary company, at the time of the Barcelona Games in 1992. The marketing program that Mars adopted was based on its view that the purchase of a chocolate bar or a snack was an impulse decision by the consumer, and Mars believed that this required a constant presence of its products or images of them, despite restrictions that had been agreed upon. We were always finding their signs, balloons and other promotional materials where they should not have been. Their people were so uncooperative that one day, shortly before the Games began, after yet another blowup with them, I called the senior person from the company headquarters to our marketing office in Barcelona and said, "If I give you your marketing rights fee back, will you go home?" It was only then that the penny dropped and their conduct thereafter complied with their contract.

We are very satisfied with our Olympic sponsors. They deliver everything we want and hope for from them, and I am proud that the Olympic movement has been able to attract and retain their support. There is, in my view, no question of there being too much commercialism on their part. They do what they do by virtue of agreements with us and with our blessing. We are not satisfied with parasite marketers, who pretend or try to create the impression that they are connected with the Games when they are not and who try to suck value out of an event to whose success they have not contributed. We do our best to create such a high level of public discomfort for them that they fold up their tents and sneak back out of town.

We were not, for example, satisfied by the ambush and street-vending programs undertaken by Atlanta, the 1996 host city, which had sought to avoid any financial responsibility for the Games yet make a profit at the expense of the organizing committee that was trying to raise enough money to pay for the Games. City facilities were used to host programs by competitors of Olympic sponsors, who had paid millions to help with the organization of the Games. The vending programs, authorized by the mayor, led to the cluttering of the Atlanta streets with shabby tents and kiosks that gave the impression of a vast MASH unit. This left a bad impression on visitors to Atlanta and, one would hope, on Atlantans themselves.

Nor was anyone else impressed with this particular aspect of Atlanta. Dick Ebersol, head of NBC Sports, the U.S. Olympic broadcaster, had a standing rule that any employee who aired a shot of the City of Atlanta, even through inadvertence, would be fired on the spot. Fortunately, therefore, not too many people were forced to see what the city looked like during the Games. But, as president Samaranch has said, Atlanta produced "exceptional" Games, a description chosen with some care, given the lack of cooperation from the city authorities, not to mention the bomb. It enraged Atlanta. Those Games are, thankfully, now well behind us. Many of the broadcast and sponsor personnel who lived through the Atlanta experience said that the most enjoyable view of Atlanta was the one that appeared in their rearview mirrors as they left. Each time we organize an edition of the Games, we learn something and we certainly learned in Atlanta.

Commercialism will be with us as long as the Games are the leading sports event in the world. Sponsors will help us keep the Games as the leading sports event in the world. We will continue controlling the level of commercial signage and identification, as well as ensuring that the decisions affecting sport are made by the responsible sports authorities and in the best interests of athletes. As for me, color me an enthusiast. Without commercial support, sport as we know it today, and the Olympic Games, would simply not exist. Trust me on this.

 Broadcast Bonanza: TV Rights

Not long before the 1960 Olympic Games, International Olympic Committee president Avery Brundage announced with great portent that the Olympics had got along very well without television for sixty years and could do so in the future as well. Famous last words! This final pronouncement on Olympic television was no sooner out of Brundage's mouth than the television coverage of the 1960 Olympics, both Summer and Winter, began a whole new era for the Games. Instead of reading about the Olympics, hearing about them on the radio, or occasionally seeing them in newsreels at the cinema, hundreds of millions of people throughout the world could suddenly experience the Games in an immediate and almost personal way. In the course of a single generation, the power of television has made the Olympic Games the most universally watched event in well over two hundred countries. Some 3.7 billion individual viewers watched the 2000 Games in Sydney, Australia.

The IOC's foray into this brave new world was tempered by Brundage's view that television was not particularly important. The IOC itself took little interest in the awarding of television rights, and virtually abdicated its position in the matter in favor of the organizing committees that had been established within the host countries of the Games. These committees negotiated the rights and gave the IOC a modest share of the rights fees, usually about a third. To be sure, the economics of the day were such that these rights fees did not warrant too much attention, especially as a percentage of the overall costs of the Games.

For broadcasting the 1960 Rome Olympics, CBS paid less than US$400,000 (all of the rights figures are in U.S. dollars) for the U.S. rights, and the worldwide total was less than $1.2 million. However, the overall amounts increased fairly quickly thereafter to $1.6 million for Tokyo in 1964, $9.75 million for Mexico in 1968, $17.8 million for Munich in 1972, and $35 million for Montreal in 1976. The really enormous increases started after the Montreal Games: $100 million for Moscow in 1980; $287 million for Los Angeles in 1984; $403 million for Seoul in 1988; $635 million for Barcelona in 1992; and more than $930 million for the Atlanta Games in 1996. The rights fees grew close to $2 billion for 2008 in Beijing.

Even as it started to grow noticeably in importance, the economic return from television did not seem to attract much attention at Olympic headquarters. What the IOC had failed to grasp in the early years was that television would become the dominant medium through which the world would experience the Olympic Games and that the television record of the Games would become a vital part of the historical tradition of the Olympic movement. Long after the IOC should have recognized the importance of television and the television rights it held as "owner" of the

Olympic Games, it contented itself with passive sharing of whatever revenues may have been negotiated by the local organizing committees. It did nothing to put an IOC stamp on the television negotiations or the broadcasts, nor to ensure that there was a reasonable promotion of the Olympic movement as part of the broadcast package. Even more importantly, it did nothing to get the permanent record of the Games into the hands and control of the IOC, which was the body responsible (or, more accurately, the body that should have been responsible) for maintaining the definitive history of the modern Olympic movement.

It was not until after the 1984 television rights to the Los Angeles Games had been negotiated that the IOC finally woke up to the economic reality, which included the disconcerting fact that the local organizing committees cared little for the IOC when negotiating television rights and were quite prepared to shade their deals in their own favor. The example that set off the alarm was the process for the U.S. television rights, which brought in U.S. rights fees of $225 million. The Los Angeles Olympic Organizing Committee (LAOOC) unilaterally decided that $125 million of this amount represented its costs of providing facilities for the broadcaster and that the "real" rights fee was only $100 million. Since the IOC was entitled to one-third of the rights fee, the L.A. committee paid the IOC $33 million and refused to discuss any other figure. There was nothing the IOC could do. The $100 million was a lot more than had been negotiated previously for U.S. rights, so it was a mixed blessing.

The other issue that finally began to emerge was that the organizing committees had had no interest in what came after their Games. They lived entirely in the present, unencumbered by any responsibility for the future; they simply wanted the money from the television rights. The contracts they negotiated did not give the IOC clear ownership of the historical material following the Games. The blame is not entirely theirs, however, because the IOC had not acted to ensure that its own interests were properly served, so it may be more equitable to lay the blame squarely at the foot of the IOC, which should have known better. ABC—which, having broadcast most of the recent Games, viewed itself as *the* Olympic network—claimed the Olympic material was its own and charged very high fees to provide the material to any other broadcasters who wanted to use it for their own reports of the Games. Not only that, but for many years, ABC would assert that no one could televise any material from those Games in the United States without its consent, since it viewed its Olympic television rights as exclusive.

• • •

I was never sure what led to my becoming responsible for the IOC's television negotiations. It came out of the blue a few years into Juan Antonio Samaranch's two-decade stretch as IOC president. Shortly after I had been elected to the IOC executive board at the 1983 session in New Delhi, Samaranch took me aside and said, "Deek, I want you to become the chairman of the IOC Television Negotiations Committee." That was the first notice I had, although I knew by then that he wanted the IOC to play a more active role in this process, especially after the Los Angeles negotiations. LAOOC basically believed that whatever the IOC received from television rights for the L.A. Games was essentially the IOC stealing some of its money, and most other Olympic organizing committees agreed. LAOOC considered that $33 million was more than enough of a windfall for the IOC and was quite unapologetic about its decision to allocate more than half of the U.S. rights total for the 1984 Games to technical assistance. On the IOC side, there were indications that the organization had no idea of the time value of money, since its counsel, who had been given an advance payment of $25 million against the total of $33 million, carried the check around with him for almost three weeks before depositing it in the IOC's account. In those days of high interest rates, the IOC lost and LAOOC gained more than $100,000 in interest. LAOOC could hardly believe its good fortune.

From the moment it was stuck with a $33-million rights cut in 1979, the IOC realized it would have to achieve greater control over the negotiations. This was easier said than done, because of the history of Olympic negotiations and the expectations of the organizing committees. Beginning with the host city contracts signed in 1981 for the 1988 Olympics, the IOC amended its rights vis-à-vis the organizing committees to provide that negotiations for television rights to the Games would be joint and that the IOC would play an active role in the process.

This development was not welcomed by the organizing committees, which bitterly resented the intrusion of the IOC into what they regarded as their territory. Even though contracts between the IOC and the host cities have always contained a general requirement for IOC approval, the host cities used to regard this as passive involvement, at best, and neither expected nor wanted the IOC to play any active role, especially in something as important as television. As the IOC began to assert itself, the broadcasters would have been keenly aware that they could not make a deal without the IOC and that the organizing committees would be gone after the Games, while the IOC would remain. So there was mainly bitching and complaining, pouting and tears. The organizing committees had allowed themselves over time to drift into the mental attitude that, because the IOC permitted them to negotiate the television rights, those rights belonged to the organizing committees, and that the perfidious IOC was taking something of "theirs" when it received its share of the rights fees.

One of the reasons behind Samaranch's decision to insert me into the process was the increasing tension between himself and Berlioux. Samaranch wanted to loosen Berlioux's iron grip on IOC activities. She had built up her power base during the largely absentee presidencies of Brundage and Killanin, and now presided over the whole matter of Olympic television. Samaranch knew that she and I did not like each other and my appointment to the position of committee chair was certain to be an annoyance to her.

Whatever the reasons, there I was, in a situation that I knew precious little about, but one that was essential to the future of the IOC. The next negotiations would be for the 1988 Winter Games in Calgary. Advising the local organizing committee, Olympiques Calgary Olympics (OCO'88), was TWI International in the person of Barry Frank, a former television executive and head of CBS Sports. Frank had encouraged OCO'88 to bank on an aggressive television budget—in excess of US$200 million for U.S. rights, well beyond anything ever seen for Winter Games. (The 1980 Lake Placid Winter Games had made only $21 million in television rights, despite the fact that they were in the United States.)

Frank and OCO'88 sat down with me to discuss the situation, which included what I thought was a justified suspicion that ABC had generated a well-beaten inside track with respect to the IOC and television rights. This had been made possible, it was suggested, by a close relationship between Berlioux and ABC's European representative, Georges Crozes. Many suspected them of discussing the bids of other networks, including what bid ABC would have to beat. This was before my time so I had no idea if it was true or not, but the perception had to be dealt with. The first objective I set for the negotiations was to assure all the networks that, even if there had been a preference in previous negotiations, under my leadership there would be a completely level playing field. I was satisfied that any one of the three major U.S. networks was perfectly capable of broadcasting the Games at a level satisfactory to the IOC.

There would be no side deals or separate contracts that might give any network an advantage, such as different rights or easier payment schedules. I said we would prepare a draft contract and send it for comments to all three networks. They would have an opportunity to comment and make suggestions, which we would collect and consider. We would incorporate those that we thought were helpful and issue a final contract, on which they could bid. I went so far as to set a condition that even to participate in the negotiations, each bidding network was required to deliver a fully executed contract to me, with only the total rights fee left blank, together with a written authorization to me to fill in the final negotiated amount in the contract signed by the winning network. If they did not agree to this procedure, they could not participate in the bidding.

The networks that had been excluded from Olympic television contracts in the past were ecstatic with the process. ABC was distinctly unhappy, especially Roone Arledge, head of ABC Sports, who maintained that ABC's experience as an Olympic broadcaster was being completely discounted and that the network should rightly be considered as *the* Olympic broadcaster. My position was firm; the credibility and fairness of the IOC in these negotiations was paramount. Even Muhammad Ali had to take off his championship belt from time to time and step into the ring, I said, to renew his claim to be the heavyweight champion of the world. This was such an occasion for ABC.

The biggest issue with OCO'88 was the timing of the negotiations. TWI believed that the longer we waited, the more valuable the rights would become. Samaranch and I both felt that the 1984 Sarajevo Winter Games would not be a success, either for U.S. television or for the U.S. Olympic team. ABC had been selling advertising time during the Sarajevo Games at large premiums, hyping them as "Miracle on Ice II" in the wake of the spectacular outcome of the ice hockey tournament at Lake Placid in 1980. We did not think lightning would strike twice. There might be a figure skating medal or two, but other U.S. pickings would be slim. For these reasons we wanted the Calgary negotiations to be held before the Sarajevo Games. But OCO'88 refused. The contract between the IOC and OCO'88 provided that the television negotiations were to be conducted jointly, so we could not proceed unilaterally. We gave our reasons for negotiating early, but OCO'88 insisted on waiting.

Finally, I went to Samaranch to say that we had an impasse and that I could see only one way out of it: let OCO'88 negotiate whenever it wanted, but I wanted to force the issue by demanding that OCO'88 guarantee the IOC its share of the minimum amount that TWI had said the organizing committee would get. As I recall, this minimum was $208 million. Samaranch agreed, and I put the proposition to OCO'88. Either it guaranteed the IOC its share of the minimum or we would negotiate in January 1984, before the Sarajevo Games. OCO'88 could not take such a financial risk and did not have the tenacity to stand up to the IOC, so, with a great deal of grumbling, agreed that we could proceed before Sarajevo. It was the best financial decision the Calgary committee ever made.

● ● ●

The bidding process for U.S. rights to the Calgary Games took place in late January 1984 in Lausanne, which ABC's Arledge scornfully dubbed "the television capital of the world." Personally, I would have preferred to meet in New York, home base for the broadcasters, but Samaranch preferred to play up the IOC's prestige at the Lausanne Palace Hotel. Bids were to be in writing, at or above amounts we specified. They went much higher that we had ever expected. CBS dropped out early, but ABC and NBC fought it out to the level of $300 million. There seemed to be no way out. I called representatives of both networks to the meeting room and said that we faced something of a dilemma. Both networks had demonstrated an interest in the rights that was far in excess of anything we had expected. The two bids were now exactly equal and I was not willing to choose one over the other. They would have to settle the matter between themselves through their bids.

Because it was already very late in the evening, I said that the bids would speed up to one every fifteen minutes and that each bid had to be $1 million higher than the other in order to be valid. Who wanted to go first? No one volunteered. Neither party was willing to cut cards either, so I suggested that we flip a coin. I told Arthur Watson of NBC to make the call while the coin was in the air, and flipped it. Watson was so nervous that he forgot to call, so we had to do it again. He won and, surprisingly, after no one had wanted to go first, said that NBC would bid first. Its bid was $304 million. ABC was advised. Its team returned at the appointed time and gave me the envelope. In it was a slip of paper that said "$309 Million." They had seen NBC's raise of $4 million, and raised it by $5 million. Bob Mulholland of NBC folded his cards and shook hands with ABC's Jim Spence.

By now it was two o'clock in the morning, but Samaranch had insisted that I call him when there was a result. I woke him up. "Is there a decision?" he asked. "Yes," I replied, "ABC beat NBC." "How much?" he asked. "$309 million," I said. "Is too much," he said, and I agreed but said I had not been able to stop the escalation. Samaranch was right. ABC ended up losing money on the Calgary Games. That is not good for Olympic business. We want our partners and sponsors to be pleased with their Olympic experience.

We had a drink with most of the participants after the harrowing process, but Arledge was so furious about the outcome that he refused to join us in the lobby for the occasion. Three or four years later, when I was in New York for some other purpose, he invited me to dinner, just the two of us, in the Jockey Club restaurant at the Ritz Carlton Hotel on Central Park South. We were talking about the Olympics in general and the future of television. No one had done more to make U.S. sports television so popular and he had done a wonderful job for the Olympics in the process, so I was delighted to have an evening by myself with this television pioneer.

I was fascinated with the history and the trade gossip that he provided, almost non-stop, throughout our dinner. In the midst of this, he asked if I remembered how angry he had been at the time of the Calgary negotiations. I told him that I could hardly forget and that I was sorry ABC had ended up losing money on the deal. But I hoped that he had come to understand my position in the matter. He said that he understood my inability and unwillingness to interfere with the process. But was I aware that ABC had been in regular contact with Barry Frank leading up to the negotiations? I was not, I said, but added that it would not have surprised me if OCO'88's agent had been doing whatever he could to encourage active bidding for the rights. It also helped to explain why the bidding started out so high and went higher.

Pound meets Pope John Paul II, Rome 1982. Also seen in the photograph are Juan Antonio Samaranch and Kees Kerdel, IOC *chef du protocole.*

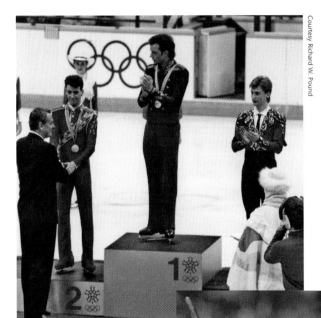

Dick Pound presents medals for the men's figure skating event—the "Battle of the Brians"—at the 1998 Calgary Winter Olympics (gold: Brian Boitano, USA; silver: Brian Orser, Canada; bronze: Viktor Petrenko, Soviet Union).

Ben Johnson of Canada wins the 100 meters in world-record time at the 1988 Summer Olympics in Seoul, South Korea. Only days later he was stripped of his gold medal in disgrace as he tested positive for anabolic steroids. Doping remains the single greatest danger that faces sport today.

Fidel Castro, President of Cuba, looks on at the opening ceremony of the 1992 Summer Olympics in Barcelona, the first Games for Cuba since Moscow in 1980.

At the 1992 Summer Olympics in Barcelona, the most poignant figure of all was Nelson Mandela, there to see South African athletes participate in the Games for the first time in thirty-two years, after the end of apartheid and the lifting of the Olympic ban against South Africa.

Barcelona 1992: King Juan Carlos of Spain presents Dick Pound with a Spanish decoration, in the presence of Queen Sofia in the foreground and Juan Antonio Samaranch in the background.

Standing: François Carrard (IOC Director General), Dick Pound, Don Petroni (O'Melveny & Myers); seated: Marcus Jurger (promoter of Olympic Spirit project), Michael Payne (IOC Marketing Director); Olympic Winter Games, Nagano 1998.

Pound and Juan Antonio Samaranch, then-President of the IOC, in Paris City Hall, 2000.

Dick Pound in a media scrum, discussing his "bronze medal" in the IOC presidential race, Moscow 2001.

Pound and Jacques Rogge in Dakar, February 2001. Rogge was elected IOC President in July of that year, becoming the fourth IOC president under whom Pound has served.

Jamie Salé and David Pelletier of Canada react with disbelief to their marks in the pairs figure skating event at the 2002 Winter Games in Salt Lake City. The audience was stunned and a public outcry over their silver-medal finish uncovered a judging scandal that made news during the Games and that continues to hang over the sport.

The International Skating Union, under pressure from the International Olympic Committee, agreed that the IOC should award a second set of gold medals in the event. Jamie Salé and David Pelletier receive their gold medals, alongside the gold medallists from Russia, Elena Berezhnaya and Anton Sikharulidze.

The opening ceremonies at the 2002 Winter Olympics in Salt Lake City. These were more welcome fireworks than those arising out of the scandal that erupted around the bidding process for the Salt Lake Games.

Dick Pound, Olympic Congress, Paris 1994.

Frank probably did not think that any other network would go higher than $275 million and from his discussions with Frank, Arledge concluded that if ABC went to $280 million, that would suffice and that I could be counted on to stop the negotiations there and declare a winner. Bidding high at each stage also made it possible that other networks would be scared off, which may have accounted for the strategy in the early rounds, and that did have the desired effect on CBS. Each time we set the new level, it was against ABC's high bid at the preceding round. The format we adopted was designed deliberately not to close out any network that was still ready to continue, and NBC hung in—just marginally above the threshold. In the discussions about what I, as chair of the negotiations, would do, they had given me a code name, said Arledge, of "Sterling." Arledge had believed that if ABC were to bid $280 million, Sterling would do his "thing" and halt the bidding. Unfortunately, Sterling did not know of any such arrangement and would not, in any event, have agreed to it.

In retrospect, it was fortunate that we had insisted on signed contracts before the bidding. I can barely imagine the grief we would have had in the face of a winning network that thought it had paid too much and had been misled in the bidding process. Now, even with a fully negotiated contract in hand, ABC still asked for a reduction in the rights fee, but we did not agree. The projected advertising rates did not materialize for ABC and inflation abated somewhat before 1988, so ABC incurred a loss that it estimated in the range of $75 million, despite successful Games in Calgary.

It is difficult to know for sure whether this figure was fully accurate, since when things go bad, it is often best to lump an assortment of other problems together and declare a single disaster. New managers in corporations do this regularly. Despite having the U.S. rights to both Sarajevo and Los Angeles in 1984, ABC soured on the Olympics after the Calgary experience and it was the network's last Games to date. From time to time, the ABC team has bid rather desultorily, but it has never been willing to go the whole way.

No other broadcaster came anywhere close to ABC in the amount of rights fees. The most disappointing outcome was when the European Broadcasting Union (EBU), a consortium of western European broadcasters, paid less than $6 million for the European rights to the 1988 Games in Calgary. This was my first close-up experience with the European negotiations, but Samaranch did not allow me to get involved in that process. He said that he understood Europe better than I did and that it was a special situation, so he would, with Marc Hodler, handle those negotiations himself.

EBU had somehow managed to convince everyone that its members—for the most part, state-owned broadcasters— could not afford to pay reasonable rights fees. They could afford to pay millions of dollars for regular episodes of programs such as *Dallas* for viewers who had to be protected from the dangers of American culture, but apparently had no money to pay for the Olympics.

They had also claimed that the costs of covering sports events on a regular basis were so high that they had no money left over for the Olympics. If they had to pay a reasonable amount for the Olympics, they could not provide sports coverage between the Games. This was ridiculous and I said as much whenever possible. It was, in fact, arrant nonsense, but Samaranch seemed to be bewitched. EBU made sure they presented him with a trophy each year for his outstanding support. In all the years I did television negotiations for the IOC, I was never allowed near the EBU discussions. All my work in getting the EBU to anything near a fair and reasonable level had to be done offstage, but I confess to having enjoyed some success over the years. Whenever there was a signing ceremony with EBU, I made a point of not being present, which seemed to make them even more nervous whenever we were together.

● ● ●

Although the Calgary and Seoul Games were awarded to their host cities at the same IOC session in Baden-Baden in 1981, it took much longer for everyone to be ready to negotiate the U.S. rights for the Seoul Games. In the first place, after the Calgary negotiations, the networks rebelled against a process that reduced the whole decision to one of money. They wanted the chance to negotiate their own contracts and to show what their plans would be for the broadcast of the Games, in the hope that some of the intangibles might make a difference. NBC also wanted to discuss the insurance of pre-Games costs. It had won the broadcast rights for the 1980 Moscow Games, and recovered its rights fees from its insurers after the boycott, since the U.S. government had not allowed the network to actually cover the Games. But NBC had forgotten to insure against its pre-Games costs, such as the travel and preparatory installations, cabling and other expenses that are incurred before the actual broadcasting of the Games.

For our part, we were very much aware in 1981 that we had scored a major coup with Calgary and that the market was unsettled in the wake of those negotiations. The certainty of the Games actually taking place in Seoul was also somewhat suspect, given the political instabilities that existed on the Korean peninsula. The change in attitude of the Soviet Union with respect to the Los Angeles Games had a negative impact, as had the Soviets' earlier shooting down of a Korean Air Lines passenger plane. North Korea had recently been implicated in a bombing in Rangoon that had killed several South Korean ministers and other officials, and meetings between the two Koreas regarding a joint team in Los Angeles broke down when the North determined to boycott the Games. It was a sobering backdrop to any television negotiations.

The negotiations were, again, held at the Lausanne Palace Hotel. This time I thought it was the right choice of location, since the Koreans would have been even more suspicious of the IOC had we agreed to negotiate on the home territory of the U.S. networks. The financial bids were very low, much lower than anyone had imagined before the negotiations. CBS was at $275 million; ABC at $300 million; and NBC at a guaranteed $325 million, with a very soft possibility of revenue-sharing if sales exceeded its estimates. There seemed to be no sign of movement. The Korean team at the negotiations was unable to make any decision. They simply said nothing. The real decision makers were not at the table. The sports minister, Lee Young-Ho, and the IOC member, Park Chong-Kyu, stayed in a separate room, so that the Koreans would have the flexibility of consultation outside the room. But even they were gofers. The real decision makers were in Korea.

Once it became clear that we were in the range of the market at the time, it was necessary to convince the Koreans that this was the case and not some nefarious plot to deceive them as Asians inexperienced in the North American market. The ostensible negotiators said nothing. I mean literally nothing, despite my efforts to get them to respond. Some of them, including Un Yong Kim, slept in their chairs. It was obvious that they would do nothing. The networks were getting impatient as the delay went on and we did not give them any indication regarding their bids.

We eventually suggested that they go to dinner while we considered the matter. I found Lee and took him aside to discuss the offers. I told him that I was satisfied that we were not going to get any more than had been offered and that I thought, disappointing as it may have been, that we should accept the NBC offer. The bid was not a bluff. The Americans were in a highly competitive environment and collusion among them to keep the price artificially low was all but impossible, not to say illegal under U.S. antitrust law. Lee, who had spent a bit of time on a course at Yale University, said he understood the Americans, that they were bluffing, and that he knew more about negotiating with them than we did. I told him that if I were in Korea and negotiating with Koreans, I would take his advice. He was adamant. I finally said that while we were sitting here doing nothing, the networks were getting angrier and angrier with the lack of response and it could be costing us millions of dollars an hour. He was unmoved.

Eventually I called Samaranch to advise him of the disappointing offers. I also told him about the apparent inability of the Koreans to give a meaningful response, which, I thought might be a result of the offers being so low that the Koreans had no power to reply. It seemed to me that we might have to get authority directly from Korea if anything was going to happen. The problem was the time difference between Lausanne and Seoul. Everyone was asleep back home, and the Koreans did not dare to wake up the president of the Republic of Korea, Chun Doo Hwan, or the president of the Seoul Olympic Organizing Committee, Roh Tae Woo (later to replace Chun as president of the republic), to get instructions. Such calls in the middle of the night were apparently regarded by the Koreans as severely career-limiting or even career-ending.

As soon as possible, Korean time, Samaranch placed a call to Roh to give him the news. Roh was surprised and disappointed. He wanted to know our opinion on whether we should accept the offer. We said he should. Roh said he would check with Chun and call back as soon as he could. By this time, we had resumed negotiations in the morning, but, as time went on, we were forced to tell the networks that we did not believe we could finish the negotiations on this occasion because the Koreans had to get instructions from Seoul and these had not yet been available. It was not until just after we had fixed a new date, this time in New York, that we finally heard back from Roh. He told us that the delegation had been instructed not to accept anything less than $550 million, which explained why they were all afraid to say anything when they saw the level of the offers. If we were certain that the offers were as high as we could get, then, relying on the IOC's advice, Roh said they would accept the highest offer with the greatest reluctance. I was forced to say that I was no longer sure that the offer was still on the table, since we had been forced to tell the networks that we had to defer the whole matter for a few weeks.

When we reassembled in New York, my worst fears were realized. NBC's minimum offer had been reduced by $25 million to $300 million. Although it was not a complete surprise, it was nevertheless quite annoying. NBC appeared to us to think it was in the driver's seat and was rubbing this in our faces; the network put us on a clock and said that the offer was good only until a certain hour that afternoon. ABC, still bruised by the Calgary negotiations, was only marginally interested. In fact, I had to practically beg them to bid at all. They cobbled together a combination of network and cable television (ESPN) to a total value approaching $300 million. That was if everything worked out, which seemed unlikely. CBS was on the fence, but still possibly interested at the $300-million level. I was angry enough at NBC that I told CBS they could have the Games if they matched NBC, but that we would have to know very quickly. Unfortunately, its most senior executives were in transit and could not be reached at the critical moment. It remained only to bite the bullet and accept the NBC offer.

The European rights fees continued to be problematic. The EBU maintained its stranglehold on Samaranch and Hodler, and it looked as if EBU would not even reach 10 percent of the U.S. total as a result of the "discussions" that proceeded in a leisurely manner. In the end, Samaranch and Hodler made a deal with EBU for $28 million. Even Japan paid more for the rights—$50 million, part of which was positioned as a special payment in view of the complicated postwar relations between Japan and Korea.

• • •

We headed straight for the Big Apple at the start of the U.S. broadcast negotiations for both 1992 Games. The IOC had awarded the 1992 Summer Games to Barcelona and the Winter Games to Albertville, France, in 1986. Once we had held the second round of the Seoul negotiations in New York, I was able to persuade Samaranch that it did not make sense to force the U.S. networks to travel to Lausanne for the process and that the IOC should, as a matter of courtesy to our biggest and most important contracting partners, visit New York for the purpose.

We had also engaged Don Petroni of O'Melveny & Myers, who had acted for the Seoul organizing committee in connection with all U.S. matters in relation to the 1988 Games, as our U.S. lawyer. He had done an excellent job for the Koreans and I thought we needed our own counsel to deal with our most important contract, in a jurisdiction that has many legal complications and a tendency to litigate at the drop of a hat. Relying on our Swiss lawyers or acting on our own account would have been reckless in the extreme. Petroni had vast experience in entertainment law and excellent judgment. Samaranch agreed that I could retain Petroni on behalf of the IOC and he has acted for us on all subsequent U.S. television contracts, up to and including the 2008 Games, and on a variety of other U.S. legal matters.

By the time we had prepared the host city contracts that were to be signed between the IOC and the winning cities for the 1992 Games, we had altered the arrangements even further, to provide that the rights would be negotiated by the IOC "in consultation with" the organizing committees. This put the legal power clearly in the hands of the IOC, but did not altogether solve the political tensions with the hosts, especially Barcelona, which still considered the television rights as theirs and the IOC as meddling in their affairs. On the other hand, by now there was at least grudging respect for the ability of the IOC to negotiate attractive contracts on their behalf. The winter rights—which went, as predicted, for considerably less than the Calgary rights—came in at $243 million, with CBS winning and with tepid interest by ABC and NBC.

But, for the Barcelona Games, NBC outbid the other networks by adding the anticipated revenues from a cable package concept called a Triplecast that it had developed. The Triplecast plan would be funded in advance, which enabled NBC to bid considerably more than a traditional network could afford to bid (which would probably have been in the neighborhood of just over $300 million), and it won with a bid of $401 million. The idea was brilliant: offering cable customers an opportunity to subscribe to one of various levels of "packages"—bronze, silver or gold—each containing access to expanded Olympic programming. The Triplecast proved to be an artistic success, but it was a financial failure. The marketing was run by television network personnel, who were not much interested in the success of a cable venture, and I think they were generally quite content for it to fail.

This did, however, drive home to us that there was great potential for additional coverage of the Games, and our contracts now require that the network broadcasts be supplemented by cable coverage. The change makes a lot of sense when you realize that there are some 3,000 hours of events during a Summer Games, and only a tiny portion can be included in traditional network coverage. If a broadcaster were willing to televise a full 18 hours of Olympic coverage per day for 17 days, that would still only amount to about 300 hours. If you allow for commentary, summaries, replays, interviews and commercial breaks, there might be about 150 hours of actual sports event coverage. This means that only about 5 percent of the sports action will be seen on the network broadcasts. Whole sports are regularly ignored and never seen at all by the viewing public.

Compared with Seoul, the Barcelona negotiations were much easier because the U.S. broadcast rights contract had been considerably improved during the Seoul line-by-line negotiations. In addition, NBC had been the previous rights holder, so it was already generally familiar with the terms of the contract. Gone, too, was the global political uncertainty that had surrounded the entire event in Seoul. We knew that the Games would take place in Barcelona. The only question was the level at which they would be organized, and this remained a factor up to and including the Games. There was almost no concern about serious boycotts. At the time, Spain was unlikely to offend anyone; any problems it might have would be internal and were considered to be manageable. The principal complicating factor in the negotiations was the U.S. Olympic Committee (USOC).

The contract was to be signed in Barcelona during the course of an IOC executive board meeting. The signing was almost aborted because of the USOC's growing demand for more control in the negotiating process, a stance that infuriated both NBC and the IOC. The USOC maintained that its consent was necessary before the word "Olympic" or any variation of the five-ring Olympic symbol could be used in the United States. This was all a part of its effort to muscle in on the Olympic television revenues. It had the chauvinistic view that the rights fees were "American" revenues, in which it had some right to participate, and that every dollar paid by a U.S. broadcaster for Olympic television rights was, somehow, a dollar ripped from its more deserving hands.

Samaranch, ever ready to avoid resolving the situation once and for all, had instructed me to negotiate with the USOC and to agree to give it some share. The USOC added nothing of substance to the negotiations except demands for more money and coverage of its own domestic events, which were combined with the desire to be involved in the selling process of advertising, so that it could leverage sponsorships from the television advertisers. This would interfere with the marketing activities of NBC, because the USOC would be trying to sell trinkets in the midst of a diamond auction. It strengthened our joint resolve to isolate the USOC as much as possible from future negotiations, and marked the beginning of increasingly difficult relations between the USOC and the IOC as well as between the USOC and NBC.

By comparison, the U.S. rights negotiations for the 1994 Games in Lillehammer, Norway, were relatively simple. We were now fully in charge of all negotiations, although we made certain that the organizing committees were kept informed and involved. CBS was happy with its Albertville rights and there would be only a two-year delay before it was back on the air with another Winter Games.

We had decided to stagger the Games, to give the Winter Games more prominence and to relieve some of the pressure on networks and sponsors, who had been having to finance two Games—Summer and Winter—in the same year. At the time of the decision to change the cycle, we had a number of good winter candidate cities, so the easiest solution was to inject a new Winter Games between the Albertville/Barcelona Games and Atlanta in 1996.

We told CBS the amount we had in mind and got indications that they would be willing to step up to it, although no commitments were made. So we told the other networks that we were ready to negotiate, at the $300-million level. Both NBC and ABC said that level was too high (ABC was still nursing its financial wounds from Calgary, and NBC was only mildly interested in winning—as long as the deal was extraordinarily low). This left only Fox, which Rupert Murdoch was in the process of turning into a network that aimed to deliver a strong sports component. He was interested in bidding, but Fox had never televised a single sports event to date and I was not willing to risk a bid from the network. So we were then free to talk with CBS alone and agreed on a price of $300 million, a considerable increase over Albertville and approaching the aberrational result of Calgary, where the Games site had been in North America. This was a good deal for CBS, since it allowed the network to keep its winter team together and would give it a chance to establish itself as the Winter Games network, with two Games in two years.

* * *

In comedy, timing is everything. This seems to be true of life in general, including most television rights negotiations. In that, Atlanta was no exception. We had a significant difference of opinion about when the U.S. rights negotiations should be held. My view, the reverse of the

Calgary situation, was that the longer we waited after Atlanta's selection as a host city in 1990, the better. These were the next Games on the horizon after Lillehammer, and most of the United States had not really focused on the 1996 Games by the early nineties, let alone the fact that they would be in Atlanta, so no real excitement had been generated yet in the American public mind. This included the potential advertisers, whose enthusiasm would drive the value of the television rights. At that time as well, the sports television market was only gradually improving from dismal to less dismal and would probably get better in the months to come.

The Atlanta Committee for the Olympic Games (ACOG) saw things differently. Apart from that, because it was an organizing committee that had no public sector financial support, it needed firm financial contracts upon which it could borrow funds to meet its operating and capital commitments. For example, it needed the U.S. television deal in order to finance the construction of the Olympic Stadium— and the construction plans left almost no room for any delays if the stadium was to be ready for the Games. Both Barry Frank, acting as ACOG's consultant, and I believed that it would be best to wait, but the Atlantans were caught between a rock and a hard place and finally decided that they could not wait. We warned them that not waiting would mean leaving significant amounts of money on the table. They insisted.

The television negotiations were held in New York in July 1993. We had the usual instant expertise of the organizing committee to deal with. Their television gurus, investment bankers Goldman Sachs, knew nothing about Olympic television and had some completely impractical ideas. As well, the organizing committee's lawyers completely rewrote the contracts we had been using, slanting them, of course, entirely in favor of ACOG and against the networks. This was contrary to all the advice we could give them about the "real world" of negotiating such contracts. We had now been through several Games and had developed forms of contract that were fair to both sides, and the networks were happy with the level of contractual detail and the ability of the IOC and the organizing committees to deliver the commitments they made. But, since we have to work with the organizing committees on a cooperative basis, I did not want to be seen to be preventing ACOG from giving the matter its best shot. So we let their lawyers draft away in their splendid theoretical isolation, knowing full well what would happen when the networks got to see the draft contract. Sometimes you have to let people make their own mistakes before they will accept that they have been dead wrong.

Actually, it did not even take that long. When we advised the networks about the dates for the negotiations, we sent out a summary of the terms that were to be contained in the contract, based upon the Atlanta draft. Frank and I hoped that the networks, as the bidders, would provide the greenhorns with a much-needed reality check. The ACOG terms drew even more flak than I had expected, and about as much as I had hoped. I had told the networks that the whole idea was ACOG's and that neither I nor Frank had any enthusiasm for it. NBC, the incumbent for the past two Games, was so furious by the one-sided terms that it said it would not even participate in the negotiations under such conditions. Furthermore, it was prepared to undertake an active campaign against the Games throughout the United States and in Japan and Europe on the grounds that the broadcasters were being exploited by Atlanta and the IOC. The other two networks were not as strident, but made it quite clear that if the deal was to be as described, their bids would be very much lower than might otherwise have been expected. So the retreat began.

In due course and after a great deal of unnecessary work, we got the networks back on track and the negotiations took place. NBC was fully represented and held the first-round lead, with a bid of $456 million and a promise of revenue sharing if gross advertising sales were to exceed $900 million. ABC was represented by Dennis Swanson, who was in a difficult position. It was the first day of work for ABC's new network chief, Bob Eiger, and he was not going to start—or perhaps end—his new career by making a huge bid for the Games, so Swanson was left more or less to twist in the wind. Between rounds, I did my best to get Swanson to step up to the NBC bid, but he was powerless to do more than make a few cosmetic adjustments. He had also been abandoned, at the last moment, by Ted Turner, who had previously indicated that there might be a joint ABC-Turner deal. CBS was not serious, having become quite satisfied with its niche role of broadcasting the Winter Games, and probably only attended the negotiations to show the flag and help us to get the best bids from the other two networks.

The $456 million was the largest Olympic contract in history, and a 50 percent increase over the "real" value of the recent Barcelona Games (that is, with the phantom Triplecast profits removed from the equation). This increase reflected the fact that the Games would be in the eastern U.S. time zone and, more importantly, in the United States itself. Believe it or not, ACOG was very disappointed with this result. Atlanta had been looking for a 50 percent increase over the Triplecast-inflated Barcelona figure and, therefore, an amount approaching $600 million. By the time we got to the negotiations, ACOG had reduced the expectation, grudgingly, to $500 million.

Atlanta Olympics chief Billy Payne said, soulfully, that it had been the worst day of his entire life. I rolled my eyes. Neither he nor ACOG had paid attention to the warnings that came from all the networks, which acknowledged that the real value of the Barcelona Games was not the $401 million paid for them, but something in the order of $300 million, given the failure of the Triplecast experiment. More extraordinarily, with the application of some bizarre logic, it became, in ACOG's tiny collective mind, the IOC's fault that their unrealistic forecast had not been achieved. I expect that ACOG's refusal to follow our suggestion and delay the negotiations probably ended up costing between $50 and $100 million. It was particularly galling for ACOG when, a year prior to the Atlanta Games, we sold the U.S. television rights to the 2000 Sydney Games in a much smaller market, halfway around the world, for $705 million.

Those Sydney Games negotiations were the occasion for what I would describe as a paradigm shift in the IOC's approach to Olympic television rights. It came as something of a surprise in August 1995 to get a call from Samaranch—who was in Sweden for the world athletics championships—saying he had just met with Dick Ebersol, Alex Gilady and Randy Falco ("this other man") of NBC and that they had made a most impressive proposal to him. He did not describe it and said only that he had told them they must speak to me and that, as I knew, he was not a person who was easily impressed. Would I be available to meet the NBC people the following morning in Montreal? I said I would make myself available.

In Montreal, they explained the offer. NBC would acquire the U.S. rights for both Sydney and Salt Lake City. There would be a combined network and cable presentation of the Games and they promised cable penetration of close to sixty million homes. In addition, NBC would offer a certain value of promotional spots to the IOC and the two organizing committees. The financial offer was the unheard-of sum of $1.25 billion. They would leave the allocation to us, but had tentatively suggested that an appropriate split might be $650 million for Sydney and $600 million for Salt Lake City. They did not know what I knew regarding the Fox network and a potential offer of $700 million for U.S. rights to the Sydney Games. Regarding the allocation, I said I would prefer that the split be $700 million for Sydney and $550 million for Salt Lake City. NBC was willing to accept that split. We had until five o'clock that afternoon to decide, the NBC people said.

I called Samaranch from another conference room and he asked me what I thought of the offer. I said I thought we should take it. I told him of the revised allocation I had suggested and he had no problem with that. We agreed that I should call the Sydney and Salt Lake City organizing committees and the USOC to advise them of what we intended, in a manner that was not to invite discussion but was to generate enthusiasm. As well it might, since the amounts allocated to each Games were well in excess of the organizing committee's budgeted amounts for U.S. television.

In the meantime we adjourned to the last smoking boardroom at Stikeman Elliott, the law firm in which I am a partner (this was prior to the time that the tyranny of the majority succeeded in preventing all smoking whatsoever on the premises), and I brought my laptop from my own office. We set about drafting a letter of intent governing our arrangement, with me typing. This is not an impressive performance, other than the opportunity it provides to brush up on scatological Anglo-Saxon as mistakes are corrected, but had at least the advantage of leading to a reasonably brief agreement, long on substance and short on boilerplate. The entire agreement, with obligations in excess of $1.25 billion, was contained in five pages.

• • •

As summer ended in 1995 we had the, by now, customary difficulties with the USOC in the negotiations of the detailed contracts, as the national committee began not only looking the extraordinary gift horse in the mouth but trying, resolutely, to become its dentist. The USOC delayed and prevaricated over the contracts until the last moment, even to the night before the scheduled formal signing in Lausanne in late September 1995. But we got it done and had a pleasant dinner that evening at the Lausanne Palace Hotel. Before the dinner and unknown to me, Ebersol had mentioned the possibility of further multi-Games arrangements to Samaranch, who took me aside after the dinner and said he would like me to consider the possibility of negotiating a further two-Game package with NBC.

Since that would have meant the Games for 2004 and 2006, it seemed to me that this would only complicate our arrangements with sponsors involved in The Olympic Program, whose contracts tracked the standard four-year Olympiad cycle. I said to Samaranch that I would be happy to consider the idea, but that I thought we should go out to 2008, so that we would track all our other contracts and complete the Olympiad. "For me, it is the same," he said, "if you can do three Games, that is fine." I said I would see what I could do, but that it would be different from most negotiations, because we would be talking about Games whose locations had not yet been determined and would not be decided, in the case of the 2008 Games, for more than six years.

"Yes, but for us, is much better to have the negotiations completed before there are organizing committees in existence to complicate the situation," he said. I told him that the biggest problem at this stage was not the organizing

193

committees, since we had demonstrated that we knew what we were doing, but the USOC. I did not want the USOC to be involved, not only because of the interference, but also because it could not be trusted to keep the discussions confidential. "Leesten, Deek," he said. "These are to be secret discussions. Not confidential. Secret. You understand?" I understood.

Easy to say, of course, but how do you negotiate agreements that are likely to run to billions of dollars when you do not know the key elements: the location of the event to be televised, the state of the world at the time the events will be held, the economic conditions that will exist, or the technological changes that will most certainly occur within an evolving industry? I met with Ebersol, Falco and Gilady the next day to see how we should proceed. We began by discussing general principles and getting agreement on them. We exchanged lists of significant points and hammered out questions such as years covered and other technical details. In the end, the U.S. rights deal involved some $2.3 billion stretching to 2008. It provided stability for the IOC, the potential host cities, the Olympic organizing committees, and for NBC. The long-term nature of the deal helped spread the risk around for everyone.

One other important dynamic has changed as a result of the new long-term television arrangements. The IOC can now advise candidate cities of the amount they would receive as their share of television rights even before they make their bids to host the Games. Thus, Athens knew in advance of its selection that it would receive in excess of $700 million from the worldwide sale of television rights. This knowledge fills in a large gap or question mark in the revenue budget of any host city and constitutes about half the total cost of organizing the Games. The IOC could also indicate with reasonable certainty that Athens would receive about $200 million from the IOC's international marketing program and that, with the IOC's permission to use the five-ring symbol for marketing purposes, it should be able to raise at least $400 million from other sponsors and at least $200 million from ticket sales. That leads to a total of US$1.5 billion, without a single dollar being required from the taxpayers of the host country. This makes the Olympics unique as a sports event: the Games can pay for themselves.

Bringing this much money to the party increases the IOC's influence and ability to define its product—the Olympic Games. We are no longer begging for candidate cities and we can assume the role of managing and promoting an extremely valuable and important franchise, instead of turning the whole thing over to the franchisees (the host cities) and crossing our fingers in the hope that they will not damage or destroy it. This is particularly important for the IOC and for the Olympic movement in general, since there can be little doubt that the engine that powers and drives the Olympic movement is its main event—the Olympic Games. The Games must, therefore, be successful and remain the leading sports event in the world. We cannot afford to make a mistake in our selection of host cities and we cannot permit each host city to redefine the Olympic movement for its own short-term existence.

There are certainly some risks attaching to long-term partnerships with broadcasters. We may have picked the wrong partners. Relationships are negotiated between people who have confidence in each other. Those people may move on and their replacements may not have the same commitment. Economic conditions may change; we may turn out to have sold for too much or too little. The television broadcast industry may evolve into something none of us could have contemplated when we made the long-term deals.

Long-term deals are relationships like any other, and as such, they take care and feeding. I am often stunned by the impression many have that, once a contract has been signed, there is nothing further to do except cash the checks. They do not seem to understand that this is just the beginning of the relationship and that the parties then have to work extremely hard to bring about the conditions that allow each to perform the obligations they have under-taken. The good part is that we now have media partners who share our interests and who can bring to bear all the communications power of television in the promotion of those interests. The tough part is that the contracts extend to periods of time and conditions within society that none of us were able to contemplate with any certainty when we signed the agreements. Who, for example, could have pre-dicted the events of September 11, 2001, and the effects they may have had in 2002, let alone 2008?

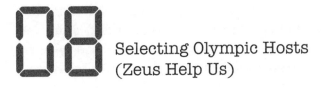

Selecting Olympic Hosts (Zeus Help Us)

The first inkling I had of the impending crisis was a call from someone in the media in Salt Lake City shortly before U.S. Thanksgiving in November 1998. A document that had been leaked to the media indicated that the child of a member of the International Olympic Committee was receiving tuition and support payments from the Salt Lake Organizing Committee (SLOC). What did I think of this and what did I counsel the person to do with that information? I said I knew nothing about the payments, but I was instantly alert to the possible ramifications. I was also smart enough to recognize the potential trap. I told the reporter that he should do what was appropriate in the circumstances. If he thought that this was a credible lead, he should follow it up. I had no interest in seeing a headline along the lines of Prominent IOC Member Encourages Cover-Up of Questionable IOC Conduct. I did not like the sound of the story and was afraid that it might well be true. I called Juan Antonio Samaranch to warn him that there might be trouble coming.

The leaked document purported to be a letter concerning tuition and other payments on behalf of Sonia Essomba, daughter of IOC member Rene Essomba from Cameroon. The leak had come from a board member of the local bid committee who seemed unwilling to make the disclosure personally and opted instead for the indirect modern method of circulating damaging information. Even though the document turned out not to have been a genuine letter, it proved to be more than enough to open the floodgates.

By the end of November, things began to heat up and one of the Salt Lake City newspapers launched a media inquiry that posed questions to Samaranch in the matter. He had a finely honed instinct for danger and self-preservation and immediately referred the issue to the IOC Juridical Commission, whose mandate is to provide the IOC with advice on matters with legal implications. It was not, however, until December 10 that the extent of the problem became known. SLOC was due to make a regular progress report to the IOC executive board in Lausanne. The evening before the meeting, the leaders of the delegation requested a meeting with Samaranch and presented him with details of a number of payments that had been made to or for the benefit of several IOC members. The extent and amounts of the payments were shocking. It was clear that a major problem was facing us, although we had no idea how serious it would become.

• • •

Choosing host cities for the Olympic Games is one of the IOC's most important responsibilities. Numerous selection criteria are considered, not all of which are equally important or perceived similarly by individual members of the IOC. We have a membership that can be likened to the standard bell curve used in statistical analysis. At one extreme of the curve might be the sport technocrats, who base their decisions almost entirely on the technical components of the bid: the facilities; the experience of the candidate city in organizing international competitions; travel times and distances for athletes; weather conditions; and so forth. At the other extreme are members who have little, if any, technical qualifications and who are likely to decide almost entirely on geopolitical considerations. In between are the great majority of members, who consider a broad range of criteria, from technical to geopolitical.

The IOC is a collection of volunteer members selected by the IOC itself to represent it in the members' countries and regions. There have been as many as 130 members at one time, but we have recently set a target of 115, to consist of 15 Olympic athletes elected by their peers at the time of the Games, 15 representatives of the international sports federations (IFs), 15 representatives of the national Olympic committees (NOCs), and 70 members selected for their particular personal characteristics. Up to 1999, members were always chosen solely for their personal qualities, but we decided that we should make sure, on a structural basis, that the membership reflected the principal constituencies within the Olympic movement, without abandoning the original catechism of individual membership and complete freedom from outside pressures.

Individual members are usually important personages in their countries and may or may not be involved in sport itself. A crude way of identifying their importance would be to consider whether, if they were to call the president or the prime minister of their country, the call would be returned. Their independence used to come from the fact that the terms were virtually for life and that it was understood that the members represented the IOC—rather than being delegates from their countries to the IOC who could be changed if they did not follow instructions from home base. Meeting together, the IOC members form the session. The session elects an executive board, whose members serve four-year terms and are eligible for re-election, but may only serve two consecutive terms before a two-year cooling-off period. In a sense, the session is like a parliament and the executive board is the cabinet that carries on the business of the IOC. The executive board and the session are chaired by the president of the IOC. Since the session normally meets only once a year and the executive board five or six times, the president has an enormous amount of residual power and influence.

Add to the unusual mix the fact that the IOC members are colleagues and often friends. They come from different continents and bring with them a sense of continental fraternity, shared languages and shared cultures. Members from smaller countries have voting equality with members from Russia, the United States or China, but quite often not the same confidence in their roles or their personal importance. Some members never open their mouths at IOC sessions, while others have an unfortunate tendency to speak at length on too many occasions.

When the process of choosing an Olympic Games host city is under way, the candidate cities make their presentations and leave the room; the IFs, NOCs and the Evaluation Commission all give their advice; and then the IOC members decide the fate of the supplicants by secret ballot. The results are often astonishing, and have been known to defy subsequent analysis. Often, they convey indirect messages. During Samaranch's presidency, for example, he was so dominant that it was impossible, or inadvisable, to challenge him directly, but members would often vote against his indicated choices when they could do so secretly. They voted against his choices of Sofia, Bulgaria, for the 1992 and 1994

Winter Games; Oestersund, Sweden, for the 1994 Winter Games; and Athens for the 1996 Games. Even he began to laugh, a bit, about it toward the end. The mice were prepared to revolt on occasion, but only in secret. Of course, when the choice really mattered to him, as in the case of Barcelona for the 1992 Games, they granted him his wish.

Offbeat results are more likely to occur in relation to Winter Games, because many of the IOC members have no particular interest in them and do not much care where they go. We nearly had such a situation during the voting for the 2010 Winter Games, when Vancouver narrowly beat out a considerably inferior bid from Pyeongchang, South Korea, even though these Games were to immediately follow another Olympic event in East Asia, the 2008 Games in Beijing. I would be surprised if Vancouver received a single vote from the African, Asian or South American members.

There is no scientifically demonstrable right choice from among candidate cities and, almost certainly, no perfect candidate. Each will have its own set of strengths and weaknesses, and many of these are subjective considerations identified by the IOC members. If we take a practical view of the situation, it is easy to see that what is more important for the IOC is not necessarily to make the right choice for a particular city but to avoid making the wrong decision. A wrong decision is to choose a city that proves to be incapable of organizing good Games. Too much rides on the celebration of successful Games to make it thinkable for the IOC to make such a mistake. The revenues from the Games keep the Olympic movement in operation for the ensuing four years. A majority of the international sports federations would be bankrupt by the time the following Games arrived if they did not receive a share of the television revenues negotiated by the IOC.

Many national Olympic committees, especially those that do not depend for their existence on government support, would be in critical condition without the television and marketing revenues generated by the IOC and redistributed to them. Sponsors and broadcasters would incur losses and be less willing to support an organization (and its main event) where that organization is so incompetent as to choose the wrong host city.

The IOC has probably always known, instinctively, that it must not make a mistake when it decides. This instinct has not, as many suggest, been the result of marketing or television issues, all of which are relatively new and seldom considered by most of the IOC members, but from a genuine desire to ensure that the Games are celebrated as planned. The sponsor and broadcast perspectives are legitimate concerns, but are largely ignored by the rank-and-file IOC members. The IOC administration, however, is not as insensitive to these and other issues and has been doing some work to try to focus the attention of members on the important factors to take into consideration when deciding.

In recent years, since organizing the Games began to be seen as potentially profitable to a host city, we have had an embarrassment of riches in terms of the number of possible candidates. We have had to develop a screening process to reduce the number of candidates to a manageable level. Nine cities, for example, have been vying for the 2012 Games. Some are not qualified and would clearly represent wrong choices, at least for purposes of the Games under consideration, and we have developed a two-stage process by which a city is first an "applicant" and only after an initial screening can it advance to the stage of being a "candidate" city. In such a process, there should probably be no more than two or three cities that become candidates, but this means that the IOC has to be ready to say no, at least for now, to some important countries and this has proven, predictably, to be politically difficult for the IOC.

Hosting the Olympic Games involves major considerations for both the host city and the host country. Virtually every recent Olympic host city has had a major construction program tied in with the Olympic Games. Even existing sports facilities need to be upgraded to modern standards and new stadiums and other facilities will be required because the existing ones are usually insufficient. These include not simply those in which the Olympic competitions will be held, but also training and practice venues. Olympic hosts are required to provide an Olympic Village for the teams and their support personnel, which means lodging for close to twenty-five thousand people. It is hard to imagine a city that would have such accommodation lying around free for the occasion.

The volume of transportation within the host city will double or triple during the Games and the people have to be moved effectively, so that athletes get to their training and competitions and spectators get to the events. Mass transit systems may or may not exist, but few if any cities would have systems with the capacity for double the normal daily requirements. Athens will likely have to locate and then deploy more than two thousand buses for the Games—and then try to ensure that there is no terminal gridlock. Very few cities are able to provide enough hotel rooms and other accommodation for the tens of thousands of visiting spectators and others working for the organizing committees, suppliers, security staff and media. Barcelona and Athens, for example, had to charter huge cruise ships to use as floating hotels, since their inventory of hotel rooms lags well behind even normal requirements in cities of their size.

The existence of these complications and expenditures often leads to the question of why any city would bother to host the Olympics, and there are good arguments for both sides of the debate. Those opposed to the Games in their city or country almost always focus on the costs, although in relation to the Winter Games there can be powerful environmental issues as well, such as the destruction of forests for ski runs, or the dangers of ammonia used for freezing bobsled and luge runs. But cost is the usual complaint. The money, it is argued, could better be spent on other projects, such as schools or hospitals. Sometimes the arguments become personal and mayors of host cities are accused of megalomania, of throwing away public funds on a two-week spectacle that leaves no enduring benefit and a pile of debt for the taxpayers to absorb.

Before the 1968 Mexico City Olympics, riots broke out in protest against the deployment of national resources for Games in the face of many other urgent needs in the country. The authorities fired upon a crowd of students shortly before the opening ceremonies, killing several people, and the resulting pall considerably diminished the joy of the occasion. It's easy to mount the "nay" side of the Olympic debate; you don't need to study anything carefully and the protest is usually emotional enough that the facts seldom get in the way of a good headline or sound bite.

There is no doubt that the Olympic Games are a unique showcase event. The host city gains an enormous visibility that would otherwise be unattainable. Outside of Norway, almost no one in the world had ever heard of Lillehammer before the 1994 Winter Games. This is obviously one of the reasons that countries and cities bid for the Games—presence on the world stage. But few if any cities would regard that as sufficient justification to bid and host. Almost every city in the past half-century or so has had far more complex reasons to become a host. Some countries, especially after the Second World War, wanted to demonstrate that they had become rehabilitated in world society—hence the Games in Rome, Tokyo and Munich. The Moscow Games were to demonstrate that the Communist system could compete with the capitalistic societies of the Soviets' political competitors. The Seoul Games grew out of a complicated mixture of goals, from beating Japan in a world forum to further isolating North Korea.

For most host cities, hosting the Games provided an extraordinary opportunity to dramatically improve the infrastructure of the city or country. In some cases, there might well be a chicken-and-egg analysis—whether the infrastructure needs drove the Olympic quest or winning the Games led to the infrastructure improvements. In a sense, the answer does not matter, provided that the resulting improvements were needed by the host city. It is only where the proverbial white elephants are created that criticism is well deserved. Montreal's beautiful but impractical Olympic Stadium—hopelessly expensive, single-purpose and poorly located—comes to mind, but there are certainly other examples that could be identified.

The great advantage of tying infrastructure enhancement to the Olympic Games is that a project of that magnitude provides an opportunity for overall assessment and planning that might not otherwise occur. The other advantage is that the very real Games deadline prevents serious diversion or postponement of the project work. Getting plans of such magnitude together generally takes longer than anticipated, so one of the critical factors in any Olympics is making sure that the construction, in particular, will be ready in plenty of time. This has led to the occasional near-miss, but, to date, no Games have been canceled for that reason.

One of the wonderful side effects of modern television, apart from the fact that billions of people throughout the world can now experience the Olympics, is that no one knows how close to disaster many Games have been. Television audiences see what appears to be a seamless presentation of flawless organization and are blissfully unaware that, behind the scenes, the whole operation is often held together with the proverbial chewing gum and baling wire. Sometimes the problems are organizational and on other occasions there is a political context that makes the very existence of the Games doubtful. I have been part of several such experiences, all of which, in the end, came off very well, but, in the process, probably accounted for a significant portion of the worldwide sales of antacid.

• • •

The Salt Lake City bidding scandal that broke in 1998 with the disclosure that payments had been made to Sonia Essomba, daughter of an IOC member, is best viewed within a larger sequence of events. Salt Lake City won its bid to host the 2002 Winter Games atypically—on the first round of voting in 1995. The spectacular nature of this competition, however, lies in the documentation of what money was spent, and to a certain extent, how it was spent to achieve the victory. Not all of it presents a pretty picture and it almost brought an end to the IOC. It also led to criminal charges against the two senior bidding committee officials. The charges were ultimately dismissed in December 2003.

The Salt Lake City bid for the 2002 Games was its second attempt. After wrestling away the incumbency of Anchorage, Alaska, as the U.S. candidate city for the Winter Games, Salt Lake City decided, unwisely in my opinion, to bid for the 1998 Games. I say "unwisely" because this competition was to be decided in 1991 at an IOC session in

Birmingham, England, less than a year after Atlanta had beaten Athens in the final round of voting to get the 1996 Games. It was highly unlikely that the IOC would award two successive Games to the United States, not only because of the country involved but also because it was already apparent that the Atlanta Games were not going to be easy. The USOC seemed resolutely unaware of the way successive bids would be perceived, and it approved Salt Lake's candidacy. The race was on. To be fair, the opposition was not overwhelming.

Early on in the campaign for the 1998 Games, I got a call from Tom Welch, who was heading up the bid committee. He wanted to come to talk to me, he said, to get some advice. I suppose he thought I might have some experience from the recent, but unsuccessful, bid by Toronto for 1996, although he would have been better advised to speak to Paul Henderson, who had run the bid almost single-handedly and had met with all of the IOC members. I agreed to meet with Welch, as I routinely agreed whenever candidate city representatives wanted advice. As an IOC member, it seemed to me that part of my job description was to help candidate cities to put forward the best possible bids, in the overall best interests of the Games. The better the bids, the better the Games; the better the Games, the better for the Olympic movement. That seemed obvious and I never doubted that it was the right thing to do.

Welch came to Montreal and we had lunch. He did not beat around the bush and said that he had been told that I would never vote for Salt Lake City, but that I would be the only member of the IOC who would give him direct and honest answers to his questions. Everyone else would give him diplomatic double-talk. I answered all his questions to the best of my ability, including suggesting the strengths and weaknesses of his own bid, as well as the same for the other bids that had been announced, and my assessment of where support for each within the IOC might be expected to come. Welch did not ask for my personal support. Nor did I promise it. I did tell him not to rely on anyone's promise of support.

The importance of the economic activity surrounding the Olympic Games makes the stakes of hosting them as big as the event itself. This has led to excesses in the costs of bidding for them and for excesses on the part of both the bidders and some members of the IOC. Part of the challenge for Salt Lake City was to get IOC members to make the long trip out there to see the place and the facilities that existed or were planned. Many IOC members have little experience with Winter Games (and some could not care less), so they would have to respond to the city and its ambience. Trips to the city were urged on members and side trips to the Grand Canyon and the Colorado River for rafting excursions were thrown in as further enticements to make a long trip. I cannot remember how many times Welch tried to get me to come out. I finally said to him, as the election day was getting closer and the bid committee needed to impress as many members of the IOC as possible, "Tom, if I promise to vote for you, will you stop calling me?" He was silent. I said, "I promise to vote for you. Now stop calling me." After a moment, Welch said that he wasn't sure what to say since I was the one who had told him not to believe such a promise from any other IOC member. But he did stop calling.

By the time the voting day arrived, it was fairly clear that Salt Lake City was an excellent candidate but was predictably short of support, for the reasons I had given Welch earlier, plus the favorite-son tendencies that occur in the early rounds of voting. IOC members like to signal encouragement for candidates from their regions and for those that are not going to win the current contest but do not wish to be humiliated. In large fields, therefore, even for the best candidates, the first couple of rounds are particularly dangerous, as proved to be the case for Salt Lake City. Other candidate cities were Nagano, Japan; Oestersund, Sweden; Aosta, Italy; and Jaca, Spain. The latter had no possibility of winning and should not have been in the contest in the first place. It would have been a classic case of a wrong choice. Samaranch, however, was urging members to give Jaca support in the first round, so that it would not be "embarrassed" by being the first to be eliminated. He asked me to vote for it as well. I said nothing. I voted for Salt Lake City.

When the results of the first ballot were announced, Aosta and Salt Lake City were tied for last place; there had to be a runoff to see which of the two would advance to the next round, and it was won easily by Salt Lake City. The IOC realized, belatedly, how close it had come to eliminating arguably the best, but certainly no worse than second-best, city in the race as a result of parochial thinking. Such an outcome would have produced a tremendous backlash, fully deserved in the circumstances. I discussed this with Samaranch, who had come to the same conclusion, and said that I bet he was glad I had not followed his advice to vote for Jaca. He said, "You did not vote for Jaca?" I said, "No, for Salt Lake City." "We were very lucky," he said.

Salt Lake City lost in the final round by a margin of four votes, to Nagano, which probably had a weaker overall bid, but which provided a plausible alternative to back-to-back Games in the United States. Its Games proved to be much better than I had thought Nagano could produce. Despite the prospect of two Games in a row in the United States, I could never satisfy myself, based on the evidence, that Nagano could do as good a job as Salt Lake City. I had never visited either city, but had confidence in the American ability to get things done, and was worried about transportation and the quality of the alpine events in Nagano. I voted for Salt Lake City on each round.

Immediately after the bid, Welch and the others from Salt Lake City were urged to bid again for 2002 and were assured that, this time, they would certainly win. They were reminded about the problem of successive Games in the United States, which would no longer be an impediment. Mainstream support would be there from the European members, many of whom were interested in the location of the 2004 Summer Games, and Asian members would, now that Nagano was a host city, be happy to support an American candidate for 2002. It was an invitation to the closest thing to a cakewalk that could be imagined. Marc Hodler, a veteran Swiss member of the IOC and the dean of the winter sports federations, made a specific trip to Salt Lake City to confirm all this.

To no one's surprise, Salt Lake City was back in the hunt. Notwithstanding the assurances given by members and Hodler's trip to repeat those assurances to the locals, the Salt Lake City plan was to take no chances and to assume that it would have to start over and win each vote. Maybe Welch remembered my advice to trust no one's promise to vote for them. It was the determination not to lose that led Salt Lake City to step over the edge of what was proper conduct for a bidding committee. The IOC also had members who stepped well over the edge of acceptable conduct. There were examples of both push and pull; the bid committee pushed members to accept benefits that were not even remotely connected with the bid, and some IOC members displayed astonishing bad faith in seeking benefits completely unconnected with their roles as members voting on the merits of candidate cities. Most of the details are now a matter of public record and do not bear repeating here, but the combination was a bomb waiting to explode.

To no one's surprise either, Salt Lake City won easily in 1995 at the IOC session in Budapest. By then, tensions were at a boiling point. Suggestions of vote-buying swirled close to public attention, not within the media, but among the Olympic insiders. Complaints were lodged—although not as heatedly as during the final stages of the 1998 contest— about the conduct of self-styled agents purporting to be soliciting funds to pay IOC members; these were vigorously denied. I had had little contact with the Salt Lake City bid for the 2002 Games because Canada, against my advice, had decided to enter its own candidate, Quebec City. It was my opinion that after the narrow loss to Nagano, Salt Lake City was almost a certainty and that a Quebec bid would have no chance of winning. Even a get-to-know-you bid would not, in my view, have had much value. It seemed to me that, if Quebec were to bid then for the 2006 Games, the city would suffer from much the same problem that Salt Lake City had experienced. Two successive Winter Games in North America was something the Europeans would never permit. It was bad enough to have the 1998 and 2002 Games outside Europe, but three in a row would be unimaginable. Quebec will be a great host city someday, but this time it had no chance. We did our best, but were outgunned and outspent by Salt Lake City at every turn. On one occasion, just to provide some flavor, Quebec had invited some IOC members to visit the city and some of them were going on to Salt Lake City as a continuation of the same trip. The members had flown on commercial carriers to Quebec. The Salt Lake City people arrived with a private jet to fly the members from Quebec to Salt Lake City and were gleeful about the effect of this putdown of Quebec.

• • •

As any athlete knows, you can have tough competition without personal animosity. During the latter stages of the 2002 bid, when it was apparent even to the Quebec bid committee that we were not making inroads into the lead that Salt Lake City had run up, I was interviewed by the media about the status of the race. In this respect I was interviewed as part of the Quebec bid committee, not as an outside independent "expert," where my assessment would have been quite different. I said that Salt Lake City had been out in the field now for six or more years and that I thought they were getting tired. They had nothing new to offer—no more magic, no more rabbits to pull out of the hat.

As anyone who has ever been connected with an Olympic bid knows, each candidate follows the news in its competitor cities closer than aging movie stars looking for mentions of their names. On a Friday evening in December 1994, shortly after my interview, the doorbell rang at home. Was this the home of Richard Pound, the IOC member? It was. Was I Pound? Yes. Here was a parcel for me. From whom? The messenger hefted a large container and tried to pass it to me. I did not let it in. What was it, I insisted. With that, he took off the cover and revealed a cage with a rabbit in it. I laughed and said that he could tell Mr. Welch to keep his rabbit. "But," the messenger protested, "there are eleven more in my truck!" I said to keep the whole dozen; I did not want them and he was certainly not going to leave them at the front door. A day or so later I sent a fax addressed to "Thomas Welch, President, Rabbit Farms U.S.A.," in which I joked that we had eaten the rabbits, and that he had better make sure he brought enough of them to Budapest, where the vote would be held in a few months.

There is a sequel to the story. In 1999, after I had been assigned the responsibility for the IOC Salt Lake City investigation, I was told that the Federal Bureau of Investigation (FBI) and the Department of Justice wanted to interview me. We agreed to meet in New York in January. Some time before the meeting, our U.S. lawyer, Jim Asperger, called me to say that the FBI had found a US$1,200 item against my name that contained only the reference "rabbits." He was most concerned that this might cause them to look at me as a possible suspect and that it could taint the whole IOC investigatory commission. I told him not to worry about it, that it was nothing. Lawyers are, however, paid huge sums of money to worry, so he worried. He absolutely had to know. So I told him. He was greatly relieved and informed the federal authorities. It is a measure of the FBI and the Department of Justice that, despite an explanation of entirely innocent behavior, received from reputable counsel, they nevertheless asked me the question during our interview and laboriously wrote down the answer, for possible future use, no doubt, against me.

●　　●　　●

The day after Salt Lake Organizing Committee (SLOC) had given Samaranch details about the bidding payments, Samaranch advised the executive board of the problem. Those of us attending the meeting listened to the delegation from SLOC, which apologized for the conduct of its own people. They hoped that the matter would not lead to withdrawal of the Games from Salt Lake City. Samaranch said we would consider the matter and advise them. After the delegation left the room, Samaranch said that the IOC would have to determine the facts and he appointed a commission of inquiry. I was to chair the commission, whose members would be Thomas Bach, Jacques Rogge, Kéba Mbaye and, later, Pál Schmitt. Mbaye was reluctant to become involved because so many of those identified were members from Africa, but he was persuaded to stay. During the morning, I examined the accounting records that the SLOC delegation had provided. The evidence looked very damning at first glance, and as someone familiar with accounting records, I could see all too easily what had happened. We agreed that it was, for all practical purposes, too late to withdraw the Games from Salt Lake City. In addition, since it seemed clear that a good deal of the problem had been created by our own members, it would be that much more difficult to justify removing the Games.

At the midday press briefing, which Samaranch sent me to chair, we confirmed that we had received the information from SLOC, that the evidence was substantial and that the IOC had established a special commission to investigate the facts and to report to the executive board as soon as possible. We also stated that we did not intend to withdraw the Games from Salt Lake City. We had been assured of full cooperation in our investigation and intended to pursue the matter as far as was necessary to determine the facts. I said that we would be meeting with the delegation at the end of the day to get as many details as we could.

As a subtext to the media briefing, that day began an extraordinary performance by Marc Hodler, the senior Swiss member of the IOC and former president of the International Ski Federation. He began holding his own series of meetings with the media, in which he said that he knew many members of the IOC who were receiving payments for their votes in favor of candidate cities. This served to pour oil on an already raging fire. Over the next several months he continued to make such statements, to the joy of the media and the despair of those of us who were trying to get the facts. We invited Hodler to one of the first commission meetings the next day, and asked him if he would be kind enough to share with us the information he had been so free in giving to the media, only to find, to our astonishment, that he had no facts whatsoever and that he had been speaking solely from hearsay. Furthermore, much of the corruption that he was ranting about turned out to relate to the ski federation, of which he had been president during the entire period that the impugned conduct had apparently occurred. The wrongdoing he railed about had not involved IOC members at all. Even though we begged him, in that case, to stop making the accusations, he persisted throughout our investigation. Because he was a quotable "source," the media egged him on, and he seemed delighted to oblige.

Our meeting with SLOC was not particularly fruitful. The members of the delegation all claimed that they had not been involved and had had no knowledge of the payments. My impression was that their main concerns were to cover their own asses and to make sure that the Games were not withdrawn. The commission also asked me to speak to Anita DeFrantz, a U.S. member of the IOC and a member of the IOC executive board (as well as a member of the SLOC board of directors and very much involved with the Salt Lake City candidacy). When I asked her whether she had any knowledge of the matters that had now come to light, she got quite defensive and demanded to know whether she was under investigation. I said that we just needed to know whether she had any knowledge that could help the IOC. She said she was completely unaware of any of the improper actions.

It was important that we get to Salt Lake City as soon as possible to see for ourselves what the records would show. By now it was mid-December 1998. SLOC said it would need a couple of weeks to get the files collected and ready for inspection. I told them that we had to get moving on this and that I wanted to be there before the end of the year. None of the other members were available during the holiday season, so I decided to go myself, but felt that it would be important to have someone else present as well, preferably a lawyer who had experience in matters of this nature. Don Petroni, who had worked with us on the U.S. television rights, suggested Asperger, who was a former prosecuting attorney from the U.S. Department of Justice and now a partner in his law firm. I called Asperger and we agreed to meet in Salt Lake City on December 27, for meetings the following day. Merry Christmas, indeed!

Asperger proved then, and thereafter, to have been a good choice. He stayed with us throughout the process and provided sound advice on the complicated process of criminal justice in the United States. We did not know, at the outset, where the matters would lead and it was important that we not get offside or do something that might, inadvertently, prove to be a breach of U.S. law. By this time, following the lead established by the IOC, SLOC had decided that it should have its own independent review board to investigate. Then the USOC, belatedly, but rightly, concerned with public perception of its own role in the bidding process, did a "me too" exercise and also appointed a commission, chaired by former senator George Mitchell, to provide yet another report. The Utah and federal departments of justice were by now indicating an interest, as was the FBI. For the latter three, the case had a wonderfully high profile and the prospect of brilliant careers and headlines proved irresistible. In the end, the federal authorities would commit more time and money to the investigation of these irregularities than they did to the April 1995 Oklahoma City bombing.

* * *

It was clear that we would have to do virtually all our work ourselves and that we would get little, if any, active cooperation from SLOC or the USOC. Tom Welch and Dave Johnson were the designated villains. They were portrayed as the persons solely responsible for any wrongdoings. The community, it seemed, knew nothing; the governor knew nothing; and, even more surprising, the chair of SLOC knew nothing. It was not a heartwarming performance and, although Welch and Johnson were the two responsible for running the bid, it strains any credulity that the other members of the bid committee, right up to the very top, were unaware of what was going on. Welch had left SLOC some time earlier as a result of publicity surrounding his domestic affairs and had, when he left, taken some of the files from his office that related to IOC members. We never saw those files. Unlike the public authorities, the IOC had no status in the United States and had no power to obtain records or information that people were not willing to volunteer.

Our own investigation had shown that SLOC had adopted a program that was targeted at IOC members who may have had no particular interest in or knowledge of the Winter Games. There was a strong element of "push" involved, occasionally on a very aggressive basis. To be sure, there were also IOC members who had their hands out and who asked for favors in a manner that brought disrepute on the IOC. The most notorious was Jean-Claude Ganga, the member from the Republic of the Congo (Brazzaville), who had led the 1976 African boycott at the Montreal Games. His conduct was outrageous. He had asked for favors for not only himself but also members of his family; had made several visits to Salt Lake City at the expense of SLOC; obtained medical treatment for himself and his family; got into land speculation with Tom Welch; and had demonstrated a host of other disagreeable tendencies. Other members asked for, or were offered, help with education, jobs for family members, and even payments to help settle personal or political debts. It was the kind of conduct that had been rumored, but for which no evidence had ever been forthcoming, despite efforts on the part of the IOC to elicit it. This was the first time that there had been documentary evidence of such conduct, and the first opportunity to show that the IOC was serious about dealing with it.

By the time I got to Lausanne for the executive board meeting in January 1999, we had settled upon recommendations that ten members should be brought before the session with the intention that they be expelled for conduct that had brought the IOC into disrepute. There were other members who still had to be cleared of allegations, but the misconduct of these ten was obvious. Some of them resigned before the session, and René Essomba, whose daughter's tuition fees had been the start of the disclosures, had died since the scandal broke. Some of the ten insisted on their right to appear in front of the session, to which they were entitled.

Since the IOC as an organization is governed by Swiss law, we had to be sure that we acted in a manner that did not give rise to any appeal before the Swiss courts. The formal charges were stated in general terms so that the untrammeled right of an association to determine and deal with its membership could not be attacked in court. We did not want to get into the niceties of deciding whether the internal rules about accepting gifts or travel restrictions were, or were not, properly adopted, so we made no reference to them whatsoever. The last thing in the world we wanted, as this controversy raged around us, was a series of dilatory appeals that would keep the pot boiling indefinitely. Everything was based on the "conduct unbecoming" aspect of the Olympic Charter and, in the end, there were no appeals, although the most egregious member of all, Jean-Claude Ganga, threatened one. It would have been great legal entertainment to watch him try to make a case that, despite his outrageous conduct, he should still be entitled to retain his membership in the IOC.

After the IOC executive board had accepted our recommendations, a special session of the IOC was scheduled for March 9, 1999, to deal with the individual expulsions. I provided a summary of the facts in each case and then the member whose charges we were studying was allowed to speak. I was astonished by the fact that a huge percentage of the members at the session had not even bothered to read the charges and the evidence we had uncovered. Here we were in the middle of a crisis that could have meant the end of the IOC and they had not made even a rudimentary effort to get their minds around the facts. I was also surprised that the votes on the first one or two members were not as overwhelming as they should have been. Then we realized that we had not followed a simple procedure that is common to such prosecutions. We had let the accused speak last and their emotional, if inaccurate, explanations had stirred sympathy among their colleagues. That was stopped when I was asked by several members, including Jean-Claude Killy and Guy Drut, both of France, to give a reply to what they had said and, thereafter, the margins for expulsion were much greater.

One of the members whose name had appeared in the Salt Lake City files was Un Yong Kim of South Korea. He had been pressuring Tom Welch to organize a visa for the daughter of the owner of a company that had recorded music played by Kim's daughter. Kim had also requested that Salt Lake City, among other candidate cities, organize concerts for his daughter. All this was highly inappropriate and would certainly have earned him a strong reprimand.

But, at a meeting in New York with the FBI and Department of Justice in January 1999, we were asked if we knew about a job that had been arranged for his son, for which the Salt Lake City bid committee had paid. This would have escalated Kim's culpability to the level of the members who were marked for expulsion. We had known nothing about this until advised, but said we would look into it.

I told Samaranch that matters regarding Kim had now become much more serious. Samaranch said I must do what I could to "save" Kim, for some unknown reason. I said that I could not, and would not, give anyone special treatment, not only because it was the wrong thing to do, but also because it would compromise the whole investigation and whatever credibility the IOC still retained. From that moment on, I had the feeling that everything we knew was also known by Kim. Samaranch could hardly wait to transfer the responsibility for the ongoing investigation from the commission that I chaired to the Ethics Commission, chaired by Kéba Mbaye. I was not a member of that. The moment the March session was completed, Samaranch disbanded my commission of inquiry, even though we were still in the process of following up the allegations against Kim and some other members. Responsibility now rested with the Ethics Commission.

Because of the seriousness of the job allegations against Kim, we had invited his son to appear before our commission, where he denied any impropriety. He said he did not know anything about the company that had paid some of the money, and his lawyers said they had been unable to locate it. When we looked, we found it with no difficulty. The FBI and the Department of Justice, who had the power to make investigations, were similarly unconvinced that Kim's son was telling the truth. They decided to prosecute him, and he fled the country just before the laying of charges for green card offenses. He was eventually arrested in Bulgaria in the spring of 2003 on an Interpol warrant issued by the United States, who wanted him extradited to face the outstanding charges and, almost certainly, to give evidence in the Salt Lake City trial that was to start in late October. These extradition proceedings were fiercely contested by lawyers representing him or the family, while he languished in a Bulgarian jail from which he was released into house arrest only after some six months.

Seen from afar, it appeared that every effort was made to try to prevent him from being in the United States during the trial of Welch and Johnson. Under oath, he would probably have been faced with the difficult choice between perjury and telling the truth regarding his job. Almost all of the surrounding details had already been provided in open court, so there was little room for further maneuver. If he had returned to the United States, he probably would not have incurred jail time, since the time he had served in the Bulgarian prison would have been taken off any sentence in the United States. Knowing this, the U.S. authorities eventually dropped the charges against the son.

It seems a shame that young Kim paid such a heavy price for a plan of action that he undoubtedly neither designed nor controlled. His father's troubles have continued to mount. At home, Kim was regarded as having scuttled his country's bid for the 2010 Winter Games by putting his personal ambitions to become IOC vice-president ahead of his country's bid. Some members may well have thought that they had done their bit for Korea by voting for Kim and felt free to vote for Vancouver in the other contest. He was subsequently arrested on bribery and corruption charges, and was forced to resign from the South Korean National Assembly; relinquish his position as president of the World Taekwondo Federation, his power base;

and has been suspended, pending final resolution of these matters, from all of his activities as an IOC member. Some conclusion as to the gravity of the matter may be drawn from the fact that the IOC Ethics Commission and the IOC executive board were both of the unanimous view that such action be taken immediately.

*   *   *

In addition to dealing with our culprits, the IOC engaged in a process of reform to deal with the many criticisms directed at it during the crisis. Some were silly, but we dealt with them anyway. When the IOC had no money at all, no one was interested in it. Now everyone wanted to see our financial statements. We had no objection, but it was amusing to see some of the media from the sports beat trying to understand them. It seemed to them to be our fault that they could not read financial statements. On this, I had no sympathy whatsoever. I did not see why we should take on the burden of educating sports writers on the subject, and told them to take the statements to their own financial reporters. They wanted disclosure. They had disclosure. If they could not understand what they were reading, that was their problem.

There were calls for structural reform even though the Salt Lake City crisis had not been the result of a structural problem within the IOC. It was not the fact that members were appointed for life, or close to life, that led to our problems. It was governance—or, more accurately, lack of governance—that created the problem. We may have had a few members who were past their prime, but they did no harm and provided a degree of stability and corporate memory for the organization. The length of appointment became a hot-button issue with the public, though, so we considered term limits. The USOC suggested that terms should last six years (coincidently, I am sure, rather like the terms of U.S. senators), which makes no sense in the Olympic four-year cycle, so we settled on renewable eight-year terms, subject to a new retirement age of seventy for incoming members, down from the limit of eighty that Samaranch had engineered for his personal electoral benefit at the same session that elected Salt Lake City. We adopted a more formal nomination process that was to include a screening to ensure that undesirable members did not slip through. It is a cumbersome process that has added little to the equation, since the initial reviews have been so perfunctory that they barely confirmed the age and address of the individuals proposed. The main protection will likely come from the new procedure by which each proposed new member is submitted to a secret ballot by the members.

The most important structural change was to move partially away from the original concept that each member of the IOC was chosen for his or her personal qualities and was regarded as a representative of the IOC in his or her country, not the delegate of the country to the IOC. The new breakdown, with specific quotas of members to be selected using different categories (athletes, IFs, NOCs, or for personal characteristics) and a new maximum number of members, will require a certain attrition to start with. The process was considered in the abstract, without much attention to the fact that the attrition might fall disproportionately in countries with major sport traditions, and I predict some difficulty in making it work so that the IOC does not get weaker, rather than stronger in the medium term.

Countries with strong sporting traditions have been involved with the Olympic movement longer, and on average their representatives are older and will be forced to retire sooner so that the wine gets watered. The usual tensions have been expressed. Each of the 35 Olympic international federations believes that it is entitled to a seat at the table; each of the 202 national Olympic committees feels the same way. The international federations would not accept being outvoted by mere NOCs. Balancing off such huge numbers with individuals would produce a huge organization, which would be impossible to govern and hugely expensive to support. It would become as paralyzed as the United Nations when faced with important issues.

One of the reasons that the IOC has worked as well as it has and been able to adapt to an astonishing array of social and political change is that the bulk of its members have come from countries that have a well-developed sport tradition. The practice of allowing a second member in countries that have hosted the Games reinforced this sport-centered approach to issues that arose. The matter of universality was addressed by appointing some members in developing countries, to be sure that such views were represented, but the IOC instinctively knew that there was a huge risk of having equal representation in every country. It did not purport to be democratically constituted, although in its internal workings it was democratic in the extreme—with equal treatment of every member, regardless of the size of his or her country.

By December 1999, the reforms were ready and a third session of the IOC was held for that year, in Lausanne, where the reforms were adopted. I think we went too far in some areas that had nothing to do with Salt Lake City and will have to deal with the consequences in due course. But in others, especially with regard to bringing on board athlete members with full voting rights, the Salt Lake City crisis was a godsend and got us further in a single year than we might have got in decades of fussing.

The final act was for Samaranch to accept an "invitation" to appear before a congressional committee in late

December and to bring an end to a potentially serious fire that had started in the U.S. Congress. Caught up in the excitement of having the IOC on the run (not yet the USOC, which would come into congressional sights four years later for its own questionable conduct and dysfunctional governance), the U.S. Congress was threatening to legislate against the IOC, tax its revenues and otherwise interfere with its activities. Samaranch was more than equal to the task and the crisis passed. The Salt Lake City affair was a much closer-run threat to the existence of the IOC than the majority of our members ever realized and only the prompt and firm actions we took prevented it from raging out of control. I hate to think what it cost the IOC during 1999, with the three sessions and the legal and public relations expenses. (The IOC refuses to release the figures.)

The Salt Lake City disaster had been in the works for years. The IOC should have seen it coming much sooner. The campaign for the 1988 Summer Games had pitted arch-rivals Japan and South Korea against each other, and money was no object where national pride—particularly with the special history between them—was concerned. Rumors were already circulating about expensive tickets being sent and not used, but cashed in. Several South Koreans were heard to boast that this scam was cheaper for them than having the members travel to their country, where they would have to be accommodated, fed and shown around. Neither Seoul nor its Japanese competitor, Nagoya, made any complaint and, to no one's surprise, none of those who may have cashed in the tickets said anything.

Gifts to IOC members took a quantum leap in the 1992 contest won by Barcelona and managed offstage by Samaranch. It was a clever gifting program, with every item having some connection to either Barcelona or Spain, but there was no question that it had moved beyond mere souvenirs. I had a particularly difficult moment with Carlos Ferrer, the suave and urbane president of the Spanish Olympic Committee and later an IOC colleague. He would invite each IOC member to lunch at his bank in Barcelona (one of many enterprises that he directed with great ability) to discuss the candidacy. I went, in my turn. Knowing that I enjoy cigars, just as I was leaving after lunch he tried to press four boxes of Cuban cigars on me. This was way out of proportion to the occasion and I said I could not accept. He persisted: they were only cigars and it was a personal gift from him. It became increasingly awkward not to give offense and I finally agreed that I would take one box, falling back on the excuse that this was the only amount I could get through Customs on my return to Canada. That should probably have been more of a warning to me than it was at the time.

As the stakes grew, so did the pressures on candidate cities and so, apparently, did the appetites of some of our members. The conduct went in the direction of the lowest common denominator. The takers were not talking, and the candidate cities did not seem to dare to speak out or complain to the IOC. Maybe they thought that the corruption went all the way to the top and were afraid that speaking out would prejudice their bids. The IOC limited itself to imposing rules that dealt with major expenses that were needlessly incurred by bidding committees, and it tried to impose limits on member visits to candidate cities and on the value of gifts. Even after-the-fact debriefings with candidate cities failed to elicit names and details of IOC misconduct. It was frustrating to be powerless, waiting for an eventual explosion. All we knew was that it would happen someday and that it would be ugly when it did. How right we were!

The new system has some advantages. It is cheaper. It seems to produce the right finalists. It saves everyone a lot of time and the expense of traveling. It puts more emphasis on the thorough review of the candidates by the Evaluation Commission. On the other hand, the contacts are so limited that candidate cities can barely speak with IOC members. I, for example, have had as much experience with candidate cities and organizing committees for both Summer and Winter Games as any member of the IOC. But no one from a bidding city can come to see me to get the benefit of my advice and I am forbidden, by the rules, from visiting any city to provide what might be useful advice. That is an example of the reforms going too far. It would be very easy to differentiate Olympic "tourism" from genuine advice-providing contacts, something that could easily be monitored by giving advance notice of a proposed contact to, say, the IOC Ethics Commission. We should be careful of cutting off our noses to spite our face. There are some IOC members who have something useful to offer by way of experience to bidding cities and others who do not. The distinction is not hard to make. I have suggested reconsideration of this matter to IOC president Jacques Rogge. Apart from all that, if candidate cities and IOC members are going to conspire and break the rules, mere prohibition of visits will not stop improper behavior. If there are unethical members and candidate cities, they will find a way.

Passing the Torch: Samaranch

Every organization relies on its leaders to provide direction and to set the standards that will establish the public face of that entity. Nowhere is this feature more apparent than with the International Olympic Committee, whose president occupies the position of virtually sole interlocutor for the organization in its many and complicated relationships, both within the sport movement and in the commercial and political spheres. On a day-to-day basis, it is the president who is the constant presence of the IOC, since the members, dispersed throughout the world, meet only once a year and the elected "government" of the IOC, the executive board, assembles four or five times a year. Even when the entire IOC is present, or the executive board meets, it is the president who provides the definitive statements and summaries of the meetings and iterates the policy of the IOC.

I have met with and have participated in the Olympic movement under the direction of four IOC presidents:

Avery Brundage, Lord Killanin, Juan Antonio Samaranch and Jacques Rogge. Each has shaped the IOC in a quite different manner, as a matter of style and as a reflection of individual character. Brundage was a powerful and forceful personality, befitting someone who was able to hold the Olympic movement together in the difficult postwar period, as the Soviet Union made its noisy entry into the movement. He eventually descended into a view of amateurism that became increasingly at odds with the manner in which sport was developing around the world and by the time he retired, he was well out of touch with the real world of sport. Killanin was a much softer man, chosen in part for that very reason over his rival, Comte de Beaumont, who was considered to be authoritarian. Killanin's style was agreeable, but the issues he faced proved too complex to be solved with a kitchen-table style of management. As the IOC moved closer to the center of the world stage, a different approach was required, and Juan Antonio Samaranch emerged on the scene.

Winston Churchill's description of Russia as a riddle wrapped in a mystery inside an enigma could well apply to Juan Antonio Samaranch, the man from the Catalonian region of Spain who became president of the IOC from 1980 to 2001. Virtually unknown outside his native city of Barcelona, Samaranch caught the attention of the IOC's then-president, Avery Brundage, who co-opted him as a second member of the IOC in Spain, despite the IOC rule that permitted only one member per country unless that country had hosted the Olympic Games. It was not the first Olympic rule to be bent for, or by, Samaranch. It was never clear what had made Brundage notice him, although Samaranch had been president of the Spanish Olympic Committee and *chef de mission* of its Olympic team. He had also been a minor governmental official under the Franco regime, of which more has been made in the media than it probably deserves. At that time, the alternatives in Spain were rather limited: one was within the regime or outside it, which in those days meant one was a Communist. Whatever he is or was, Samaranch was not a Communist.

He did possess considerable ambition, coupled with superior organizational skills and a work ethic that would have made Hercules blush with shame. From his first day as an IOC member—encouraged along the way, perhaps, by Brundage's observation that he might, one day, make a good IOC president—Samaranch worked assiduously to bring himself close to the center of IOC power; to be seen with those in power; to build alliances with those in a position to help him in his ambition; to not make waves; to not be out in front of issues, but to stay behind; and to offend no one.

It was too soon to make a move in 1972, when Brundage retired and the battle was between the powerful Comte de Beaumont of France and Michael Morris, the Lord Killanin, of Ireland. Samaranch's tendencies in the quest to become president were reinforced when the bland Killanin triumphed over the more severe de Beaumont. As it became increasingly clear in the late 1970s that Killanin would not seek a second term, Samaranch's campaign began to roll out. He managed to be appointed as Spanish ambassador to the Soviet Union and stationed in Moscow, the host city for 1980, he made a point of meeting every Olympic person of influence that visited Moscow, as well as to solidify the support of the Soviet bloc members. He had left the executive board in 1978 at the end of his four-year term, but his ambitions made it essential that he get back on in 1979, since it would have been difficult to become president from outside the IOC's inner sanctum.

The 1979 session in Montevideo, Uruguay, was my first as an IOC member. I saw how the political machinery came together to elect Samaranch to the executive board and Alexandru Siperco of Romania to the vice-presidency to pacify the Soviet bloc, which was important for Samaranch's campaign.

Once back on the board, Samaranch made sure he attended all the major Olympic gatherings, including the meeting of national Olympic committees (NOCs) in Puerto Rico later that year—which created the Association of National Olympic Committees (ANOC), presided over by the Mexican Mario Vázquez-Raña—and the Pan American Games. There was not much visible politicking at the 1980 Winter Games in Lake Placid, because everyone was more concerned about the possible effects of the U.S.-led boycott of the 1980 Summer Games in Moscow.

By the time I arrived in Moscow for the traditional IOC session preceding the Games, the ducks were all in order and Samaranch, supported by a well-organized campaign that had been several years in the making, was poised for a first-round victory, almost unheard of in IOC elections. Not only that, but the positions for the vacant executive board seats had all been determined in advance, to the point that not only were the players identified, but also the order in which they would be elected—all this by secret ballot, as well.

The bulk of Samaranch's electoral support came from Africa, Asia and Eastern Europe, with very little from mainstream Europe, where the votes were split between Marc Hodler of Switzerland, Willi Daume of Germany and, to a lesser extent (among the Scandinavian members), Jim Worrall of Canada. This was also a time when the leadership of international sport was changing from what had been largely Anglo-Saxon: the soccer federation FIFA (Fédération Internationale de Football Association) ousted its British president and replaced him with Joao Havelange of Brazil; the ANOC had elected Mario Vázquez-Raña of Mexico; the

International Amateur Athletic Association (IAAF) chose Primo Nebiolo of Italy; swimming picked Javier Ostos of Mexico; and so forth. Samaranch's accession to the presidency of the IOC gave more momentum to this development.

The evening before the election, David McKenzie of Australia and I had been having dinner in the dining room of the Moskwa Hotel, where the IOC members were housed, when Norma Macmanaway, Killanin's secretary, came in and said that the president was all by himself in his room. Would we be willing to come up and spend some time with him? We were happy to do so and he invited us in for a "jar" or two and we chatted about the elections the following day. Although he had not been a powerful president and was well over his head in many of the complicated international problems that arose on his watch, Killanin was a thoroughly nice man and excellent company.

He was in a reflective mood that evening and may have been a bit hurt by the fact that none of his long-standing friends were with him, but he was pleased to have a couple of the junior members for company. I had, indeed, been the last member to be co-opted under his presidency, just three years earlier. We said it appeared that Samaranch was going to win, despite the late attack being launched by Hodler (who had repeatedly said he would not be a candidate) and Killanin agreed with that assessment. I said I did not know Samaranch well at all and asked what he was like. "Will he make a good president?" I asked. "He will be better than you think," said Killanin, a prediction that certainly proved to be correct.

After the election, I wrote to Samaranch, congratulating him on his victory and offering to be of whatever help he might wish. I was the junior member of the IOC at the time, but told him I had a certain amount of energy and that I thought I wrote pretty well and that I was willing to work hard in the interests of the Olympic movement. I also noted that he was inheriting many problems within the organization. His reply took the form of a short letter of acknowledgment and a request for clarification. So I thought that I might as well let him know exactly what I meant and wrote that the IOC had not shown itself to be collegial, but, instead, composed of highly disciplined blocs, which risked turning it into an ineffective mini-United Nations. I described how I had seen the elections unfolding precisely as programmed. His reply was largely dismissive, and his suggestion that I would naturally have voted for my Canadian colleague showed that he realized I was not without sin myself. Samaranch, of course, had benefited from the highly disciplined bloc votes. Indeed, the vote count had been one short of what his handlers had expected and a serious effort was made to find out who might have defected.

It was generally understood that the members from the Soviet sphere of influence, including the Soviet members themselves, had no choice but to follow whatever instructions they received from the political masters. It was always a sign of the good personal relations between the IOC members that they understood the situation and cheerfully ignored most of the blatant political posturing. The IOC was quite careful to make sure that the membership did not get over-balanced with political hostages who had to follow orders, so that it was able to get its business done despite the occasional anvil chorus of overwrought political speeches.

I have always maintained, publicly and privately, that Samaranch was one of the three great IOC presidents, the other two being Pierre de Coubertin and Brundage. De Coubertin had the vision and energy to establish the IOC and to bring back the Olympic Games as an international festival. Brundage held the Olympic movement together, almost by the sheer force of his personality, during the difficult postwar period when it could easily have split apart. He also possessed a sophisticated mind, and an ability to deal with difficult political problems that many people—particularly if they remember only his last years and, especially, Munich—might not fully appreciate.

It was Samaranch, however, who brought the IOC into full bloom, so that it was ready to play a meaningful role on the international stage in the latter part of the twentieth century. He brought a breadth of ambition and understanding of politics, tempered with a realization of the need to understand both the upper and lower limits of what was possible for the IOC. Each limit proved to be beyond what anyone could have imagined when he came to power in Moscow just before his sixtieth birthday in July 1980. He added to this a remarkable level of self-discipline and a work ethic that had never been seen in any sports leader. He had, as does everyone, his faults and his blind spots, some of which would lead to serious problems for the IOC, but these were far overshadowed by the successes that his leadership created. Since both had far-reaching consequences for the IOC, they both deserve consideration in any assessment of him.

•　•　•

The IOC holds occasional Olympic congresses, in addition to its regular sessions. They had been sporadic, to the point where several decades had elapsed prior to the congress in Varna, Bulgaria, in 1973. Another congress had been scheduled for Baden-Baden the year after Samaranch assumed the presidency. It would be important for him to demonstrate his grasp of the portfolio here and also to begin healing some of the wounds created by the Moscow boycott. One signal that Samaranch had come to grips with his new job was the IOC session's choice of the 1988 Olympic host cities. Both Canada and Korea had boycotted the 1980 Games. Making sure that the Olympic family did not lose its resolve and collapse under the political pressure that the United States had exerted on would-be participants to the Moscow Games had taken its toll on the IOC.

The Olympic movement knew that the Soviets would be aware that it had helped prevent the ignominy of canceling or postponing the Games. So the IOC had no compunction about going against the express wishes of the Soviets and announcing that the 1988 Games were awarded to South Korea.

Oddly enough, the political interests of the Soviet Union and Japan, which had been at severe odds in 1980, now coincided, and the Soviets were set up to pose what they and the Japanese thought would be a killer question designed to sink the South Korean bid. Interestingly, the topic was not the recent military coup in South Korea, which might well have deserved more attention than it got, but rather the economic conditions in South Korea that required massive borrowings by its government. The question was posed at the congress by Yuri Titov, the Soviet president of the International Gymnastics Federation (FIG), but the Koreans had anticipated it and an expert in their delegation demolished the suggestion by showing that such borrowings were perfectly normal for developing countries and that this same technique had also been heavily relied upon by Japan during the postwar reconstruction period. It was a tremendously embarrassing moment for the Japanese, because of both the substance of the matter and the obvious political dimension.

That message delivered by the IOC session, the congress then considered the importance of reinforcing the unity of the Olympic movement. Recruitment of several prominent Olympic athletes, led by Sebastian Coe, the great British middle-distance runner and Olympic champion, was an important initiative that Samaranch had already started establishing. It would lead to the creation of a special Athletes Commission within the IOC and, eventually, to the inclusion of active athletes as full IOC members. The athletes at the congress proved to be effective communicators and gathered a great deal of attention to athlete-related issues, including the use of performance-enhancing drugs; the athletes underlined the fact that the sports authorities had already let the doping situation get out of hand, with precious more than lip service being paid to the problem. The congress was well managed and there was little doubt that Samaranch was firmly in control of the IOC and, through it, the movement as a whole.

I must have made some impression on Samaranch by then, perhaps as president of the Canadian Olympic Association (COA) on behalf of the Calgary bid for 1988 and perhaps as a result of my opposition to the management style of Monique Berlioux, the director of the IOC, who was already in the process of becoming Samaranch's arch-enemy. Unlike the previous IOC presidents, for whom the job was part-time, he decided to live in Lausanne and to become a full-time president. This, of course, cut hugely into the authority exercised by Berlioux, who was not at all pleased with the new regime, even though it was generally believed that she had been in favor of Samaranch as the new president during the electoral campaign.

The tensions between them began to grow almost immediately and eventually led to her dismissal four years later prior to a session in East Berlin. Samaranch had it all set up the previous year in Sarajevo, but she was saved by the intervention of the long time Romanian member, Alexandru Siperco. The most delicious rumor that circulated was that Samaranch and Berlioux had each bugged the other's office.

237

Samaranch was constantly asking me what legal grounds existed to fire her and what the consequences might be for the IOC if it were to do so. I had told him he could always fire her and that the only liability was the balance due to her under her contract, which, to everyone's surprise and Samaranch's annoyance, Killanin had renewed shortly before the expiry of his term as president.

My suggestion to Samaranch was that all he had to do was tell her that the contract would be honored, in its entirety, but that she did not have to bother showing up for work. I doubt if we could have got away with that, but there would have been much pleasure in it for Samaranch. In any event, the only exposure was money. The major worry for Samaranch was that she might write some form of memoir that would put him in a bad light, so once she had been dealt with, the terms of her settlement provided that she would do nothing detrimental to the IOC. After her departure, whenever there was some thought that she might be dealing with a publisher, we wrote to the publisher to say that there was a non-disclosure contract and that they would be involved in assisting with the breach of that contract if they were to publish any Olympic-related book written by her. None was ever published.

My own relationship with Berlioux had been uneasy from the moment I first encountered her imperious style leading up to the Games in Montreal in 1976. I had said to Samaranch on several occasions that one of the difficulties for the IOC was that, by the time the Games in any city were over, everyone involved hated the IOC and the reason for this was Mme Berlioux. It was not the IOC members, who were perhaps a bit doddery on occasion but were generally gentle souls who worked hard at giving no offense to their hosts. One example was her view of the ownership of the pictograms that portray each of the sports at the Games.

Montreal had bought the rights to the 1972 Munich pictograms and transferred them to the COA once the 1976 Games were over. Berlioux disputed this ownership and claimed that the Munich organizers had transferred them to the IOC, before the organizers had assigned the rights to Montreal. This was complete nonsense, so we pressed for documentary evidence that the copyright had been transferred to the IOC. After extensive stalling, she finally said that the assignment had been made verbally at an IOC executive board meeting. It was such a spurious position as to be ludicrous. In the meantime she had purported, on behalf of the IOC, to enter into a long-term licensing arrangement with a third party, thereby exposing the IOC to extensive and expensive litigation in the U.S. and Swiss courts.

I remember an occasion at the 1979 session, held in Montevideo, Uruguay, where I was to be sworn in as a member. I had been co-opted at the Athens session the year before and had not attended as it might have been seen as presumptuous for me to have been there, anticipating the result of the election, especially at my precocious age of thirty-six. At each session the members show they belong to the IOC by wearing badges that bear the session design and have white ribbons attached. Participants with other affiliations—such as IFs and NOCs—have different-colored ribbons attached. I had received mine, from Berlioux's office, and was wearing it. Berlioux instructed one of the junior staff members to come to me to say that I could not wear it, as I had not yet been sworn in, and that the young lady was to return it to Berlioux, who certainly knew better than to make the demand in person.

Knowing that the staff member would be in deep trouble if I gave her the answer I would have given Berlioux, I returned it, in exchange for a badge that had no ribbon. I got a piece of white paper, cut it into the shape of the ribbon and sported it, for the twelve "illegal" hours, to the great amusement of my colleagues (to whom I made a point of telling the story) with the inscription I LOVE MONIQUE written on it. In many ways, it was a pity that she was so abrasive. She was possessed of much ability and was an efficient and tireless worker. She was the top female sports administrator in the world and could, no doubt, have continued in her position had she not offended so many people and, most importantly, had she been able to adjust to the fact that the new IOC president was simply a horse of a different color.

In 1982 Samaranch suggested that I should run for the executive board. I said that I had seen what happened to David McKenzie, who had run early in his career and been soundly defeated. I observed that the IOC seemed to be an organization that devoured its young and that I had no desire to be the hors d'oeuvre of the season. I would be willing to run only if he were to put his own authority behind my candidacy, and obviously there was not enough time for him to do so for the 1982 session in Rome. He said he would think about it for the following year, in New Delhi, and it was there that I was first elected to the executive board, where I would remain, officially and unofficially between terms, until 2001. Early on, I think he wanted some people who would be able to think for themselves, and I was someone representing the Anglo-Saxon tradition in an international sport leadership that was becoming increasingly Latin.

As a president, Samaranch had a very clear idea of what he wanted to do and he always made sure that there would be a majority of members on the executive board who would do what he wanted, in case of a vote. He was prepared to encourage the members he wanted on the board to run and willing to tell others not to run if he did not want them. If anyone decided to run against his advice, he made his views known to the members and the results of the elections accorded with his wishes. After only a couple of years, he got the executive boards he wanted and they were suitably subservient whenever decisions were required.

I once asked him why, if he were in a position to choose his executive boards, he did not get the best members for the purpose. He said he did not want a board filled with people like me who would be willing to challenge his ideas (not all of which were equally good) and offer different proposals, but preferred to be able to count on the majority who would agree with him, no matter what he wanted. "Leesten, for me, it is important to know that I will always have a majority to support me." Most decisions were made by consensus, however, and it was rare that there was sufficient divergence of opinion to require a vote. When he sensed that there could be a serious division, Samaranch usually postponed the decision—"We are not in a hurry"— either because it could be put off, or until he had a chance to make his minions aware of exactly what he wanted if there was to be a vote. When an issue could not be put off and actually required detailed study, a plethora of IOC commissions was available to do the work. They were all advisory bodies, with no power to act, and all of them were appointed by the president.

Pursuing his idea of increased unity among the Olympic movement, Samaranch established a new tripartite commission, which he named the Commission for the Olympic Movement, composed of equal numbers of IOC members (basically the executive board), and representatives from the IFs and NOCs. Ostensibly created to provide a forum for discussion of common concerns between Olympic congresses, it was almost entirely symbolic. I always thought that it was a singularly useless commission and no one took it at all seriously. Its main virtue was that it existed and could therefore be used if ever there was a matter that might appear to call for such an impressive consideration. The solution would, however, have already been found long before the commission were to meet and solemnly decide to decide what had already been decided.

Samaranch was an effective chair and enjoyed the role. Although he asserted himself in executive board meetings, he rarely played an active role in the full sessions of the IOC, leaving the bulk of the reporting to the chairs of the various commissions and to staff members with specific responsibilities. He expected the executive board to act in much the same way, so that unless one was reporting as chair of a commission, one was expected not to be active in the sessions. This meant that the sessions were very dull, since we had reviewed all the reports beforehand (more than once, if you happened to be a member of a commission) and had to sit through them once again. It also meant that the bulk of any discussion was carried by the IOC members at large who were the most unfamiliar with the issues and the background.

There were few opportunities for the sessions to consider broad matters of principle and they became mere reporting occasions, affording little satisfaction to any of the members. The virtual monopoly of detailed knowledge of the issues held by the executive board caused a widening gap between the board and the general IOC membership and a growing resentment that simmered just beneath the surface. Samaranch was so powerful that this could only be demonstrated indirectly, such as in the secret ballots to choose host cities.

A particular skill that Samaranch had mastered was the ability to have many short, but productive, meetings. In the course of ten or fifteen minutes, he could receive, welcome, listen to and dispose of the issues raised by the various penitents who sought audiences with the IOC president. My experience was that almost everyone who had such meetings came away satisfied that their point had been made and understood. In many cases, the fact that such meetings took place was often more important than the outcome. The ability to return home and say that a particular matter had been discussed directly with the IOC president, provided status to the person or organization that had sought the meeting. The great percentage of matters were little more than special pleading, by a sport seeking admission to the Olympic program; an organization hoping for IOC recognition; an individual hoping to become an IOC member; or someone merely ranting about some small, insoluble problem. The usual coded answers would be provided: "Yes," which, as all diplomats know, means maybe; "maybe," which means, in the same lexicon, no; and "we will study," which means that the answer is almost certainly no, but that some hope might be held out that something might, possibly, happen before hell freezes over.

It was Samaranch's idea to try to create an international political status for the IOC. He retained his Spanish ambassadorial rank, which entitled him to be addressed as "Your Excellency." Although he did not refer to himself in that manner, he made sure it was clear that others should, and at all formal occasions, he was referred to accordingly. Within the sport community, it was viewed as rather pompous, but for protocol purposes it could sound suitably statesmanlike. Later, when he was named Marquis ("El Marqués de Samaranch") by King Juan Carlos, I asked him whether he was going to insist on being called by that title. He replied that the Spanish king would be very disappointed if he did not. I think, however, that he got the point and he did not generally use the title, although formal correspondence and official documents were an exception. In the quest for improving the diplomatic status of the IOC, he made a point of meeting the heads of state and political leaders in each of the countries he visited, so that he had reasonable access to them if the circumstances warranted it in future. Nor was he shy about using the access and he maintained the ties, expressing best wishes, condolences and congratulations on appropriate occasions.

Since the cold war was very much a part of sport in his early years as president, he always attended the annual meetings of the socialist sports ministers and was given the opportunity to speak, usually in bland generalizations, a feature of almost all his public utterances. Part of his routine was also to try to meet separately with each of the ministers so that he knew the micro, as well as the macro, issues that they considered important. The symbolic point was that he was there, representing the IOC, and his presence undoubtedly diminished the chances of any extreme positions being adopted. The fact that he had been ambassador to the Soviet Union added to his credibility at these meetings. The socialist ministers knew that he had been in Moscow and was familiar with the issues that were important to the Soviets. It was also advantageous that they knew he understood that they had very little room for individual maneuver as countries under the Soviet rule.

On a personal basis, Samaranch had a travel schedule that would have killed someone without his iron constitution. He attended all major meetings of IFs and NOCs, world and regional championships, continental Games and other prestigious events such as Wimbledon and the French Open tennis championships in Paris. Naturally, he was front and center at each event, and this was precisely the effect he sought: the IOC was everywhere, at every major sport (and other) happening, and he was the IOC.

In this pursuit, Samaranch always wanted to have representatives of the IFs and NOCs, in such capacity, as members of the IOC. This, too, was symbolic, merely intended to show that the IOC embraced those other pillars of the Olympic movement. The IOC membership would probably have accepted the idea, but for the choice of representatives he had in mind. The IF representative he wanted was Primo Nebiolo, president of the International Amateur Athletic Federation (IAAF) and the NOC representative was Mario Vázquez-Raña, president of the ANOC. Nebiolo was Italian and Vázquez-Raña was Mexican. Each of those countries already had two IOC members, so the pair could not be coopted in their own right. None of the existing members from those countries was willing to step aside for them, and efforts within Italy to persuade the senior member to resign in return for a financial consideration had failed, so Samaranch was searching for another solution. His principal problem was that the IOC membership as a whole had so little regard for the two individuals that they resisted the idea. Samaranch knew they were disliked, but the symbolism of their positions was nevertheless important to him, and he wanted them inside the tent, even though he would, personally, have been much happier with other people.

Had the individuals been different, I am certain that the principle would have been accepted with no difficulty. It was one of the few defeats he experienced within the IOC, but, typical of Samaranch, he kept working at it until he achieved success. For some reason, which none of us ever figured out, Nebiolo seemed to have him in some sort of thrall, and Samaranch never put an end to a continuing series of posturing and threats about removing athletics from the Olympic Games.

Nebiolo would complain that the Olympics cost the IAAF so much money that they were not a worthwhile event; that athletics needed more prestige; that athletes should be paid to attend; that he did not have to provide a schedule that could be used by the television broadcasters to plan their Olympic coverage; that because of the Olympics, he could not sell his world championship events to broadcasters, so the Olympic contracts should include compulsory coverage of the world championships (at an exorbitant price compared with their market value); and on and on. Always behind this was the implied threat that he would withdraw athletics from the Games and thus effectively destroy them. Instead of calling this foolish bluff, Samaranch's interim response was to throw money at the problem, in the form of greater shares of Olympic television revenues. He also ensured that Nebiolo was elected as the president of Association of Summer Olympic International Federations (ASOIF), by discouraging others from running for the position and using all his influence to get votes for Nebiolo, who could easily have been defeated. Samaranch seemed blind to the fact that athletics needed the Olympics at least as much as the Olympics needed athletics and that the IAAF would have got rid—in a nanosecond—of any president who actually purported to boycott the Olympic Games.

The other IFs put up with Nebiolo because he was getting them more money and, frankly, they could not have cared less whether he became an IOC member or not. Their power bases were their control of their sports, and a minor role in the IOC might have added status but did nothing extra for them. For the rest of us, it was nothing more than an amusing spectacle of a comedic pursuit of power, but it seemed really to matter to Samaranch and he became increasingly desperate to make it happen. He had changed his approach slightly to say that he wanted to have the presidents of ASOIF and the Association of International

Olympic Winter Sports Federations (AIOWF) as IOC members so long as they held such office.

It was not until the IOC session in Albertville, France, before the Winter Games in 1992, that he got his first breakthrough, after two or three failures. Perhaps he was worried about the Barcelona Games coming up later that year, but he was determined to try again and this time I decided to help him. The debate on the issue in the session was going back and forth, mainly against the general idea (the argument being that having members coming from a particular constituency—known as representative members—was contrary to the fundamental idea of IOC individual members acting in a disinterested manner for the best interests of the Olympic movement), but, in fact, in full knowledge that we were discussing Nebiolo. Since the decision would involve an amendment to the Olympic Charter, it needed a two-thirds majority, which, based on the discussion, was very unlikely to be achieved.

I signaled to Samaranch that I would like to speak and indicated that he should wait until near the end. When he called upon me, I said that, as IOC members, we should give considerable deference to the requests made by the president, who was the person responsible for the operations of the IOC. If he thought that he needed this change in order to manage the Olympic movement more effectively, we should give the most careful consideration to that request, even if we did not fully comprehend the need for the amendment. Even if we might be concerned about the principle (we never mentioned Nebiolo), what the president suggested would only involve a maximum of two extra members, which was less than 2 percent of the total membership, and could not, therefore, adversely affect any decisions of the regular IOC members. He got the necessary majority and Nebiolo's current wish came true. The new-comer proved to be no problem within the IOC.

• • •

I do not wish to suggest that Nebiolo was without merit. He was, in fact, a very able sports administrator, who accomplished a great deal for the IAAF as well as for the International University Sports Federation (known by its French acronym, FISU). Apart from his limitless ambition, which he wore on his sleeve for all to see, he was an amusing character and I would have cheerfully spent an evening with him more than with some of my colleagues who detested him. He was short, oily, bald, spoke with a raspy voice, and people said he looked like Mussolini. He once said that before he got out of bed in the morning, he would spend at least five minutes determining how he could achieve some personal advantage for himself that day.

I remember that during the World Athletics Championships in Rome in 1987, Nebiolo had arranged a visit to Castel Gandolfo, the Pope's summer residence, for an audience with John Paul II on the regular rest day in the middle of the competitions. When he presented the delegates to the Pope, he announced in his inimitable style that in honor of the visit he had canceled the world championship competitions for the day. Gary Hite, then a vice-president of Coca-Cola involved with the Olympic sponsorship, was astounded. "Did you hear that? Primo's lying to the Pope!" It is probably not the first fib His Holiness had ever heard.

I had a delightful encounter with Nebiolo just prior to the Barcelona Games, after he had been elected at the Albertville session. I was running for election to the executive board, having sat out a mandatory one-year period of ineligibility after completing a four-year term as vice-president. We were entertaining all our marketing partners at a reception in a historic ship shed on the Barcelona waterfront and during the reception, Nebiolo's wife, Giovanna, came over and said that Primo wanted to speak with me. I followed her over to where he was. He took my arm and we paced back and forth the length of the shed while he told me that he had many friends in the IOC and that he could be quite influential. He thought I was a swell fellow and said that he would convince all his friends to vote for me. I said that was very kind of him and thanked him very much. But our walk was not over. He repeated that he would do all this for me and I repeated my thanks. He continued as if I had said nothing and said, ". . . and maybe someday, you will be able to do a little favor for me." I said that I thought I already had—at Albertville. "Heh, heh," he chortled, and persisted, ". . . and maybe someday you can do a little favor for me." "Primo," I said, "this sounds like something out of *The Godfather!*" "Heh, heh, but as I say, maybe someday . . ." He was cheerfully incorrigible.

Nebiolo had, unfortunately, only a few years to live and died in November 1999. We had all known that he was seriously ill, but his death came as something of a surprise nonetheless. As soon as I had learned of it, I called Samaranch to find out what had happened. He said, "This man, he is so lucky." "Lucky?" I said. "For God's sake, Juan Antonio, he's dead!" "Yes," said Samaranch, "but he died as president [of the IAAF]." It was an indication of what he was thinking for himself. He later said to me, discussing his own plans, "Anyway, it is better to die as president than as past-president."

•　•　•

As a political realist, Samaranch knew that money was power. He must be credited with going about the business of putting the IOC on a sound financial footing for the first time in its history. When I joined in 1978, all the IOC members had to pay their own travel expenses and hotel accommodations for IOC sessions or the Olympic Games. I was lucky that the Canadian Olympic Association was willing to pay the airfare to IOC sessions for the Canadian members. The IOC had perhaps US$250,000 as its total assets, all kept in a bank owned by the Comte de Beaumont, one of its members. The only revenues came from television rights, which had not begun to reach the levels of today. NBC had bid US$85 million (again, all TV rights figures are in U.S. currency) for the worldwide television rights for the Moscow Games in 1980, Samaranch's first year as president. Despite the Moscow boycott, NBC paid the IOC almost $12 million of its share of the television revenues it would have received from the Games, had NBC broadcast them. That meant that the IOC finally had enough money to begin to pay the travel costs of its members to sessions. This fit in well with Samaranch's objective of making the IOC more universal, since it meant that individuals from developing countries did not have to be wealthy in order to become IOC members. This money was not, however, enough to create any meaningful independence.

In 1982 he had decided to establish a new commission with the ponderous title of Commission for New Sources of Financing, the mission of which was to propose new methods of raising funds for the IOC. To have an economic model for an organization that depended on a single source of revenue (television) and of which some 90 or 95 percent came from a single country (the United States) was reckless. Especially when that country had just done everything it could to ruin your principal event and had prevented its own broadcaster from covering the Games. It was this commission that eventually developed the idea of an international marketing program, which I describe elsewhere.

Samaranch was quite willing to buy the loyalty of the IFs and NOCs and knew that, if the IOC had no money, it would have little or no influence within the Olympic movement. It was a two-edged sword, however, since once you create an appetite among the mob, you create expectations and, eventually, dependence. Less than a quarter of a century after his election, the great majority of Olympic IFs could not survive without the television money that the IOC provides from the Olympic Games. Their sports would all but disappear if ever they were to come off the Olympic program. The domino effect would be precipitous: they would drop off regional and continental games, and they would cease to get national funding from most governments. Young athletes would not enter the competitive structure of sports that did not offer an Olympic goal and sponsors would have no interest in sports that had no future.

The keeper of the purse held the balance of control over Olympic events. And Samaranch knew that the only purpose of having power was to wield it. I had a conversation with him one time and we were discussing Manfred Ewald, the East German sports minister who was widely acclaimed for the extraordinary success of the East German athletes (in the days when it was not considered polite to suggest that they were filled with performance-enhancing drugs). Sport was an East German national priority and was virtually the only foreign policy it was able to exercise under the stern gaze of the Soviet Union. Ewald was reported to have said that there were two elements involved: power and glory. He did not care, he said, who got the glory, as long as he had the power. "No, no," said Samaranch. "You do not understand. The power *is* the glory."

Power is often a quality that is perceived more by the holder than the observer. I was witness to an amusing occasion in the early 1990s, when the centenary of the IOC was approaching and we had decided to have an international contest to see who could design the logo that we would use during the period leading up to the event. We received entries from several countries and designers and had organized a jury consisting of recognized international figures, including David Ogilvy, founder of the Ogilvy & Mather advertising agency. He was an interesting, if opinionated, character, possessed of a towering ego that had not been assuaged when we decided against his personal choice of design. At a lunch in the IOC cafeteria that was hosted by Samaranch, who had not participated in the morning's judging, I was seated beside Ogilvy, who had been given the place of honor directly across from Samaranch. The air was heavy with the two egos, but, as is often the case, neither paid much attention to the other. About halfway through lunch, Ogilvy turned to me and motioned his head toward Samaranch. "Who," he asked in the loud voice of the hard of hearing, "is that odious little man?" Fortunately, Samaranch was also slightly hard of hearing, or may not have been aware that he was being discussed. I told Ogilvy that the person was none other than the IOC president. He absorbed the news with no particular interest and the two continued to be unimpressed with each other.

• • •

One particular blind spot Samaranch had was his fixation on the power, as he saw it, of the IFs. Nebiolo had an inordinate influence on him, from which we could not shake him. When the IAAF announced that it would hold world championships the year before the 1984 Olympics, you might have thought the world was going to end. I said they would be nothing more than a warm-up for the Olympics, but Samaranch saw it as the beginning of a long, slippery slope toward the Olympics becoming a non-prestigious event. You can imagine his angst when Nebiolo, even more self-inflated with the success of his event, later decided that he would hold world championships every two years. This time, he was convinced, the world really was going to end. I told Samaranch this was even better for the Olympics and that the best thing Nebiolo could do would be to hold his damn championships every year, or every six months. They would become an endless and boring blur and no one would pay the slightest attention to them. The Olympics would become even more important, not less.

It was the same, to varying degrees, with the other IFs. This may have hearkened back to the days when the IFs, organized by Thomas Keller—the Swiss president of the world rowing federation, FISA (it is known by the French acronym)—tried to capture control of the Olympic movement. The setting was the 1973 Olympic Congress in Varna, Bulgaria, during Killanin's presidency. Keller was beaten off, although he won a partial seat at the table when Killanin agreed to establish the Tripartite Commission (a precursor to the Commission for the Olympic Movement), ostensibly to prepare for the next congress. Keller had no regard for the IOC or for the NOCs, and thought that the Olympic movement would be much better off in the hands of the IFs, who controlled the sports and without whom the Games would not be possible. It was a crude position, inelegantly expressed, but one that had to be taken seriously and defended against.

IFs are inherently technical organizations, each concerned solely with its own sport. They can be visualized as a series of silos, vertically organizing their sports and their competitions throughout the world. There are very few similarities between swimming and rowing or between tennis and field hockey. About their only common need is for money. They do not have a common or shared philosophy about sport in general or its place in society. There is nothing inherent in their operations that would lead to any unity or effective joint programming. The NOCs have different problems, but are at least connected with each other and the IOC through the commitment to the principles of promoting the Olympic movement in their countries. They provide a link with the national sport federations affiliated to the IFs and integrate them all into the national sport structure. But they do not control the national federations, which are under the jurisdiction of the IFs. The only time they do is in the selection of the participants for the Olympic Games, which occasionally leads to friction with the IFs, who believe they are better equipped to make such decisions. The NOCs are the only organizations entitled to use the Olympic five-ring symbol in their countries, which gives them the best opportunity to raise funds, which again is often a sore point with their own national federations, who are not allowed to use it.

Samaranch, though, had little, if any, regard for the NOCs. "We can organize the Olympic Games tomorrow without the NOCs," he would often say. The NOCs were a nuisance that had to be accommodated and the great utility of Mario Vázquez-Raña was that, under his presidency of ANOC, they would never be sufficiently organized to create any problems. "As long as Mario is president, there will be no difficulties with the NOCs," Samaranch repeated many times. Even assuming he might have been right about being able to organize Games without NOCs (which I doubt), Samaranch never seemed to understand that it was national sentiment and identification that makes the Olympic Games so special. If there were to be no national team participating at the Games, but simply a series of world championships, public interest in such events would be marginal in comparison to the Games. They would have quickly degenerated into the lukewarm spectacle of the now-defunct Goodwill Games, which were first organized by Ted Turner as a U.S. television event in the expectation that it would be a profitable venture. The event was neither a sport nor a commercial success.

Samaranch also overlooked the fundamental importance of the NOCs as the means by which the Olympic movement was presented, interpreted and delivered in each country. Individual sport federations had neither the interest nor ability to do this. They cared only about their own sport. The entire emotional quotient was brought by the NOCs and the Olympic team, bound to the magic of the five-ring Olympic symbol and the mystery that make the Olympics greater than the sum of their parts. Had he managed to get rid of the NOCs, he would have had to immediately re-invent them.

• • •

Samaranch quietly arranged for the age limit of IOC members to be extended from seventy-two to seventy-five during the IOC session in East Berlin in 1985. The move did not attract much attention amid the sensation of the termination of Berlioux's employment as director of the IOC, but it was essential to Samaranch, who was already thinking about successive terms as IOC president. I did not have any objection to the three-year extension, and IOC members were not selected for their athletic ability, but for experience and judgment. It was, however, a good lesson in advance planning, since Samaranch was barely halfway through his first term as president.

His first term was destined to run for nine, rather than the usual eight, years, to avoid the difficulties of electing presidents at the session immediately preceding the Olympic Games. Since the outgoing president remained in office until the end of the Games, there had always been an awkward relationship between the incoming and the outgoing presidents. Traditionally, the new president was elected during the session just before the Games, to take office immediately after the close of the session. But the theory was that the session was still technically "in session" until the closing ceremony of the Games (in case decisions needed to be taken, for example), so you ended up with the "old" president still being there during the Games and the new one in limbo until the end of the Games. De Beaumont proposed the nine-year term, and it was immediately accepted as a major improvement. Subsequent presidential terms were each four years, with no limit as to the number of terms. Increasing the age limit to seventy-five took care of the elections that would occur in 1989 and 1993. The rules at the time allowed a member to be elected to a position and to serve out the term in that position even if he or she reached the age limit during that term. Samaranch was born in 1920, so he was secure up to 1997.

Well before his third term drew to a conclusion, he decided he would like to run again. The problem was his age and the Olympic Charter requirement that he retire in 1997, by which time he would be seventy-seven. There was no doubt that he wanted to continue. The question was how to arrange it. I thought he should retire and told him so, but suggested that, if he wanted to continue, all he had to do was ask the IOC session, if it was willing to have him continue as president, to make an exception to the age limit in his case. I thought that the lesser evil was to have only one person go on to eighty, rather than all the old dears.

For some reason, he did not want to be an exception. He engaged in a "consultation" with all the members, asking them to advise him whether they wanted him to continue. An overwhelming majority appeared to want him to continue, but, of course, most would not have the courage to tell him if they did not want him to do so. Once he knew where I stood, he did not discuss his strategy with me, but relied on one of his longtime confidants, former judge Kéba Mbaye, to develop it. When the matter was raised at the session in Budapest in 1995, Mbaye had made it so complicated that the members did not understand it and voted against all four of the scenarios that Mbaye had proposed. It was a disaster for Samaranch, since it could mean that he would have to retire, which was not at all what he had had in mind. During the night, however, he got his minions together and they demanded a reconsideration of the matter, with an extension of the age limit for all IOC members to eighty years.

Members were pressured to sign a "spontaneous" resolution to this effect. Even members privately opposed to the idea signed, lest they be identified as having opposed Samaranch once the smoke had cleared. Interestingly enough, no one approached me to sign the resolution. The pressure tactics continued with their insistence on a vote by show of hands, rather than by secret ballot. I was astonished, but probably should not have been, by the small number of members willing to oppose the measure, especially those who should have shown some leadership. I was the only one at the executive board level who raised his hand against the proposal, and a handful from the regular members followed suit. The new measure succeeded, but Samaranch lost a great deal of the high ground he had previously occupied. It was by now clear that he was willing to do anything to stay in power.

We spoke afterward and I said that, although normally I viewed part of my job as keeping him out of trouble of this nature, he had seemed content with the advice he was getting from Mbaye so I had not felt it necessary to intervene, even though it had been clear to me that the advice was tactically wrong. I have seen other cases of judges or former judges who think that knowing some law means that they can be good practicing lawyers, without realizing that the skill sets are significantly different. One way or another, however, Samaranch was embarrassed by the whole manner in which his supposed acclamation was achieved and he was furious with me for showing that I was opposed to his second effort after the debacle of the previous day. I would see the first manifestation of that displeasure the following year in Atlanta when I was a candidate for election as a vice-president.

I was completing a four-year term as a member of the executive board and had been appointed by Samaranch as chair of the coordination commission for the 1996 Atlanta Games, the functions of which were assumed by the executive board once it assembled in Atlanta prior to the Games. The other member whose term was also coming to an end was Ashwini Kumar of India, then almost seventy-six years old and in indifferent health. Earlier in the year, at a meeting in Athens to commemorate the hundredth anniversary of the original modern Games in April, we had spoken and I asked him whether we would be running against each other for the vice-presidency. He assured me that he would not be running: he was old and at the end of his career and I had a great future in front of me, so he would not be contesting the position. I said that was very generous of him and thanked him for letting me know.

I assumed that he would, as I would have done, honored his commitment and I did nothing by way of campaigning for the position. When we had been in Atlanta for a few days, someone asked me why I was not "working the room" with respect to the elections. I said that I had spoken with Kumar several months ago and that he said he was not running. Well, I was told, this was not true: Kumar was running and, indeed, looked as if he might be successful. I found Kumar and asked if, despite our agreement, he was running. Yes, he admitted, the president had encouraged him to do so. Samaranch had put Kumar up to running against me as a payback for my not voting for raising the retirement age limit. I said to Kumar that I was disappointed with him on two counts: one, that he had broken the commitment he had given me, and two, that he had not given me the courtesy of advising me of the change in circumstances. He had no answer.

Whether or not I became vice-president was not the end of the world for me. I could see why Samaranch would want to teach me a lesson about opposing him, to show that he was the boss and that you did not cross him without paying a heavy price. Above all, you did not publicly oppose his plans for personal continuance as president and embarrass him by showing that he was willing to continue all members until the age of eighty for the sole purpose of making it possible for him to remain in office. I understood all of this and, if that was the price for standing up for what I believed, it would be one that I would happily pay.

The only thing he had to understand was that, were I to lose, I would immediately resign my positions as chair of the television rights negotiations committee and the Marketing Commission. The political tradition in my country was that an electoral loss under such circumstances would be regarded as a vote of nonconfidence in what I had been doing and, consistent with such tradition, the proper thing to do would be to resign.

I told him that were I to lose to a seventy-six-year-old in poor health who did almost nothing for the IOC, it would not be possible to continue to deal with television and corporate executives as the chief representative of the

IOC. That, too, was not the end of the world, I said, because Samaranch could almost certainly find someone else to take on those responsibilities. François Carrard, the director general, was sent to try to talk me out of resigning, should the electoral results play out that way. The IOC members were emotional creatures, he said, and often did not understand the full implications of their votes. I should not take this personally and I should, whatever happened in the election, stay in the positions where I was much needed. I said that it was time the members did understand the consequences of their actions and that I was firm in my resolve to resign in the event of a loss.

Samaranch then realized what the external perceptions would be among the IOC's television and corporate sponsors, as well as in the media, were his vindictive effort to succeed, in addition to the fact that I would no longer be handling the marketing and television matters, in which I had enjoyed some considerable success on behalf of the IOC. He had, however, a good idea of the individual votes and suggested that I speak to a couple of members to explain what I proposed to do if I lost, which I did. These contacts were enough to enable me to win by a two-vote margin in an election that had nothing to do with the merits of the contributions of the candidates, but solely the anger of the president from the prior year. I don't think he ever forgave me for not supporting him in Budapest.

•   •   •

For a man who was, generally, remarkably savvy about politics, Samaranch had an odd view of the media and their role. He thought of the media as an extension of the communications arm of the IOC, whose responsibility was to promote the IOC and the Olympic movement, and not to criticize him. His detractors took this to be evidence of his fascist background during the Franco regime in Spain, but I always thought it was more of a generational gap and an inability to understand what had become the place of media in society. He was, except on rare occasions, not a good communicator in his own right. He worked at making his news conferences stultifying and dodged any difficult questions, either by giving off-topic replies or by answering a different question from the one that had been asked; he also practiced a strict policy of not allowing follow-up questions from the same reporter. ("Mr. President, is it true that the IAAF threatened to withdraw from the Olympics unless the IOC provided a greater share of the television revenues?" "The IOC has excellent relations with all the IFs, and athletics is the most important sport on the Olympic program." "Mr. President, is it true that the Athens Games are so far behind schedule that the IOC may withdraw the Games and return them to Sydney or Seoul?" "We are working very closely with our Greek friends.") Within the IOC communications department, at least one full-time employee was assigned the task of following all the news agencies and major publications and to provide Samaranch with hard copies, as reports came in, with his name highlighted in pink and any aspects of the stories that might be of interest highlighted in yellow.

I remember a particular period, before the 1994 Olympic Winter Games in Lillehammer, when the Norwegian press, not known for its self-restraint, was particularly down on him. Probably a combination of factors was to blame— including the north-south tensions in Europe; his patrician attitude; a dispute with Johann Olav Koss, the famous Norwegian speed skater; not to mention general prickliness—but, whatever the cause, he got nothing but bad press. He complained to the president of the organizing committee, Gerhard Heiberg, and ordered him to stop the press from writing such articles. Heiberg had no idea what to do about these orders. I told Heiberg not to worry about it and to do nothing. It would have been like pouring oil on a fire for Heiberg to have gone to the media to say that they should stop criticizing Samaranch. When I spoke with Samaranch about the coverage, I said there were, perhaps, four million people in the whole world who could read Norwegian. Why was he worrying about what they might write? He said that someday, they might be writing stories like that about me and then I would understand. I replied that, should that happen, I would not waste my time reading them, let alone having someone come to me every couple of hours with translations of the articles.

There was another area of Samaranch's life that attracted unfavorable media attention. Especially in his later years as president, when much of the bloom had come off the rose, the media were constantly "reporting" on the lavish lifestyle that Samaranch maintained. Most of this was greatly exaggerated or deliberately false.

Samaranch's discipline carried over into his personal life. He maintained a room at the Lausanne Palace Hotel that served as a sitting room, and had a bedroom attached, which the IOC paid for if he was in Lausanne and did not pay for if he was not there. The Lausanne Palace is a fine hotel, although not, in my view, the best in Lausanne. When I decided that I would be a candidate for the IOC presidency, I joked with some members by saying that I thought my chances would be greatly improved if I were to make the central plank in my electoral platform the promise that, if elected, I would transfer the IOC business to the Beau-Rivage Palace, on the shores of Lac Léman, next to the Olympic Museum in which the IOC now houses its heritage.

Samaranch's quarters were modest; the sitting room was filled with mementos from his many trips and featured a large television set on which he followed sports and world events. He did not occupy anything grand, such as the owner's suite on the top floor. He was as likely to have his dinner in his room as in the hotel restaurant, unless there was an official function or dinner, which he would attend but invariably leave early. He hated long dinners and speeches. He ate simply, and food for him was merely fuel, the ingestion of which gave him no particular pleasure. He seldom took wine with meals and, if so, never more than a glass. He did not smoke, having given it up many years earlier, and was religious about daily exercise, which helped his stamina with the impossible schedule he maintained. It was the same with his apartment in Barcelona, which he had owned for many years. His bedroom was more like a monastic cell than an ordinary bedroom. He was very religious and often made arrangements for private masses whenever he traveled.

I remember one time during a summer when I had had to be in Lausanne for a series of meetings and Samaranch had suggested that we have dinner. I agreed. He said we would meet in his room at 8:00 that evening. I said no, we would go out for dinner. He wanted to know where. I said I had a great place in mind and that he should arrange for the hotel's car to be ready to leave at 7:45. He was dubious, but agreed that we would go out for dinner. I had selected the Hôtel du Monde in Grandvaux, between Lausanne and Montreux, in the vineyards that may well be the most scenic country in the world. The hotel terrace provides an incomparable view over the entire Lac Léman, from Geneva to the right to Montreux and the Rhône Valley on the left, and looks over to Evian to the south. We had a delightful evening that enabled us to watch a storm develop over the lake, with stupendous lightning working its way toward us. Samaranch paid for the dinner with his credit card from the savings bank of which he was president, La Caixa of Barcelona. He said it was the first time he had ever used the card. We would never have gone out of the Lausanne Palace had I not forced the issue and I think he had a wonderful time. I was often worried that he spent too much time by himself.

*   *   *

I never thought of Samaranch as particularly reflective, as opposed to tactical. In the tactical sense, he was brilliant and he had certain strategic strengths as well. What I never found was a philosophical commitment to any basic principles. He would be ready to compromise whatever might be necessary to accomplish a particular objective. I have often said that hardly a day went by when I did not learn something from watching Samaranch, even though it might well have been something I did not really want to learn or was something that I would never want to do myself. He had a highly developed cynicism regarding the motives of others, which were more than matched by his own. He knew, as do all leaders, that those who came to him generally wanted either to attain advancement for themselves or to bring damning commentary down on others.

My guess is that history will be kinder to Samaranch at a distance than it has been to date. Certain issues will fade into their proper perspective—the scandals toward the end of his term in office; his particular manipulative style; some of the dubious people he promoted to prominence; and the combination of duplicity and blandness that seems to be required of certain leaders—and a longer view of his accomplishments will emerge. As someone who worked with him on almost a daily basis throughout his presidency, I can say that he was unique and that, on balance, his presidency of the IOC was by far the most important of any to date. The IOC and the Olympic movement generally could not have developed to the extent they have without his leadership. He left office having accomplished the three objectives he had brought with him when he assumed office: the Olympic movement was united, it was universal, and it was solvent.

All this said, I did not much care for the excesses that marked the end of his presidency, especially the many staged events in Moscow in 2001. There were so many elements of a cult of personality that it smacked of the retirement of the Sun King, with medals struck, obsequious speeches, photo ops with Moscow mayor Yuri Luzhkov, galas and banquets that, in the end, became offensive. I was generally aware of all of the pomp and circumstance, but was in the middle of a campaign, ultimately spectacularly unsuccessful, to become president of the IOC, and did not pay too much attention to the departing monarch, although it was difficult to remain unaware of the adulation poured upon him.

I had decided, not without some misgivings, that I would become a candidate to succeed Samaranch as president of the IOC. The misgivings were not about my ability to do the job, since I knew more about every issue facing the IOC than any of the other candidates and knew everything about the nature of the IOC's operations. They related, instead, to what I would have to give up to do the IOC president's job properly, including the practice of law, which I enjoyed very much; the loss of considerable income, since I believe that the IOC president should be regarded as a volunteer; the loss of my involvement with McGill University, of which I was chancellor; the inability to be independent, instead of politically correct in the role of IOC president. There would have been a difficult adjustment for my family, since most of the time that was not spent traveling would have had to be in Lausanne, taking care of business. I was also aware that I was not very "polit-ical" by nature and that I had not spent much time cultivating the IOC members. Most of my time, even when there were members around, had been spent taking care of sponsors and broadcasters, rather than being charming to IOC colleagues. My hope was that the election would be based on issues and experience. In fact, that was the only basis on which I would have had a chance to win, since my record was far better than that of any other candidate.

For a non-European to win was, at best, a long shot. Almost 50 percent of the votes lie with European members. The voting regulations, devised by Kéba Mbaye as chair of the IOC Ethics Commission, prevented any candidate from raising money to travel to meet other IOC members and prevented candidates for, arguably, the most important sports position in the world, from publishing their elec-toral platforms. There was, in my case, only one voting IOC member within a 5,000-kilometer radius of Montreal, com-pared with about seventy members within the same radius of Brussels or Budapest, the homes of the two European candidates. It was not difficult to see what was intended by the Ethics Commission. My friend and colleague, Kevan Gosper, from Australia, ventured the view that he thought I was the best candidate for the position. He was castigated by the same Ethics Commission for expressing such an opinion publicly, while those members who said, equally publicly, that it was imperative that the president of the IOC must always be European slipped under the watchful radar of the same commission.

If you add to this my general non-disposition toward schmoozing, the odds were not great and, had I been forced to handicap the race, I suppose I would have had to cede the advantage to Jacques Rogge. The hill became steeper when Un Yong Kim decided to become a candidate.

By this time, even Samaranch, who had used his best efforts to keep Kim from being expelled from the IOC as a result of his misconduct in the Salt Lake City bidding scandal, had come to understand that if Kim were to become IOC president, the IOC would be hopelessly compromised. He worked to make sure that Kim would not succeed and the way he chose to do so was to say that, to stop Kim, members should support Rogge, not me. I suppose he thought that the European vote was strong enough to stop Kim, but it was disappointing, considering all I had done for Samaranch, including saving his skin over the Salt Lake City scandal, that he worked against me in the election.

The outcome of the election, namely the win by Jacques Rogge, was not altogether surprising and I had been resigned to that result, especially with Samaranch working for him. But I was insulted by the fact that someone such as Un Yong Kim, who had barely avoided expulsion from the IOC over the Salt Lake City fiasco, had received more votes than I had. This did little to increase my respect for the members who seemed unable to differentiate our respective contributions to the Olympic movement and the IOC. I was even less impressed to learn, in 2004, that Kim still had on hand, in cash, more than two years after the election, some $1.5 million in contributions to his candidacy to become president of the IOC. Whatever the playing field we may have been on, it was far from level.

• • •

Jacques Rogge is now entering into the fourth year of his first term as president, and he is settling into his new role. I think he has found the "business" of the IOC to be far more complex than he expected and, while he keeps his own counsel on this, he has probably also found it much less fun than he had hoped. The IOC is a several-billion-dollar undertaking and the IOC's success is vital to the financial health of the Olympic movement as a whole, from Olympic organizing committees to international federations to national committees and the IOC itself. Rogge has taken over as chair of the television rights negotiations commission and has changed the basic structure of the marketing portfolio by acquiring full ownership of Meridian Management, the marketing agency we had established following our escape from the clutches of ISL in 1995. François Carrard was unwilling to become a full-time director general and has been replaced by Urs Lacotte of Switzerland. Carrard will continue to be available for special mandates, but his experience and judgment on a daily basis will be sorely missed. In general, Rogge has imposed a financial and management style that is much lower key than that applied during Samaranch's rule, which included construction of modern expanded headquarters next to the old Château de Vidy in Lausanne, and the enormously expensive, but stunning, Olympic Museum and Studies Center, also in Lausanne, the latter costing well in excess of US$100 million. Rogge has established a goal of creating a reserve fund that will see the IOC through a four-year period, in case an edition of the Games is canceled and we lose the revenues normally arising from the related television and marketing activities.

He also wants to see how the costs and complexity of the Games can be reduced and, to formalize the process, he established the Olympic Games Study Commission (OGSC), which he asked me to chair. Our first meeting was at the Salt Lake City Games in 2002 and we were required to report to the 2003 session in Prague. After a preliminary presentation of the directions we were pursuing during a special session in Mexico late in 2002, our final report was delivered and accepted on schedule. We had many recommendations, the most important of which focused on the need to plan for the after-use of Olympic construction and not to build facilities that were too big for subsequent use by the host community. This, combined with doubling up on Games use by proper scheduling of events and using temporary facilities, could easily result in savings of up to hundreds of millions of dollars. Limiting the number of accreditations, which have grown to more than 200,000 for Summer Games, can also bring down costs, as can reducing service levels for sponsors, broadcasters, the Olympic family and spectators to levels that are more comparable to other international events. It was a good exercise and one that was much needed.

It is too soon to conclude what the defining character of Rogge's presidency will be, but it is already quite different from any of his immediate predecessors. He seems content to work with any members elected to the executive board, unlike Samaranch, who decided on the makeup of the team he needed to accomplish his mandate and, in effect, told the IOC that, if you want me to do this job, I need to have the people around me who will make it possible. Rogge is more fiscally responsible than Samaranch, who favored the *grand geste* and was obsessed with the prestige of the organization. He is very much committed to the fight against doping in sport, a matter on which Samaranch was equivocal, at best. He is more concerned with rationalizing the structure of the IOC administration than Samaranch, who regarded the administration as a mere tool to make his life easier and who had not the slightest hesitation in ignoring the supposed lines of decision making and even of deliberately setting off one part against the other for whatever purpose he may have had in mind.

Regardless of who may occupy the position of IOC president, there is an ebb and flow in international affairs from which sport and the Olympic movement are not immune. The IOC, under Samaranch and now Rogge, has selected host cities for future Games that provide opportunities for continuation of its mission to contribute to the betterment of the world, but no one can predict what events may overtake these choices.

Italy is muddling along in preparation for the 2006 Winter Games and China is charging headlong into its own preparations for 2008. No one in the world has the slightest doubt that China will be ready in plenty of time, and that the spectacle will be stupendous. By the same token, no one has the faintest idea of how China will deal with the challenges of human rights that have attracted world attention, nor how its relations with Asia, the United States and the rest of the world will develop in future. Any of these factors could have a significant impact on the Beijing Games.

The Vancouver-Whistler Games in 2010 will, I predict, be a great success and the IOC should regard itself as fortunate to have made that choice in 2003. It will not be long before the IOC will gather in Singapore to choose the host city for the 2012 Games. In this process all but one of the nine candidates, several of which are world capitals or otherwise well known, will be disappointed and the IOC will, once again, cross its fingers and hope that it has not made a mistake.

But the universe will unfold as it should and the historians are already working on the first rough drafts of their chronicles. I count myself among their members.

Conclusion

The modern Olympic movement is currently robust—and it is fragile. The Olympic Games, its major showpiece, have become the most celebrated event in history, experienced by more people than the founders could ever have imagined in their wildest dreams. The Olympic family has taken largely positive steps toward internationalizing sport and making it as accessible to as many people and countries as possible. Yet, despite the astonishing strength the movement has shown under external pressures, it is vulnerable to forces from both within and without.

World events may shape society in ways that we cannot anticipate. War, disease, politics and economics may determine how the world develops. Changes may affect the way in which we communicate, interact, travel, eat, live and play. As long as the human race is constituted the way it is today, people will play games. If the collective memory of the human race were suddenly to be erased, and with it, the knowledge of all games now played, it would take almost no time at all for people to begin throwing, kicking or hitting objects, to run, to swim, to compete, to invent games of skill, and to develop certain rules that would apply to the "new" conduct. In time, this conduct would become organized and spread through communities and beyond. Communities would compete with communities and eventually, countries with countries. There is nothing to suggest that something approximating what exists today could not recur. Whether the same ethical values would be reflected is less clear, but there would undoubtedly be some innate sense of order, the structure that societies require in order to exist.

How well, and even whether, the modern Olympic movement will survive ultimately depends on its integrity. It is that integrity which creates a desirable set of values that youth and society in general can accept and emulate. Remove it and the structure will quickly become unstable and collapse. Those charged with the direction of the Olympic movement must be vigilant in maintaining its integrity and fearless in rooting out any conduct that may compromise its foundation.

Officials must demonstrate that accountability starts at the top. Their own conduct in the management of sport must be, and like Caesar's wife, be seen to be, above reproach. They have a responsibility to act fairly, impartially and within the letter and spirit of the governing rules. We have all seen what happens when officials fail to act in such manner. The Salt Lake City judging scandal in ice skating was a perfect example of reprehensible conduct that tarnished a very popular sport, spread to the Olympics where it happened, disillusioned athletes, cast doubt on the character of all officials, and offended the public's sense of decency and fair play. If the officials show no respect for the sport, how can the athletes and the public be expected to observe higher standards?

Salt Lake City also provided a graphic reminder of what happens when the moral compass of sport leaders is ignored. I have never commented too much on the actions of the bidding committee for the 2002 Games, since whatever their transgressions may have been, the situation would never have developed had there not been International Olympic Committee members who were greedy and tasteless and who lost sight (assuming they ever had it) of their own duty to be incorruptible in the exercise of their functions. Everyone should have their own smell test for what is beyond normal courtesy and hospitality as part of an inspection visit and there should never have been the slightest thought of asking for favors. The IOC should accept its full responsibility for what occurred and, if some of the bidders went too far, it is only because they were led to believe that the IOC condoned the conduct. The media blitz and the political carpet bombing that descended on the IOC provided a major wake-up call that was overdue. The IOC had failed to practice what it preached and showed that its standards had fallen well short of acceptable for an organization that purported to head an ethically based sport movement. The reforms were put in place remarkably quickly, but they are structural only and must now be lived.

The same sport leaders must also demonstrate their commitment to the philosophical foundation of the Olympic movement, making sure that their actions support the principles of nondiscrimination and mutual respect. It is not enough to talk about the principles. The talk must be combined with action. The Olympic movement did just that with regard to apartheid and was a major contributor to its eventual dismantlement. It has combined the talk and action in its promotion of sport for women, but thus far with less success and genuine conviction than might be hoped. It has done so in its efforts to make sure that the Olympic movement is open to all, and has reached solutions to complex issues that have confounded political authorities, as in the case of the two Chinas, the 1988 Games in South Korea, and in enabling some Yugoslavian athletes to participate in Barcelona in 1992. This kind of challenge will constantly occur and firm judgment must be exercised on each occasion to be certain that expediency does not become an easy substitute for maintaining the principles.

The Athens dice are cast. On March 7, 2004, the Greeks elected yet another government, to see the Games through to their conclusion. The IOC and the international sports organizations are already turning their eyes forward to Turin in 2006, Beijing in 2008, Vancouver in 2010, and the site of the 2012 Games (to be chosen in 2005). Each will have its own set of logistical and political challenges, and solutions will have to be found for them, as has been done in the past. We are getting somewhat better at anticipating the logistical problems and can therefore head off difficulties before they arise. The whole concept of the Olympics as a franchise, granted temporarily to each host, has led the IOC to adopt a more vigorous approach to the organization and a much better transfer of information to each new set of organizers. It is often said, only partly in jest, that the last remaining amateurs in the Olympic movement are the organizers. Each host city is a novice and the only time it knows everything it needs to know is the day after the closing ceremony. Getting them all started in the right direction and posting guidelines for the achievement of steps along the way is an important way of helping to ensure that the franchise is well delivered.

We must be careful in our selection of host cities. This may be easier said than done, especially since we choose them seven years in advance, which can be several political lifetimes in some countries. The IOC has made occasional risky choices, as was the case with Seoul in 1988, with Atlanta in 1996 and Athens in 2004. It has made choices that were sound at the time, such as that of Moscow for 1980, but which were overtaken by events with the invasion of Afghanistan and the U.S.-led boycott. In most other cases, the choice has been mainstream and generally cautious. I have always maintained that the IOC does not necessarily have to be able to identify the best city in the competition, which is, in any event, an art and not a science, but that it does have to find a way not to make a mistake. Under our new rules of not visiting candidate cities, this means we have to be able to rely more and more on our evaluation commissions, which in turn means that they have to be much more clear and judgmental. We can no longer accept vanilla-flavored reports, filled with coded nuances, in which we have to search for Delphic meaning between the lines.

The IOC has accumulated a large staff whose mandate is the management of the Games, which starts with the selection process, and the IOC members should have the advantage of knowing precisely what they think about the specific questions they have been asked to research. The cities have put themselves forward in a competition and, like the athletes who may one day compete in their cities, they have to expect to be measured. Some will be better than others and they must accept the risk of favorable as well as unfavorable judgment. I do not want our IOC staff to be presenting reports that try to second-guess the political sensitivities of the various choices and to report on the basis of their views as to the electability of the various candidates. We can manage the politics ourselves.

It would be naive to think that terror will disappear from our world in the short to medium future. It would be unrealistic to think that the Olympic platform will not be irresistible to shady groups that want to be on the world stage, acting, of course, through surrogates. Every organization connected with the Games needs to be especially vigilant, to ensure that anyone contemplating terror on behalf of others knows that there will be no free ride but that there will be a high degree of risk of being caught before he or she can act. Boycotts, the other way of drawing attention to oneself, are ineffective, since the only countries hurt will be those who use the technique, not the supposed target. The main thing to remember is that vigilance will now be required, as never before, to ensure that the peaceful gathering of the Olympics can remain what it should be.

One of the most exciting possibilities, for me, that arises from reducing the costs of organizing the Games is that the revenues may well continue to expand. This means that we may be able to take a new look at how the Olympic revenues could be divided. Instead of the roughly 50:50 split we now have, if the costs are reduced, host cities may require less from the IOC than at present, perhaps even nothing, provided ticket sales and local marketing efforts are sufficient to cover all the operating costs. Perhaps when bidding, cities should be required to say how much they will need from the IOC, which can then agree to provide that amount and retain all other revenues for redistribution within the Olympic family, concentrating on areas needing development. I would not be inclined to have a fixed formula for any incremental revenues, but to concentrate instead on development programs that will best serve the Olympic movement as a whole.

We have allowed a climate of entitlement to shares of Olympic revenues to build up, with no accountability for sensible application of those revenues. The image that comes to mind is a nest of young birds, blind, with their mouths open, into which the parents stuff food. I would insist on timely receipt of audited financial statements from any organization that seeks Olympic revenues, so that I could see exactly what was being done with them. I would also institute program audits to assess the effectiveness of the activities. I have a feeling that there is considerable wastage and duplication and that far less of the resources get down to the level of the athletes than would be reasonable to expect. I want to reduce the gap between the developed countries and the developing countries and I am convinced that the means exist to do that, if we are willing to make the commitment—and it is essential to make that commitment.

In keeping with another commitment—to the ethical values of the Olympic movement—there is a need to continue the fight against doping in sport. This is, in my view, the single greatest danger that faces sport today. It is the fight against doping in sport that distinguishes Olympic sport from entertainment sport and, if we do not pursue this fight and win the war, I do not believe that true sport can survive. Sure, we may have a class of twenty-first-century gladiators who perform in arenas for the amusement of the masses, but, whatever that may be, it will not be sport. Ordinary people will not aspire to it; parents will not want their children to enter into the downward spiral that leads to it; the public will eventually have no respect for it. I do not want my grandchildren to have to become chemical stockpiles in order to be successful in sport. Sport should be uplifting, a celebration of humanity and a joy of effort. It should be a source of pride, not something to be hidden from view, like the picture of Dorian Gray.

One of the dangers I see before us is the *success* to date of the World Anti-Doping Agency (WADA). With the adoption of the WADA World Anti-Doping Code, the temptation for many will be to declare the war won. The real danger will be that the international sport federations could use the adoption of the code as an excuse to stop their own activities and lay them off on WADA, disclaiming further responsibility while still claiming full power and autonomy over their sports. Not only that, but they will try to find some way to blame WADA for the continuing phenomenon of doping, yet be unwilling to take their own actions to prevent or detect doping.

Even before the full adoption of the WADA code, there were efforts to use it as a pretext for abandoning testing programs or for enforcing anti-doping rules. Instead of becoming an additional weapon in the fight, the code has been used by some international federations as a pretext for reducing sanctions they would otherwise have been bound to institute. Some sports, cycling in particular, have shown a degree of institutional denial regarding the prevalence of doping that exists within the sport that is almost clinical.

Their response has been to shoot the messenger that reports on the extent of doping in the sport, a phenomenon that goes back more than a century, rather than to admit the problem and to take serious measures to combat it. This is yet another example of needing an independent agency not only to harmonize anti-doping rules, but also to monitor compliance with them and to report on the abandonment of responsibility when infractions occur. WADA will have the right to appeal to the Court for Arbitration for Sport (CAS) if the sanctions are—as is likely—too weak, and urge CAS to impose what should have been the correct penalty. Ultimately, this will be the real means of ensuring that rules are applied evenly in all countries and in all sports.

I am determined that WADA will exercise this right on a proactive basis, because I believe that many international federations lack the courage or the will to take effective measures on their own to clean up their sports. But, if they will not do it, WADA will—with the help of the independent view of CAS as to what is appropriate in the circumstances. And WADA will have no compunction about reporting on international federations or countries that do not comply with the anti-doping code, which will have consequences for the Olympics and other events. I am not willing to declare the war against doping in sport won until 99.9 percent of athletes and their entourages do not dope because it is wrong to do so, and they can be assured that the 0.1 percent who may break the rules will be caught and sanctioned. This is not going to be an easily achieved victory, but it is too important for the future of sport for us not to be uncompromising in pursuing it.

I believe that sport, and particularly the Olympic movement, can provide an extraordinary values system for today's and tomorrow's youth. We live in a world that has lost its ethical path, in which values that enabled society to develop in the confidence that they were doing the "right" thing are no longer unshakable, no longer reliable guides. Evidence of ethical failures is all around us—in business, in politics, in science, in education and in religion. There is moral decay in sport as well, as a subset of the same society. But the ethical framework of sport is still clear and still accepted by the vast majority of participants, and its values are worthwhile in their own right as well as being portable across the full range of social activity. It is this ethical platform that can provide a valuable tool to society as young people look for guidelines that will help them adapt to a world that changes in some aspect every day. Our choice of Athens for 2004 was a first step in renewing the commitment to these values. I believe you *can* go home again.

Sports Organization Acronyms

ACOG	Atlanta Committee for the Olympic Games
AIBA	Association Internationale de Boxe Amateur
AIOWF	Association of International Olympic Winter Sports Federations
ANOC	Association of National Olympic Committees
ASOIF	Association of Summer Olympic International Federations
COA	Canadian Olympic Association (renamed COC in April 2002)
COC	Canadian Olympic Committee
CAS	Court of Arbitration for Sport
FIFA	Fédération Internationale de Football Association (soccer)
FIG	International Gymnastics Federation (known by French acronym)
FINA	Fédération Internationale de Natation (Swimming, diving, water polo, synchronized swimming)
FIS	International Ski Federation (known by French acronym)
FISA	Fédération Internationale des Sociétés d'Aviron (rowing)
FISU	International University Sports Federation (known by French acronym)
IAAF	International Association of Athletics Federations (formerly International Amateur Athletic Federation)
ICAS	International Council of Arbitration for Sport
IFS	international sports federations
IIHF	International Ice Hockey Federation
IOC	International Olympic Committee
ISU	International Skating Union
IWF	International Weightlifting Federation
LAOOC	Los Angeles Olympic Organizing Committee
MLB	Major League Baseball (American League and National League)
NBA	National Basketball Association
NFL	National Football League
NHL	National Hockey League
NOCs	national Olympic committees
OCO'88	Olympiques Calgary Olympics '88 (Calgary organizing commitee)
OGSC	Olympic Games Study Commission
PGA Tour	Professional Golfers' Association Tour
SANOC	South African National Olympic Committee
SANROC	South African Non-Racial Olympic Committee
SLOC	Salt Lake Organizing Committee
SLOOC	Seoul Olympic Organizing Committee
TOP	The Olympic Program
UCI	International Cycling Union (known by French acronym)
USATF	USA Track & Field
USOC	United States Olympic Committee
WADA	World Anti-Doping Agency
WNBA	Women's National Basketball Association

Olympic Games Host Cities

1896 Athens
1900 Paris
1904 St. Louis
1908 London
1912 Stockholm
1920 Antwerp

Summer		Winter
Paris	1924	Chamonix
Amsterdam	1928	St. Moritz
Los Angeles	1932	Lake Placid
Berlin	1936	Garmisch-Partenkirchen
London	1948	St. Moritz
Helsinki	1952	Oslo
Melbourne	1956	Cortina d'Ampezzo
Rome	1960	Squaw Valley
Tokyo	1964	Innsbruck (replacing Denver)
Mexico City	1968	Grenoble
Munich	1972	Sapporo
Montreal	1976	Innsbruck
Moscow	1980	Lake Placid
Los Angeles	1984	Sarajevo
Seoul	1988	Calgary
Barcelona	1992	Albertville
—	1994	Lillehammer
Atlanta	1996	—
—	1998	Nagano
Sydney	2000	—
—	2002	Salt Lake City
Athens	2004	—
—	2006	Turin
Beijing	2008	—
—	2010	Vancouver

Index

Index

Index

Index